Body Consciousness

Contemporary culture increasingly suffers from problems of attention, over-stimulation, and stress. We are plagued by a growing variety of personal and social discontents generated by deceptive body images. This book argues that improved body consciousness can relieve these problems and enhance one's knowledge, performance, and pleasure. The body is our basic medium of perception and action, but focused attention to its feelings and movements has long been criticized as a damaging distraction that also ethically corrupts through self-absorption. In *Body Consciousness*, Richard Shusterman eloquently refutes such charges by engaging the most influential twentieth-century somatic philosophers and incorporating insights from both Western and Asian disciplines of body-mind awareness. Rather than rehashing intractable ontological debates on the mind-body relation, Shusterman reorients study of this crucial nexus toward a more fruitful, pragmatic direction that reinforces important but neglected connections between philosophy of mind, ethics, politics, and the pervasive aesthetic dimensions of everyday life.

Richard Shusterman is the Dorothy F. Schmidt Eminent Scholar in the Humanities and Professor of Philosophy at Florida Atlantic University, Boca Raton. Educated at Jerusalem and Oxford, he is internationally known for his contributions to philosophy and his pioneering work in somaesthetics, a field of theory and practice devoted to thinking through the body. A recipient of senior Fulbright and National Endowment for the Humanities fellowships, Dr. Shusterman has held academic positions in Paris, Berlin, and Hiroshima and is the author of several books, most recently *Surface and Depth* and *Performing Live*. His *Pragmatist Aesthetics* has been published in thirteen languages.

Body Consciousness

A Philosophy of Mindfulness and Somaesthetics

RICHARD SHUSTERMAN

DEFINED — P 19

CAMBRIDGE
UNIVERSITY PRESS

CAMBRIDGE UNIVERSITY PRESS
Cambridge, New York, Melbourne, Madrid, Cape Town, Singapore, São Paulo, Delhi

Cambridge University Press
32 Avenue of the Americas, New York, NY 10013-2473, USA

www.cambridge.org
Information on this title: www.cambridge.org/9780521858908

First published 2008

Printed in the United States of America

A catalog record for this publication is available from the British Library.

Library of Congress Cataloging in Publication Data

Shusterman, Richard.
Body consciousness : a philosophy of mindfulness and somaesthetics / Richard
Shusterman.
p.   cm.
Includes bibliographical references (p.) and index.
ISBN 978-0-521-85890-8 (hardcover) – ISBN 978-0-521-67587-1 (pbk.)
1. Body, Human (Philosophy)   2. Aesthetics–Physiological aspects.   I. Title.
B105.B64S38   2008
128'.6 – dc22   2007034891

ISBN   978-0-521-85890-8 hardback
ISBN   978-0-521-67587-1 paperback

In memory of J.W.S.,
whose body gave me life, love, and consciousness.

> *. . . her pure and eloquent blood,*
> *Spoke in her cheeks and so distinctly wrought,*
> *That one might almost say, her body thought.*
> *She, she, thus richly, and largely housed, is gone.*
>> *John Donne, "Of the Progress of the Soul:*
>> *The Second Anniversary"*

"The human body is the best picture of the human soul."

Ludwig Wittgenstein, *Philosophical Investigations*

"The body is to be compared, not to a physical object, but rather to a work of art."

Maurice Merleau-Ponty, *The Phenomenology of Perception*

"Monks, one thing, if practiced and made much of, conduces to great thrill, great profit, great security after the toil, to mindfulness and self-possession, to the winning of knowledge and insight, to pleasant living in this very life, to the realization of the fruit of release by knowledge. What is that one thing? It is mindfulness centered on body."

The Buddha, *Anguttara Nikāya*

"Besides, it is a shame to let yourself grow old through neglect before seeing how you can develop the maximum beauty and strength of body; and you can't have this experience if you are negligent, because these things don't normally happen by themselves."

Socrates, from Xenophon's *Memoirs of Socrates*

Contents

vii

Preface

Contemporary culture increasingly suffers from problems of attention, overstimulation, and stress. We are further plagued by a growing variety of personal and social discontents generated by deceptive body images. This book argues that improved body consciousness can help relieve these problems and enhance one's knowledge, performance, and pleasure. If body consciousness is a topic unlikely to comfort conventional philosophical tastes, this is not because philosophy has always ignored the body, as too many somatic advocates are fond of complaining. The body in fact exerts a very powerful (though generally negative) presence in philosophy's persistent privileging of mind and spirit. Its dominantly negative image – as a prison, distraction, source of error and corruption – is both reflected and reinforced by the idealistic bias and disregard for somatic cultivation that Western philosophers generally display.

We must not forget, however, that philosophy in ancient times was practiced as a distinctly embodied way of life in which somatic disciplines frequently formed an important part, even if such disciplines sometimes assumed a more body-punishing character in philosophies where mind and soul were thought to achieve more freedom and power through severe somatic asceticism. Plotinus, for example (according to his admiring biographer Porphyry), was so "ashamed of being in the body" and so keen to transcend it that he not only drastically limited his diet but even "abstained from the use of the bath." Today, when philosophy has shrunk from a global art of living into a narrow field of academic discourse, the body retains a strong presence as a theoretical (and sometimes potently political) abstraction. However, the idea of using its cultivation for heightened consciousness and philosophical insight would probably strike most professional philosophers as an embarrassing aberration. I hope to change this prejudice.

Unlike philosophers, artists have generally devoted a very adoring, revering attention to the body. Realizing how powerfully and precisely our mental life is displayed through bodily expression, they have shown how the most subtle nuances of belief, desire, and feeling are reflected in the postural and gestural attitudes of our figures and facial countenance. However, in their idolizing love of the human body, artists have usually preferred to portray it as the attractive object of another person's consciousness rather than the radiating expression of the somatic subject's own probing consciousness of embodied self. Women, particularly young vulnerable women, are the frequent subjects of such objectification, portrayed as lusciously sensuous and obligingly passive flesh for the viewer's devouring delectation. The artistic yearning to glorify the body's beauty as desired object often results, moreover, in stylistic exaggerations that propagate deceptive images of bodily ease and grace.

Such problems can be detected in the illustration that adorns the cover of this book, the famous *Valpinçon Bather* (1808) of Ingres, one of his series of acclaimed Turkish bath and harem paintings portraying naked odalisques (female slaves or concubines of the harem). The young woman here, passively posed on a luxuriously bedded and curtained interior, is fresh and naked from her bath and thus ready for her required sexual service. She presents a deliciously lovely and luminous backside of flesh. But in her static pose, with her head turned away in darker shadow and her gaze and facial expression invisible, we get no sense of her having any active, thoughtful consciousness at all. She even seems unconscious of the close presence of the implied viewer, who sees her in almost total nakedness, apart from the turban on her bound hair and the sheet wrapped around her arm – both more suggestive of her bondage than of protective covering. Ingres, moreover, intensifies the woman's visual beauty and erotic charge by putting her in a postural constellation of legs, spine, and head that highlights her figure's graceful long limbs and curving lines but that in fact is anatomically far from a posture conducive to comfort, let alone effective action. What a shock to learn that the marketing department had selected this beautiful but painfully misleading image for the cover of my book on body consciousness! As a critic of media culture's deceptive objectifications of the body, but also as a Feldenkrais practitioner sensitive to the strain and suffering of the spine, I voiced my objections but was decisively told that the vast majority of my potential readers would only be attracted to the beauty of the Ingres and never notice its unsightly social and somatic import. If that indeed is true, then this book's arguments are all the more needed to open their eyes to other

forms and beauties of body consciousness. Do not judge this book by its
cover.

We can easily appreciate, however, why artists would focus on beautifying the body's external form and why philosophers would find body
consciousness a disconcerting matter and prefer to think of mind. As
bodies are the clearest expression of human mortality, imperfection, and
weakness (including moral frailties), so body consciousness, for most of
us, primarily means feelings of inadequacy, our falling far short of the
reigning ideals of beauty, health, and performance – a point that also
indicates that body consciousness is always more than consciousness of
one's own body alone. Moreover, despite its share of intense pleasures,
body consciousness is perhaps most acutely and firmly focused in experiences of pain. Embodiment thus suggests a discomforting vulnerability or
evil, epitomized in Saint Paul's declaration that "nothing good dwells in
me, that is, in my flesh." Cultivation of body consciousness has thus been
repeatedly attacked as a psychological, cognitive, and moral danger, even
though philosophy's commitment to self-knowledge would surely seem
to entail the exercise of heightened somatic awareness. Kant, for example, though affirming self-examination as a crucial duty (and despite his
meticulous personal attention to details of diet and exercise), sharply
condemns somatic introspection for generating melancholia and other
corruptions. William James likewise warns that heightened consciousness
of the bodily means of action leads to failure in achieving our desired
ends.

Do our bodies really function best when we most ignore them rather
than mindfully trying to guide their functioning? How should we rec-
oncile this incentive for nonthinking with philosophy's ideal of critical
reflection? Without critical somatic consciousness, how can we correct
faulty habits and improve our somatic self-use? If philosophy remains
committed to the maxim "know thyself," how, then, can we better know
our somatic selves, feelings, and conduct? If philosophy is likewise committed to the goal of self-improvement and self-care, could enhanced
skills of somatic awareness enable better ways of monitoring and directing our behavior, managing or diminishing our pain, and more fruitfully multiplying our pleasures? How to distinguish between helpful and
unhelpful forms of body consciousness? How to combine critical body
mindfulness with the demands for smooth spontaneity of action? Are
there special principles or methods of somatic introspection for improving body consciousness and then using such enhanced awareness for
better cognition and sensorimotor performance? How do these methods

relate to the struggles of individuals whose bodies serve to underline their subordinate social status? How does somatic proprioception expand our traditional picture of the senses and their role in cognition and coordinated action? Is body consciousness nothing more than an awkward term for denoting the mind's reflective consciousness of the body as an external object, or are there truly bodily forms of subjectivity, intentionality, and awareness?

Such questions, and many others related to body consciousness, will be addressed in this book, which is a product of at least a decade of struggling both theoretically and practically with this topic. Though the struggle continues, this book marks a significant measure of progress in my ongoing project of somaesthetics that grows out of earlier work in philosophical pragmatism as a philosophy of life. The pragmatism I advocate puts experience at the heart of philosophy and celebrates the living, sentient body as the organizing core of experience. Underlining the body's formative role in the creation and appreciation of art, my *Pragmatist Aesthetics* (1992) included the arts of self-styling. The body is not only the crucial site where one's ethos and values can be physically displayed and attractively developed, but it is also where one's skills of perception and performance can be honed to improve one's cognition and capacities for virtue and happiness. In that context, *Practicing Philosophy: Pragmatism and the Philosophical Life* (1997) introduced the notion of somaesthetics as a field of theory and practice, which was later elaborated in *Performing Live* (2000). This book is a further extension of the somaesthetic project, with much more detailed attention to issues of body consciousness and to their problematic treatment by past masters of twentieth-century philosophy. I often prefer to speak of *soma* rather than body to emphasize that my concern is with the living, feeling, sentient, purposive body rather than a mere physical corpus of flesh and bones. In fact, were I not worried about burdening this book with an awkwardly technical title, I might have called it "somatic consciousness" or even "somaesthetic consciousness" to avoid the negative associations of the term "body."

***

I gratefully acknowledge the munificent support of my research provided through Florida Atlantic University's Dorothy F. Schmidt Eminent Scholar Chair in the Humanities that I am truly fortunate to hold. Three other institutions were also particularly supportive of my work on this book. The University of Oslo kindly invited me to spend the month of May 2006 sharing my somaesthetic research with their interdisciplinary study group on literature and disease (special thanks here to Knut Stene-Johansen and Drude von der Fehr). In the fall semester of 2006, the Université de Paris 1 Panthéon-Sorbonne graciously hosted (through the good offices of Dominique Chateau, Marc Jimenez, and Jacinto Lageira) a series of lectures in which I could test the book's final arguments in a foreign language. Earlier, Hiroshima University (on the suggestion of Satoshi Higuchi) generously invited me to spend the entire academic year of 2002–2003 as a visiting professor (with no teaching duties) to pursue my research in somaesthetics, affording me a much closer view of Japan's extraordinary body-mind disciplines, from meditation to the martial arts. The highlight of that year was the time I lived and trained in a Zen cloister, the Shorinkutsu-dojo, set on a hill by the coastal village of Tadanoumi on the beautiful Inland Sea. I am extremely grateful to my Zen Master, Roshi Inoue Kido, for his superb instruction, which amazingly combined uncompromising discipline with affectionate kindness. It was not an easy time; there were moments of struggle, frustration, failure, shame, and pain. But I cannot remember a more perfect happiness or greater perceptual acuity than what I experienced through Roshi's guidance.

This experience of Zen practice reinforced my faith that despite the problems and risks of somatic consciousness, its disciplined cultivation (in the proper forms, foci, and contexts) can prove an invaluable tool for pursuing a philosophical life of self-discovery and self-improvement that also takes one beyond the self. I first acquired this conviction through my four-year training and subsequent professional work in the Feldenkrais Method of somatic education and therapy and through some earlier instruction in the Alexander Technique. These body-mind disciplines taught me other important lessons: that philosophical understanding of body consciousness can be enhanced through practical training in disciplines of reflective somaesthetic awareness; that our somatic consciousness is typically flawed in ways that systematically hamper our performance of habitual actions that should be easy to perform effectively but yet prove difficult, awkward, or painful; and that somaesthetic insight can provide us with creative strategies to overcome such faulty habits and other disorders involving somatic, psychological, and behavioral problems. Body consciousness is therefore not, as many have complained, something whose cultivation speaks only to the young, strong, and beautiful. Though aging and infirmity bring a disconcerting somatic consciousness we are tempted to shun, the older and weaker we get, the more we need to think through our bodies to improve our self-use and performance for the effective pursuit of our daily activities and the goals we strive to realize. I know this not only from my Feldenkrais experience in caring for others but also from my personal experience of aging.

***

I am grateful not only to my teachers in somatic disciplines of mindfulness but also to the many scholars who have helped refine, develop, and extend the field of somaesthetics through critical analysis and exploratory interpretations, in fields ranging from dance and performance art to feminism, drug education, sports, and spirituality. Confining myself to a sample of published English texts, I wish in particular to acknowledge the discussions of Jerold J. Abrams, Peter Arnold, Deanne Bogdan, Jon Borowicz, Liora Bressler, David Granger, Gustavo Guerra, Casey Haskins, Kathleen Higgins, Robert Innis, Martin Jay, James Scott Johnson, Thomas Leddy, Barbara Montero, Eric Mullis, Richard Rorty, Simo Säätelä, Shannon Sullivan, Ken Tupper, Bryan Turner, and Krystyna Wilkoszewska. I also acknowledge my debt to the talented philosophers whose work in translating my texts on somaesthetics often prompted me to refine and rethink my views: Jean-Pierre Cometti, Peng Feng, Wojciech Małecki, Fuminori Akiba, Nicolas Vieillescazes, Heidi Salaverria, Robin Celikates, Alina Mitek, József Kollár, Satoshi Higuchi, Emil Visnovsky, Ana-Maria Pascal, Jinyup Kim, K.-M. Kim, and Barbara Formis.

In testing out the book's ideas in preliminary papers, I was fortunate to receive helpful comments from too many colleagues to mention here. But I am happy to acknowledge those of Roger Ames, Takao Aoki, Richard Bernstein, Gernot Böhme, Peg Brand, Judith Butler, Taylor Carman, Vincent Colapietro, Arthur Danto, Mary Devereaux, Pradeep Dhillon, George Downing, Shaun Gallagher, Charlene Haddock-Seigfried, Mark Hansen, Cressida Heyes, Yvan Joly, Tsunemichi Kambayashi, Hans-Peter Krüger, Morten Kyndrup, José Medina, Christoph Menke, James Miller, Alexander Nehamas, Ryosuke Ohashi, James Pawelski, Naoko Saito, Manabu Sato, Stefan Snaevarr, Scott Stroud, John Stuhr, and Wolfgang Welsch. I am thankful that Chuck Dyke and Jerold J. Abrams read an early draft of this book and offered very valuable comments, as did two readers for Cambridge University Press (who were later identified to me as Robert Innis and Shannon Sullivan). Marla Bradford was helpful in preparing the bibliography, Giovanna Lecaros assisted with proofreading, and Wojciech Małecki very generously offered to work on the index.

Some of the book's arguments have already been rehearsed in articles published in *The Monist, Hypatia, The Philosophical Forum, The Cambridge*

Companion to Merleau-Ponty, and *The Grammar of Politics: Wittgenstein and the Political* (Cornell University Press). I am grateful for the opportunity to use some of this material, which has been significantly revised and expanded, to help shape a much more developed, sustained, and unified book-length study. It is a privilege to have Beatrice Rehl of Cambridge University Press as my editor, and I thank her for thoughtful advice and encouraging support. My wife Erica Ando and our daughter Talia Emi have continuously inspired my work through graceful intelligence in action and cheerful beauty in repose. This book could not have been written without them.

Richard Shusterman
Boca Raton, May 2007

Introduction

I

Body consciousness (a term of multiple meanings with widely ranging applications) forms the central focus of this book. In exploring various forms and levels of body consciousness and the diverse issues and theories through which twentieth-century philosophy has tried to explain the body's role in our experience, the book also advocates greater attention to somatic self-consciousness both in theory and in practice. I make the case for heightened somatic consciousness not simply by refuting influential philosophical arguments against the value of such consciousness, but also by outlining a systematic philosophical framework through which the different modes of somatic consciousness, somatic cultivation, and somatic understanding can be better integrated and thus more effectively achieved.

That disciplinary framework, somaesthetics, is explained in the book's first chapter, and its concepts and principles continue to shape my subsequent arguments. For the moment, we can briefly describe somaesthetics as concerned with the critical study and meliorative cultivation of how we experience and use the living body (or soma) as a site of sensory appreciation (aesthesis) and creative self-fashioning. Somaesthetics is thus a discipline that comprises both theory and practice (the latter clearly implied in its idea of meliorative cultivation). The term "soma" indicates a living, feeling, sentient body rather than a mere physical body that could be devoid of life and sensation, while the "aesthetic" in somaesthetics has the dual role of emphasizing the soma's perceptual role (whose embodied intentionality contradicts the body/mind dichotomy) and its aesthetic

uses both in stylizing one's self and in appreciating the aesthetic qualities
of other selves and things.[1]

Before going any further, readers might already object: Why advocate
any more attention to body consciousness and even develop a systematic discipline for it? Is not our culture already far too body conscious,
excessively fixated on how our bodies look, how much they weigh, how
alluringly they smell, how stylishly they are decorated, how powerfully
they can be made to perform athletically through drugs and intensified
disciplines of training? Are we not, then, suffering from a monstrously
overgrown body consciousness whose irrepressible surge is even infecting
fields like philosophy that are traditionally respected as devoted to mind
in contrast to body? If so, this book would seem more the sad symptom of
cultural and philosophical malaise than an instrument for improvement.

A further objection is likely. Our perceptual powers are already fully
occupied with more pressing matters than cultivating somatic consciousness. Transformed by the continuing information revolution, inundated
by increasing floods of signs, images, and factoids, we already have too
much to attend to in the surrounding environments of our natural, social,
and virtual worlds of experience. Why, then, devote a portion of our limited and overstretched capacities of attention to monitor our own somatic
experience? How can we afford to do so? Besides, our bodies seem to
perform perfectly well without any somatic reflection or heightened consciousness. Why not simply leave our bodily experience and performance
entirely to the automatic mechanisms of instinct and unreflective somatic
habits, so that we can focus our attention on matters that really call for
and deserve full conscious attention – the ends we seek and the means,
instruments, or media we need to deploy to achieve those ends?

Responding to such questions with one of this book's guiding principles, we should recall that the body constitutes an essential, fundamental dimension of our identity. It forms our primal perspective or mode
of engagement with the world, determining (often unconsciously) our

---

[1] Although I introduced the term "somaesthetics" to propose a new interdisciplinary field
for philosophical practice, "somaesthetic" (or as it is more frequently spelled, "somes-
thetic") is a familiar term of neurophysiology, referring to sensory perception through
the body itself rather than its particular sense organs. The somaesthetic senses are often
divided into exteroceptive (relating to stimuli outside the body and felt on the skin),
proprioceptive (initiated within the body and concerned with the orientation of body
parts relative to one another and the orientation of the body in space), and visceral or
interoceptive (deriving from internal organs and usually associated with pain).

choice of ends and means by structuring the very needs, habits, interests, pleasures, and capacities on which those ends and means rely for their significance. This, of course, includes the structuring of our mental life, which, in the stubbornly dominant dualism of our culture, is too often sharply contrasted to our bodily experience. If embodied experience is so formative of our being and connection to the world, if (in Husserl's words) "the Body is ... the *medium of all perception*," then body consciousness surely warrants cultivating, not only to improve its perceptual acuity and savor the satisfactions it offers but also to address philosophy's core injunction to "know thyself," which Socrates adopted from Apollo's temple at Delphi to initiate and inspire his founding philosophical quest.[2]

The body expresses the ambiguity of human being, as both subjective sensibility that experiences the world and as an object perceived in that world. A radiating subjectivity constituting "the very centre of our experience," the body cannot be properly understood as a mere object; yet, it inevitably also functions in our experience as an object of consciousness, even of one's own embodied consciousness.[3] When using my index finger to touch a bump on my knee, my bodily subjectivity is directed to feeling another body part as an object of exploration. I thus both *am* body and *have* a body. I usually experience my body as the transparent source of my perception or action, and not as an object of awareness. It is that *from which* and *through which* I grasp or manipulate the objects of the world on which I am focused, but I do not grasp it as an explicit object of consciousness, even if it is sometimes obscurely felt as a background condition of perception. But often, especially in situations of doubt or difficulty, I also perceive my body as something that I *have* and *use* rather than *am*, something I must command to perform what I will but that often fails in performance, something that distracts, disturbs, or makes me suffer. Such discord encourages somatic alienation and the familiar denigrating objectification of the body as just an instrument (lamentably

command

[2] Edmund Husserl, *Ideas Pertaining to a Pure Phenomenology and to a Phenomenological Philosophy*, trans. R. Rojcewicz and A. Schwer (Boston: Kluwer, 1989), 61. The italics are Husserl's. Hereafter my book will note only when I add italics to quotations.

[3] See Maurice Merleau-Ponty, *The Phenomenology of Perception*, trans. Colin Smith (London: Routledge, 1986), 71. William James describes the body in the same terms of centrality, as "the storm centre" and "origin of coordinates" in our experience. "Everything circles round it, and is felt from its point of view." "The world experienced," he elaborates, "comes at all times with our body as its centre, centre of vision, centre of action, centre of interest." William James, "The Experience of Activity," in *Essays in Radical Empiricism* (Cambridge, MA: Harvard University Press, 1976), 86.

weak and vulnerable) that merely belongs to the self rather than really constituting an essential expression of selfhood.

However, even if we objectify or instrumentalize the body (and to some extent we must for pragmatic purposes of somatic care), this is no reason to regard it as not needing or deserving our attentive consciousness. For even if construed as an instrument of the self, the body must be recognized as our most primordial tool of tools, our most basic medium for interacting with our various environments, a necessity for all our perception, action, and even thought. Just as skilled builders need expert knowledge of their tools, so we need better somatic knowledge to improve our understanding and performance in the diverse disciplines and practices that contribute to our mastery of the highest art of all – that of living better lives. A more discerning awareness of our somatic medium can improve its use in deploying all our other tools and media; for they all require some form of bodily performance, even if it is the mere pushing of a button or blinking of an eye.

The body's role as our primordial instrument or *ur*-medium has long been recognized; the basic somatic terms of "organ" and "organism" derive from the Greek word for tool, *organon*. Yet, Greek philosophy's aristocratic tendency to champion ideal ends while disparaging material means as mere menial necessity has resulted, with Plato and subsequent idealists, in condemning rather than celebrating the body as medium, while using its very instrumentality to exclude it from what is essential and valuable in human being. A medium or means (as etymology indicates) typically stands between two other things between which it mediates. Being in the middle, an interface with two faces, a medium connects the mediated terms, yet also separates them by standing between them. This double aspect is also present in the instrumental sense of medium as means to an end. While being a way to the end, it also stands *in* the way, a distance to be traveled between purpose and its fulfillment.

Plato's seminal condemnation of the body as medium in the *Phaedo* (65c–67a) concentrates on the negative interfering aspect. Prefiguring today's dominant lines of media critique, it argues that the body distracts us from reality and the search for true knowledge by interrupting our attention with all sorts of sensational commotion and diverting our minds with all sorts of passions, fancies, and nonsense. Moreover, our somatic sensorial medium distorts reality through its flawed perception. The body is even portrayed as a multimedia conglomerate of different sensory modalities and technologies (such as eyes, ears, feeling limbs, etc.), and such plurality and divisibility of parts provide all the more reason for Plato to degrade it by contrast to the indivisible soul that seeks the truth despite its confinement in the body's distortive prison.[4]

These ancient lines of critique, adopted by Neoplatonism and integrated into Christian theology and modern philosophical idealism, have waxed enormously influential in our culture, as has another Platonic argument (from *Alcibiades* 129c–131d) to denigrate and alienate the body as instrument. We clearly distinguish between a tool and the user of the tool, between instrument and agent; so if the body is our tool or instrument (no matter how intimate and indispensable), then it must be altogether different from the self who uses it, for which it must therefore be a mere external means. It follows (so goes the argument) that the true self must be the mind or soul alone, and consequently that self-knowledge and self-cultivation have nothing to do with cultivating bodily knowledge and consciousness. More generally, the idea of the body as an external instrument used by the self is easily translated into the familiar image of body as servant or tool of the soul. This further promotes the disparaging identification of the somatic with the dominated serving classes (including women), an association that reciprocally reinforces the subordinate status and disrespect for all the associated terms.

Yet Plato's reasoning can surely be challenged, even by extending its basic argument, with its dichotomizing objectifications, into a *reductio ad absurdum*. We clearly use more of ourselves than our bodies alone. We use our minds to think and our souls to will, hope, pray, decide, or exercise virtue. Does the use of one's mind or soul likewise entail its being a mere external instrument rather than an essential part of one's identity? If we strip everything that the self uses from belonging to the real self, we are left with nothing at all; for we indeed use our selves, whenever we use other things and even when we do not. Self-use is not a contradiction in terms but a necessity for living, and to show why heightened somatic consciousness can improve one's use of the self is a major aim of this book. Nor does this express a joyless instrumentalism, because improved self-use surely includes a greater ability to enjoy oneself, with the soma clearly a key experiential site (rather than a mere means) of pleasure.

---

[4] For a more detailed critical discussion of Plato's argument and its reflection in contemporary debate concerning the body's relationship to the new media, see my chapter on "Somaesthetics and the Body-Media Issue," in Richard Shusterman, *Performing Live* (Ithaca, NY: Cornell University Press, 2000), ch. 7.

II

Contemporary culture undeniably lavishes enormous and, in some ways, excessive attention to the body. But it is not the sort of attention that this book is most keen to advance. Social theorists and feminist critics have convincingly exposed how the dominant forms in which our culture heightens body awareness serve largely to maximize corporate profits (for the massive cosmetics, dieting, fashion, and other "body-look" industries) while reinforcing social domination and inflicting multitudes with self-aversion. Ideals of bodily appearance impossible for most people to achieve are cunningly promoted as the necessary norm, thus condemning vast populations to oppressive feelings of inadequacy that spur their buying of marketed remedies.[5] Distracting us from our actual bodily feelings, pleasures, and capacities, such relentlessly advertised ideals also blind us to the diversity of ways of improving our embodied experience. Somatic self-consciousness in our culture is excessively directed toward a consciousness of how one's body appears to others in terms of entrenched societal norms of attractive appearance and how one's appearance can be rendered more attractive in terms of these conventional models. (And these same conformist standards likewise impoverish our appreciation of the richly aesthetic diversity of other bodies than our own.) Virtually no attention is directed toward examining and sharpening the consciousness of one's actual bodily feelings and actions so that we can deploy such somatic reflection to know ourselves better and achieve a more perceptive somatic self-consciousness to guide us toward better self-use.

Such improved self-use, I should reiterate, is not confined to mere practical, functional matters but includes improving our capacities for pleasure, which can be significantly enhanced by more perceptive self-awareness of our somatic experience. We can then enjoy our pleasures "twice as much," insists Montaigne, "for the measure of enjoyment depends on the greater or lesser attention that we lend it."[6] Too many of our ordinary somatic pleasures are taken hurriedly, distractedly, and almost as unconsciously as the pleasures of sleep. If this dearth of somaesthetic sensitivity helps explain our culture's growing dependence on increasing stimulation through the sensationalism of mass-media entertainments and far more radical means of thrill taking, then such a diet

[5] See, for example, Susan Bordo, *Unbearable Weight: Feminism, Western Culture, and the Body* (Berkeley: University of California Press, 1993).
[6] *The Complete Works of Montaigne*, trans. Donald Frame (Stanford, CA: Stanford University Press, 1965), 853.

of artificial excitements can conversely explain how our habits of perception (and even our sensorimotor nervous system) are transformed in ways that elevate the stimulus threshold for perceptibility and satisfaction while diminishing our capacities for tranquil, steady, and sustained attention. Somatic reflection's cultivation of more refined somatic self-consciousness can address these problems by providing more rapid and reliable awareness of when we are overstimulated by a surfeit of sensory excitements so that we know when to turn them down or switch them off to avoid their damage. Such heightened, attentive awareness can also teach us how to tune out disturbing stimulations by means of cultivated skills in redirecting control of conscious attention in one's own experience, as disciplines of mindfulness have clearly shown.

Our culture's general indifference to this cultivated form of somatic self-consciousness is also expressed in philosophy's continued disregard of its importance, even in philosophers who champion the body's essential role in experience and cognition. This book tries to trace and explain this omission in twentieth-century somatic philosophy and to make a case for the philosophical appreciation and cultivation of this neglected type of somatic self-awareness or reflection, whose value is contrastingly advocated by a wide variety of somatic theorists, educators, and practitioners outside the institutional framework of philosophy.

Though I write this book as an academic philosopher, I should confess from the outset that my perspective on body consciousness has been deeply influenced by my practical experience of various somaesthetic disciplines. Most instructive has been my training and professional experience as a certified practitioner of the Feldenkrais Method, a form of somatic education for improved self-awareness and self-use that has inspiringly successful and wide-ranging therapeutic applications, but also an uncompromising integrity whose refusal of commercialized simplification has denied it the popularity and market share it deserves. I also acknowledge my debt to other disciplines that promote heightened somatic consciousness and body-mind attunement: from yoga and t'ai chi ch'uan to *zazen* and Alexander Technique.

While providing a critical study of contemporary philosophy's most influential arguments against the heightened consciousness of somatic reflection, this book also makes a case for somaesthetics as a general framework in which the cultivation of such consciousness (as well as other forms of somatic training) can best be understood and pursued. This project involves a phenomenological study of body consciousness that probes the different kinds, levels, and values of somatic self-awareness – from essentially unconscious motor intentionality and unfocused automatic reactions involving unreflective somatic habits or body schemata to explicitly thematized body images, somatic self-awareness, and reflective somatic introspection. It also means exploring the ways these different modes of somatic consciousness can be related and collaboratively deployed to improve our somaesthetic knowledge, performance, and enjoyment. A key argument in the condemnation of cultivating somatic self-consciousness is that any sustained focus on bodily feelings is both unnecessary and counterproductive for effective thought and action. Attentive self-consciousness of bodily feelings (or, for that matter, of bodily form or movement) is thus rejected as a distracting, corruptive obstacle to our essential cognitive, practical, and ethical concerns, a retreat into ineffectual self-absorption. Our attention, it is argued, must instead be directed exclusively outward for our engagement with the external world.

The book's defense of reflective or heightened somatic self-awareness will show, however, that such intensified body consciousness need not disrupt but rather can improve our perception of and engagement with the outside world by improving our use of the self that is the fundamental instrument of all perception and action. Indeed, I contend that *any acutely attentive somatic self-consciousness will always be conscious of more than the body itself.* To focus on feeling one's body is to foreground it against its environmental background, which must be somehow felt in order to constitute that experienced background. One cannot feel oneself sitting or standing without feeling that part of the environment upon which one sits or stands. Nor can one feel oneself breathing without feeling the surrounding air we inhale. Such lessons of somatic self-consciousness eventually point toward the vision of an essentially situated, relational, and symbiotic self rather than the traditional concept of an autonomous self grounded in an individual, monadic, indestructible, and unchanging soul.

III

For treating all these diverse and complex issues, six twentieth-century philosophers are especially important: Maurice Merleau-Ponty, Simone de Beauvoir, Michel Foucault, Ludwig Wittgenstein, and two pragmatist philosophers whose writings also stretch back to the late nineteenth century, William James and John Dewey. These renowned thinkers are exemplary, not only for their influential somatic theorizing but also for the striking way they represent today's most powerful Western philosophical traditions: phenomenology, analytic philosophy, pragmatism, existentialism, hermeneutics, poststructuralism, and feminism.[7] In engaging their theories, this book is thus not simply dealing with past historical products but with perspectives that continue to shape the orientations and command the commentary of today's body philosophers. Each of these master thinkers forms the primary focus of one of the book's six chapters, but their arguments will be interrelated in terms of the following narrative.

The first chapter introduces the field of somaesthetics and the book's major issues through a study of Michel Foucault's distinctive and influential somatic philosophy. Advocating the body as an especially vital site for self-knowledge and self-transformation, Foucault argues that self-fashioning is not only a matter of externally stylizing oneself through one's bodily appearance but of transfiguring one's inner sense of self (and thereby one's attitude, character, or ethos) through transformative experiences. Central to this experiential transformation, according to Foucault, is the experience of bodily pleasures. Because their predictable stereotypes and conventional limits, however, constrain our possibilities of creative self-fulfillment and growth, he explicitly urges the pursuit of unorthodox somatic practices to make the body "infinitely more susceptible to pleasure." Yet, the range of pleasures that Foucault in fact advocates remains paradoxically narrow, essentially confined to the most intense delights of strong drugs and transgressive sex, epitomized by his ardent affirmation of consensual, homosexual sadomasochism. The body, however, enjoys many other pleasures that are less violent and explosive without being so boringly conventional that they blunt self-awareness and self-development. Tranquil practices of meditative awareness in breathing, sitting, and walking can generate subtle streams of deep delight and initiate radical transformations, often burgeoning into experiences of intensely exhilarating, yet quiet, joy.

---

[7] I recognize that my choice of thinkers and movements does not cover the full spectrum of influential twentieth-century somatic philosophy. One major philosophical movement not examined here but often rich in somatic insight is *Philosophische Anthropologie*, represented by Max Scheler, Arnold Gehlen, and Helmut Plessner (with some phases of Ernst Cassirer's work also somewhat linked to this trend). For a contemporary version of philosophical anthropology based on a systematic reconstruction of Helmut Plessner's work (which is enjoying an especially vibrant renaissance in Europe), see the important two-volume study of Hans-Peter Krüger, *Zwischen Lachen und Weinen*: vol. 1, *Das Spektrum menschlicher Phänomene* (Berlin: Akademie, 1999), and vol. 2, *Der dritte Weg Philosophische Anthropologie und die Geschlechterfrage* (Berlin: Akademie, 2001).

Why are such gentler practices and subtler, quieter delights ignored when Foucault's goal is to maximize our capacities for pleasure? More than merely a personal problem of Foucault's tortured psyche, this neglect reflects our culture's general insensitivity to the subtleties of somatic sensibility and reflective body consciousness, a numbness that promotes the quest for sensationalism. And this general cultural deficiency finds salient philosophical expression even in the most progressive twentieth-century thinkers who affirm the body's crucial role. We can better understand Foucault's deafness to subtle somatic pleasures and gentle body disciplines by tracing his impaired body consciousness to a strongly entrenched philosophical tradition that rejects somatic reflection even when celebrating the body.

Chapters 2 and 3 therefore address the philosophies of Maurice Merleau-Ponty and Simone de Beauvoir who form a significant part of the French philosophical background from which Foucault's somatic thinking emerged. Merleau-Ponty is treated first, since Beauvoir's account of our bodily existence explicitly draws on him and since Foucault confessed to have been "fascinated by him."[8] Examining how Merleau-Ponty and Beauvoir affirm the body's intentionality and essential role in our personal development, these chapters also explain the ways they resist, for different reasons, the affirmation of *reflective* body consciousness as a means of enhancing one's powers, emancipatory development, and self-understanding. In showing the limitations of their arguments, I demonstrate how Merleau Ponty's insights about the primacy of unreflective consciousness and Beauvoir's concerns about the objectification and exploitation of female bodies need not be sacrificed by recognizing the value of reflective body consciousness. Though Beauvoir's arguments against somatic self-cultivation (including not only somatic self-consciousness but also the cultivation of external bodily form and performance) are most potently expressed in her feminist classic *The Second Sex*, they also appear in her subsequent book on old age, which merits our attention for its extensive treatment of this important somatic issue that most philosophers have failed to theorize in a systematic way (including the other five past masters discussed here).

The next chapter turns to a key figure in analytic philosophy of mind. Ludwig Wittgenstein is famous for his vigorous arguments against using bodily feelings as philosophical explanations of key mental concepts such

---

[8] See his remark in Claude Mauriac, *Et comme l'espérance est violente* (Paris: Livre de poche, 1986), 492.

as emotion, volition, and our sense of self. A closer reading of his work, however, reveals his recognition of other, nonexplanatory, uses for reflectively attending to somatic feelings. The chapter then shows how Wittgenstein's limited and fragmentary acknowledgments of somatic reflection can be expanded and pragmatically employed in key questions of ethics and aesthetics that he links to the body in brief but cryptic remarks whose meaning can be fruitfully developed in terms of enhanced somatic consciousness. One important issue that this chapter investigates is the problem of ethnic and racial intolerance in terms of its visceral roots, and its need for somaesthetic remedies.

The final two chapters engage the principal pragmatist treatments of body consciousness as exemplified in William James and John Dewey. James, the main target of Wittgenstein's arguments against the philosophical misuse of somatic reflection, persistently argues that bodily feelings are crucial in explaining almost all areas of mental life. He even associates our most basic inner sense of self with bodily feelings in the head that he detects through somatic introspective. Only the will is held to reside "exclusively within the mental world" devoid of an essential somatic component. James, moreover, displays extraordinary mastery in the introspective observation and phenomenological description of bodily feelings alleged to be involved in thought and emotion. However, despite his use and advocacy of self-conscious somatic reflection in his theoretical work, James paradoxically argues against such reflection in the actual practice of living. Urging that effective action instead demands the same sort of uninhibited, unthinking spontaneity advocated by Merleau-Ponty, James further condemns reflective somatic self-consciousness for generating psychological and moral problems of depression. Besides refuting James's arguments, this chapter explains the underlying cultural and personal reasons for his resisting the role of somatic reflection in practical life.

The book concludes with a chapter on John Dewey, showing how he develops the essential somatic orientation of James while removing some of its troubling dualisms and one-sided limitations. After explaining Dewey's improvements to James on such theoretical issues as the body's role in will, emotion, thought, and action, the bulk of the chapter gives special attention to Dewey's vigorous case for self-conscious somatic reflection in the realm of concrete practice. As this advocacy is intimately connected to Dewey's work and friendship with the somatic educator F. M. Alexander, the chapter includes a critical analysis of the impressively original methodology of bodily awareness and self-use now known as the Alexander Technique. The problems with Alexander's approach (such as its excessive cephalic-centrism and rationalistic denigration of sex and passion) will be shown to be reflected in the limitations of Dewey's theorizing of the body, which (like James's) sadly neglects the erotic, whose importance for somatic philosophy is rightly emphasized by Merleau-Ponty, Beauvoir, and, of course, Foucault. Nonetheless, Dewey provides what is probably the most balanced and comprehensive vision among twentieth-century somatic philosophies, because he appreciates the value of reflective somatic consciousness along with the primacy of spontaneous, unreflective bodily perception and performance, while also providing conceptual clues for understanding how the reflective and unreflective can best be combined for improved use of ourselves. Dewey's account of self-consciousness and self-cultivation, moreover, cogently underlines the essentially situated and environmentally constituted and interactive nature of the self.

IV

Dewey died more than fifty years ago (in 1952), long before the new microchip technologies accelerated the successive information revolutions that define today's globalized culture. Is this book – with its focus on the past century's somatic philosophy, with its appreciation of ancient Asian somatic disciplines of heightened consciousness, and with its worries that our powers of attentive somatic awareness are being threatened by the sensationalism and informational overload of the new media age – then simply outdated, a backwardly old-fashioned reflection of philosophy's characteristic conservatism? Though rooted in the past, this study is nonetheless forward-looking in its concern for heightened somatic self-consciousness in our increasingly mediatic lifeworld.

There is no compelling reason to believe that our new technologies will render our bodies obsolete and our somatic consciousness gratuitous. As I argue in *Performing Live*, the more the new communications media strive to free us from the need for physical bodily presence, the more our bodily experience seems to matter. The most advanced technologies of virtual reality are still experienced through the body's perceptual equipment and affective sounding board – our sensory organs, brain, glands, and nervous system. So even the highest flights of technological fantasy (such as William Gibson's vision of the Matrix) portray their fictional heroes as physically drained from their harrowing escapades in cyberspace, since their intensely stressful emotions, though virtually induced, must be somatically grounded to be experienced as strong emotions at all.

The more information and sensory stimulation our new technologies provide us, the greater the need for cultivating a somaesthetic sensitivity to detect and deal with threats of stressful overload. We cannot simply rely on further technological instruments to do our somatic monitoring for us, because we need our own body sensitivity to monitor the performance of those devices whose functioning and fit are always fallible. Patients who use monitoring devices in or on their bodies are therefore urged to be vigilantly attentive to whether these instruments are causing discomfort or showing other signs of malfunction. More generally, any use of new tools and technologies involves new uses (and postures and habits) of the body, which means new possibilities of somatic strains, discomforts, and disabilities resulting from inefficient body use that cultivation of heightened somatic self-consciousness could help us to reveal, remedy, or avoid. We already know how extended computer use has generated a multitude of somatic problems, ranging from eyestrain and back and neck pain to varieties of tendonitis, carpal tunnel syndrome, and other repetitive stress disorders that typically result from bad posture and habits of somatic misuse that could be detected through improved somatic self-awareness and self-monitoring. Better ergonomic design can help to some extent but even such design, which itself depends on enhanced somatic self-consciousness, cannot overcome the abuses of bad postural habits.

We cannot simply trust our habits to correct themselves through unconscious trial and error or through eventual evolutionary adjustments. That attitude of unthinking trust in ourselves and our future, rather than the critical somatic self-consciousness here advocated, is more truly labeled old-fashioned for its expression of a traditional unquestioning faith in divine or natural providence. Unreflective trial and error and evolutionary adjustment not only leave too much to unreliable blind chance but also work far too slow to ensure the individual's well being and to keep up with the rapid pace of new technological inventions, which will require ever new somatic adjustments. Even if a familiar action can be performed more quickly and reliably through unconscious habit than through somatically self-conscious attentiveness, such mindful consciousness is important for learning new skills and necessary for properly identifying, analyzing, and rectifying our problematic bodily habits so as to render them more appropriate to our changing conditions, tools, and tasks and more in harmony with the changing needs and health of our basic bodily instrument. As long as our future involves transformations in bodily use and experience, somatic self-consciousness should play a central role in tracking, guiding, and responding to these changes.

1

Somaesthetics and Care of the Self

The Case of Foucault

I

Among the many reasons that made Michel Foucault a remarkable philosopher was a doubly bold initiative: to renew the ancient idea of philosophy as a special way of life and to insist on its distinctly somatic and aesthetic expression. This double dimension of Foucault's later work (elaborated not only in the three volumes of his *History of Sexuality* and his final courses at the Collège de France but also in a variety of interviews and short articles) is pointedly expressed through his central ideas of the "aesthetics of existence," the stylizing "technologies of the self," and the cultivation of "bodies and pleasures."[1] This chapter examines Foucault as an exemplary but problematic pioneer in a field I call somaesthetics, a discipline that puts the body's experience and artful refashioning back into the heart of philosophy as an art of living. A long dominant Platonist tradition, intensified by recent centuries of Cartesianism and idealism, has blinded us to a crucial fact that was evident to much ancient and non-Western thought: since we live, think, and act through our bodies, their study, care, and improvement should be at the core of philosophy, especially when philosophy is conceived (as it used to be) as a distinctive way of life, a critical, disciplined care of the self that involves self-knowledge and self-cultivation.

Even in today's atmosphere of heightened body consciousness, most theorists have followed Pierre Hadot in treating the philosophical life

---

[1] The quotations are from Michel Foucault, *History of Sexuality*, trans. Robert Hurley, vol. 1 (New York: Vintage, 1980), 157; vol. 2 (New York: Vintage, 1986), 89; and "Technologies of the Self," in *The Essential Works of Michel Foucault, 1954–1984*, ed. Paul Rabinow, trans. Robert Hurley, vol. 1 (New York: New Press, 1997), 223–251.

as a one-sided life of the mind.[2] Hadot, who first revived contemporary interest (including Foucault's) in philosophy as a way of life, defines this life in terms of its programmatic practice of therapeutic disciplines (e.g., "meditations," "therapies of the passions," and "self-mastery"), which he pointedly calls "spiritual exercises" and which he defines in sharp contrast to bodily exercises and needs. Tracing these exercises back to Socratic dialogue and focusing primarily on the "Stoico-Platonic" tradition, Hadot even more tellingly defines their spiritual character and philosophy's essential goal in terms of the *Phaedo,* Plato's most body-despising dialogue. Here Plato portrays philosophy's life as a training in death, through the exercise of "separating the soul as much as possible from the body . . . until it is completely independent."

   Glossing these famous words to express the soul's spiritual striving "to liberate itself" from the body's passions and senses "so as to attain to the autonomy of thought," Hadot sees spiritual exercise as the tool through which "philosophy subjugates the body's will to live to the higher demands of thought," "an attempt to liberate ourselves from a partial, passionate point of view" linked to the senses and the body "so as to rise to the universal, normative viewpoint of thought," to embody our pure essence of reason. Noting that these spiritual exercises to strengthen the soul can be seen as a form of "spiritual gymnastics" analogical to physical exercises to bolster the body, Hadot even recognizes that "the gymnasion, the place where physical exercises were practiced, was the same place where philosophy lessons were given." Yet, he strangely seems unwilling to countenance the idea that both these activities could be fruitfully combined by the ancients in pursuing philosophy as a way of life. Though awed by Hadot's superior scholarship in ancient philosophy, I dare to think this combination can be detected if we look beyond the imposing antisomatic

---

[2] See Pierre Hadot, "Spiritual Exercises," in his *Philosophy as a Way of Life,* ed. Arnold Davidson (Oxford: Blackwell, 1995), 81–125, citations here from 84, 94, 102. Hadot's one-sided emphasis on the mind is clearly echoed in the accounts of philosophical living offered by Stanley Cavell, Martha Nussbaum, and Alexander Nehamas. In *Practicing Philosophy: Pragmatism and the Philosophical Life* (New York: Routledge, 1997), where somaesthetics is introduced to provide a more body-friendly account of philosophical living, I critique Cavell and Nehamas for ignoring the body and defining the philosophical life wholly in terms of words, especially the textual exercises of reading and writing. Martha Nussbaum's study of *The Therapy of Desire* (Princeton, NJ: Princeton University Press, 1994) exhibits the same intellectualist one-sidedness in limiting philosophical life to "the technique" of "rational argument" (5–6, 353–4). She moreover follows Hadot's focus on the Stoics and a one-sided emphasis on the medical-therapeutic model of philosophical life as opposed to the aesthetic model that Foucault, Nehamas, and I advance.

shadow of Platonist idealism and its enormously influential expression in the *Phaedo*. In the *Timaeus*, for instance, Plato urges "an equal and healthy balance between [body and mind]. So anyone [like the philosopher] engaged on mathematics or any other strenuous intellectual pursuit should also exercise his body and take part in physical training."[3]

If we look beyond Platonic sources, we will be reminded that Socrates "took care to exercise his body and kept it in good condition" by regular dance training. "The body," he declared, "is valuable for all human activities, and in all its uses it is very important that it should be as fit as possible. Even in the act of thinking, which is supposed to require least assistance from the body, everyone knows that serious mistakes often happen through physical ill-health." Socrates was not the only ancient philosopher to celebrate physical health and advocate somatic training and refinement. Before him, Cleobulus, a sage "distinguished for strength and beauty, and ... acquainted with Egyptian philosophy," "advised men to practise bodily exercise." Aristippus (hedonistic pupil of Socrates and founder of the Cyrenaic school) claimed "that bodily training contributes to the acquisition of virtue," while Zeno, founder of the Stoics, likewise urged regular bodily exercise, claiming that "proper care of health and one's organs of sense" are "unconditional duties." Though rating mental pleasures above mere bodily ones, Epicurus still affirmed "health of body and tranquillity of mind" as the twin goals of philosophy's quest for "a blessed life."[4]

Diogenes, founder of the Cynics, was still more outspoken in advocating bodily training as a necessary key to developing virtue and the good life: "And he would adduce indisputable evidence to show how easily from gymnastic training we arrive at virtue."[5] Practicing the somatic discipline he preached, he experimented with a variety of body practices to test and toughen himself: from limiting his diet and walking barefoot in the snow, to masturbating in public and accepting the blows of drunken revelers.

Recognition of somatic training as an essential means toward philosophical enlightenment and virtue lies at the heart of Asian practices of hatha yoga, Zen meditation, and t'ai chi ch'uan. As Japanese philosopher Yuasa Yasuo insists, the concept of "personal cultivation," or *shugyō* (an

---

[3] *Timaeus* (88), trans. H. D. P. Lee (London: Penguin, 1965), 116–117.

[4] See Diogenes Laertius, *Lives of Eminent Philosophers*, trans. R. D. Hicks, 2 vols. (Cambridge, MA: Harvard University Press, 1991), vol. 1: 91, 95, 221; vol. 2: 215, 653; cf. 1: 22, 153, 163; and Xenophon, *Conversations of Socrates* (London: Penguin, 1990), 172.

[5] Diogenes Laertius, *Lives of Eminent Philosophers*, 2: 71–73.

A in a "conception of philosophy"
a bold manifesto for all philosophers

obvious analogue of "care of the self"), is presupposed in Eastern thought as "the philosophical foundation" because "true knowledge cannot be obtained simply by means of theoretical thinking, but only through 'bodily recognition or realization' (*tainin* or *taitoku*)."[6] From its very beginnings, East–Asian philosophy has insisted on the bodily dimension of self-knowledge and self-cultivation. When the Confucian *Analects* advocate daily examining one's person in the quest for self-improvement, the word translated as "person" is actually the Chinese word for body (*shen* 身). Arguing that care of the body is the basic task and responsibility without which we cannot successfully perform all our other tasks and duties, Mencius claims, "The functions of the body are the endowment of Heaven. But it is only a Sage who can properly manipulate them."[7] The classic Daoist thinkers Laozi and Zhuangzi similarly urge the special importance of somatic care: "He who loves his body more than dominion over the empire can be given the custody of the empire."[8] "You have only to take care and guard your own body… [and] other things will of themselves grow sturdy;" "the sage is concerned… [with] the means by which to keep the body whole and to care for life"; "being complete in body, he is complete in spirit; and to be complete in spirit is the Way of the sage."[9]

This is not the place to explore these ancient and non-Western philosophies of somatic self-care, nor to explain somatic philosophy's eclipse in modernity and its displaced resurgence in twentieth-century body theorists-cum-therapists like Wilhelm Reich, F. M. Alexander, or Moshe Feldenkrais. However fascinating these topics are, I prefer here to focus on developing a conception of philosophy as a distinctively embodied and somatically self-conscious practice of transformative cultivation of the self by exploring Foucault's rich but controversial contributions to this

---

[6] Yuasa Yasuo, *The Body: Toward an Eastern Mind-Body Theory*, trans. S. Nagatomo and T. P. Kasulis (Albany: SUNY Press, 1987), 25. In Yuasa's later book, *The Body, Self-Cultivation, and Ki-Energy*, trans. S. Nagatomo and M. S. Hull (Albany: SUNY Press, 1993), the term *shugyo* is translated as "self-cultivation." Derived from combining the two Chinese characters that respectively stand for "mastery" and "practice," *shugyō* literally means to "master a practice," but the idea that this requires self-cultivation and self-mastery is implicit and essential.

[7] See *The Analects of Confucius: A Philosophical Translation*, trans. Roger Ames and Henry Rosemont, Jr. (New York: Ballantine, 1999), 72; *Mencius*, trans. W. A. C. H. Dobson (Toronto: University of Toronto Press, 1963), 144; cf. 138.

[8] *Tao Te Ching*, trans. D. C. Lau (London: Penguin, 1963), 17 (XIII).

[9] *The Complete Works of Chuang Tzu*, trans. Burton Watson (New York: Columbia University Press, 1968), 120, 135, 313.

idea.[10] First, I propose somaesthetics as a systematic framework in which his work can be usefully situated. I then consider important objections both to Foucault's specific somaesthetic program and more generally to the idea of somaesthetics as a field of theory and practice: these include charges of narrowness, sensualism, hedonistic triviality, and apolitical narcissism.

II

Somaesthetics can be provisionally defined as the critical meliorative study of one's experience and use of one's body as a locus of sensory-aesthetic appreciation (aesthesis) and creative self-fashioning. It is therefore also devoted to the knowledge, discourses, and disciplines that structure such somatic care or can improve it. If we put aside philosophical prejudice against the body and instead simply recall philosophy's central aims of knowledge, self-knowledge, right action, happiness, and justice, then the philosophical value of somaesthetics should become evident.

1. Since knowledge is largely based on sensory perception whose reliability often proves questionable, philosophy has long been concerned with critique of the senses, exposing their limits and avoiding their misguidance by subjecting them to discursive reason. Western modernity has essentially confined this philosophical project to the analysis and critique of sensory propositional judgments that defines traditional epistemology. The complementary route offered by somaesthetics is to correct the actual performance of our senses by an improved direction of one's body, since the senses belong to and are conditioned by the soma. If the body is our primordial instrument in grasping the world, then we can learn more of the world by improving the conditions and use of this instrument. A person unable to turn her head to look behind her because of a stiff neck (typically caused by bad habits of clenching the upper body, which hinders the shoulders and ribs from swiveling) will see less and

---

[10] This work includes not only Foucault's three volumes of *The History of Sexuality*, but also his numerous short essays, lectures, course summaries, discussions, and interviews dealing with body practices, sexuality, and the ethics and technologies of self, many of which are collected in Sylvère Lotringer, ed., *Foucault Live: Collected Interviews, 1961–1984*, trans. Lysa Hochroth and John Johnston (New York: Semiotext(e),1996), hereafter FL; and in the three volumes of Paul Rabinow, ed., *The Essential Works of Michel Foucault, 1954–1984*, trans. Robert Hurley and others (New York: Free Press, 1997), drawn from the more complete collection, *Dits et Ecrits*, ed., D. Defert and F. Ewald, originally published in four volumes by Gallimard in 1994. I refer below to the more recent Quarto edition (Paris: Gallimard, 2001).

perceive less reliably. If our hand muscles are too tightly contracted, we are less able to make fine perceptual discriminations of the qualities of soft or subtle surfaces that we touch. As Socrates recognized that physical ill health (through consequent organ malfunctioning or mental fatigue) could cause error, so disciplines like the Alexander Technique and the Feldenkrais Method (and older Asian practices of hatha yoga and Zen meditation) seek to improve the acuity, health, and control of our senses by cultivating heightened attention and mastery of their somatic functioning, while also freeing us from the distorting grip of faulty bodily habits that impair sensory performance.

2. If self-knowledge is a central aim of philosophy, then knowledge of one's bodily dimension must not be ignored. Recognizing the body's complex ontological structure as both material object in the world and intentional subjectivity directed toward the world, somaesthetics is concerned not only with the body's external form or representation but also with its lived experience; somaesthetics works toward improved awareness of our feelings, thus providing greater insight into both our passing moods and lasting attitudes. It can therefore reveal and improve somatic malfunctions that normally go undetected even though they impair our well-being and performance. Consider two examples. We rarely notice our breathing, but its rhythm and depth provide rapid, reliable evidence of our emotional state. Consciousness of breathing can therefore make us aware that we are angry or anxious when we might otherwise remain unaware of these feelings and thus vulnerable to their misdirection. Similarly, an unnecessary chronic muscular contraction that not only constrains movement but also can result in tension or even pain may nonetheless go unnoticed because it has become habitual. As unnoticed this chronic contraction cannot be relieved, nor can its resultant disability and discomfort. Yet increased somaesthetic awareness of our muscle tonus can reveal such unconscious habits of chronic contraction that unknowingly cause discomfort, and once such somatic malfunctioning is brought to clear attention, there is a chance to modify it and avoid its unhealthy consequences.

3. A third central aim of philosophy is right action, for which we need knowledge and self-knowledge but also effective will. Because action is only achieved through the body, our power of volition – the ability to act as we will to act – depends on somatic efficacy. Knowing and desiring the right action will not avail if we cannot will our bodies to perform it; and our surprising inability to perform the most simple bodily tasks is matched only by our astounding blindness to this inability, these failures resulting from inadequate somaesthetic awareness and control.

Consider the struggling golfer who tries to keep her head down and her eyes on the ball and who is completely convinced that she is doing so, even though she miserably fails to. Her conscious will is unsuccessful because deeply ingrained somatic habits override it, and she does not even notice this failure because her habitual sense perception is so inadequate and distorted that it feels as if the action intended is indeed performed as willed. This golfer lifts her head against her will. But no one is forcing her to lift it, nor is there any wired-in instinct that makes her lift it. So her head lifting is not involuntary in these senses; yet, it is not what she consciously wills. Her free will is thus blocked by the oppressive habits of misuse and misperception of her body. In too much of our action, we are like the "head-lifting" golfer whose will, however strong, remains impotent by lacking the somatic sensibility to make it effective. Such misperception and weakening of the will stunts virtue. Advanced today by body therapists outside the bounds of legitimized philosophy, this line of argument has ancient philosophical credentials. Diogenes the Cynic was not alone in employing it to advocate rigorous body training as "that whereby, with constant exercise, perceptions are formed such as secure freedom of movement for virtuous deeds."[11]

4. Pursuit of virtue and self-mastery is traditionally integrated into ethics' quest for better living. If philosophy is concerned with the pursuit of happiness, then somaesthetics' concern with the body as the locus and medium of our pleasures clearly deserves more philosophical attention. Even the joys and stimulations of so-called pure thought are (for us embodied humans) influenced by somatic conditioning and require muscular contraction; they can therefore be intensified or more acutely savored through improved somatic awareness and discipline. Even ascetics who castigate the flesh to seek their higher happiness still must make their bodies crucial to their pursuit. Recent philosophy has strangely devoted so much inquiry to the ontology and epistemology of pain while so little to its psychosomatic mastery or transformation into pleasure.

5. Beyond these four important but much neglected points, Foucault's seminal vision of the body as a docile, malleable site for inscribing social power reveals the crucial role the soma can play in political philosophy and the question of justice. It offers a way of understanding how complex hierarchies of power can be widely exercised and reproduced without any need to make them explicit in laws or to enforce them officially; they are implicitly observed and enforced simply through our bodily habits,

---

[11] Diogenes Laertius, *Lives of Eminent Philosophers*, 2:71; cf. 1:221; 2:119 for Aristippus and Zeno.

including habits of feeling that have bodily roots. Entire ideologies of domination can thus be covertly materialized and preserved by encoding them in somatic social norms that, as bodily habits, are typically taken for granted and so escape critical consciousness. The norms that women of a given culture should speak softly, eat daintily, sit with closed legs, assume the passive role in copulation, walk with bowed heads and lowered eyes, are embodied norms that both reflect and reinforce such gender oppression. Domination of this sort is especially hard to challenge because our bodies have so deeply absorbed it that they themselves revolt against the challenge – as when a young secretary involuntarily blushes, trembles, flinches, or even cries when trying to raise a voice of protest toward someone she has been somatically trained to respect. Any successful challenge of oppression should thus involve somaesthetic diagnosis of the bodily habits and feelings that express the domination as well as the subtle institutional rules and methods of inculcating them, so that they, along with the oppressive social conditions that generate them, can be overcome.

However, just as oppressive power relations are encoded and sustained in our bodies, so they can be challenged by alternative somatic practices. Fruitfully embraced by recent feminist and queer body theorists, this Foucauldian message has long been part of the psychosomatic program of thinkers like Reich and Feldenkrais. Affirming deep reciprocal influences between somatic and psychological development, such theorists explain somatic malfunctioning as both a product and reinforcing cause of personality problems, which themselves typically require re-educating the body for their proper remedy. Similar claims are made by yogis and Zen masters but also by bodybuilders and martial arts practitioners. In these diverse disciplines, somatic training forms the heart of philosophy's care of the self, a prerequisite to mental well-being and psychological self-mastery.

The multifaceted dimensions and somatic nexus of these philosophical concerns led me to propose somaesthetics as an interdisciplinary field of study. For despite today's palpable increase of theorizing concerning the body, it tends to lack two important features. First, a structuring overview or architectonic to integrate its very different, seemingly incommensurable discourses into a more productively systematic field, some comprehensive framework that could fruitfully link the discourse of biopolitics with therapies of bioenergetics or connect the ontology of supervenience with the bodybuilding methods of supersets. The second thing lacking in most current philosophical body theory is a clear pragmatic orientation – something that the individual can directly translate into a discipline of

are the simple moments at... WIP SG MUCH GIVEN To FOUCAULT? IS THAT IFE IS THE

improved somatic practice. Inspired by Foucault's embodied vision of care for the self, somaesthetics seeks to remedy both these deficiencies.

ONLY MODERN (1960 - 1990) PHILOSOPHER TO GET WITH IT? ✱ III GIVES SO MUCH To FOUCAULT

1. Somaesthetics, as I conceive it, has three fundamental branches, all powerfully present in Foucault. The first, *analytic somaesthetics*, is an essentially descriptive and theoretical enterprise devoted to explaining the nature of our bodily perceptions and practices and their function in our knowledge and construction of the world. Besides the traditional topics in philosophy of mind, ontology, and epistemology that relate to the mind-body issue and the role of somatic factors in consciousness and action, analytic somaesthetics also includes the sort of genealogical, sociological, and cultural analyses that Foucault so powerfully introduced into contemporary philosophy and that has helped shape the somatic theory of Pierre Bourdieu and feminist theorists such as Judith Butler and Susan Bordo. Such studies show how the body is both shaped by power and employed as an instrument to maintain it, how bodily norms of health, skill, and beauty, and even our categories of sex and gender, are constructed to reflect and sustain social forces.[12] Foucault's approach to these somatic issues was typically *genealogical*, portraying the historical emergence of various body doctrines, norms, and practices. This descriptive approach could be extended by a comparative analysis that contrasts the body views and practices of two or more synchronic cultures or even an analysis that focuses on the somatic complexity of a single culture with its variety of subcultures and classes. But the value of such historico-cultural studies does not preclude a place for more general analyses of embodiment, whether ontologically or phenomenologically oriented or from perspectives involving the biological and cognitive sciences.[13]

2. In contrast to analytic somaesthetics whose logic (whether genealogical or ontological) is descriptive, *pragmatic somaesthetics* has a distinctly

---

[12] Among the wealth of excellent research in this area, I should at least note two pioneer works that are similarly titled but very different in content: sociologist Bryan Turner's *The Body and Society: Explorations in Social Theory* (Oxford: Blackwell, 1984) and historian Peter Brown's, *The Body and Society: Men, Women, and Sexual Renunciation in Early Christianity* (New York: Columbia University Press, 1988).

[13] There is an encouraging convergence of such orientations particularly in recent research relating to embodied cognition, as exemplified in the work of Francisco Varela, Evan Thompson, Eleanor Rosch, George Lakoff, Mark Johnson, Antonio Damasio, Brian O'Shaughnessy, Shaun Gallagher, John Campbell, Alva Noë, and others.

III should have been started on p 22

BUT THIS IS DANGEROUS!

normative, prescriptive character by proposing specific methods of somatic improvement and engaging in their comparative critique. Since the viability of any proposed method will depend on certain facts about the body (whether ontological, physiological, or social), this pragmatic dimension will always presuppose the analytic dimension, though transcending it not only by evaluation but also by meliorative efforts to change certain facts by remaking the body and society. Over the course of history, a vast variety of pragmatic methods have been designed to improve our experience and use of our bodies: various diets, forms of grooming and decoration (including body painting, piercing, and scarification as well as more familiar modes of cosmetics, jewelry, and clothing fashions), dance, yoga, massage, aerobics, bodybuilding, calisthenics, martial and erotic arts, and modern psychosomatic disciplines like Alexander Technique and Feldenkrais Method.

These different methodologies of practices can be classified in different ways. We can distinguish between practices that are holistic or more atomistic. While the latter focus on individual body parts or surfaces – styling the hair, painting the nails, tanning the skin, shortening the nose or enlarging the breast through surgery – the former practices are emphatically oriented toward the whole body, indeed the entire person, as an integrated whole. Hatha yoga, t'ai chi ch'uan, and Feldenkrais Method, for example, comprise systems of integrated somatic postures and movements to develop the harmonious functioning and energy of the body as a unified whole. Penetrating beneath skin surfaces and muscle fiber to realign our bones and better organize the neural pathways through which we move, feel, and think, these practices insist that improved somatic harmony is both a contributory instrument and a beneficial by-product of heightened mental awareness and psychic balance. Such disciplines refuse to divide body from mind in seeking the enlightened betterment of the body-mind of the whole person.

Somatic practices can also be classified in terms of being directed primarily at the individual practitioner herself or instead primarily at others. A massage therapist or a surgeon standardly works on others but in doing t'ai chi ch'uan or bodybuilding, one is working more on one's own body. The distinction between self-directed and other-directed somatic practices cannot be rigidly exclusive because many practices are both. Applying cosmetic makeup is frequently done to oneself and to others; and erotic arts display a simultaneous interest in both one's own experiential pleasures and one's partners' by maneuvering the bodies of both self and other. Moreover, just as self-directed disciplines (like dieting or bodybuilding) often seem motivated by a desire to please others, so other-directed practices like massage may have their own self-oriented pleasures.

Despite these complexities (which stem in part from the deep inter-dependence of self and other), the distinction between self-directed and other-directed body disciplines is useful for resisting the common pre-sumption that to focus on the body implies a retreat from the social. My work as a Feldenkrais practitioner has taught me how important it is to pay careful attention to one's own somatic state in order to pay proper attention to one's client. When I give a Feldenkrais lesson of Functional Integration, I have to be aware of my own body positioning and breath-ing, the tension in my hands and other body parts, and the quality of contact my feet have with the floor in order to be in the best condition to gauge correctly the client's body tension and ease of movement.[14] I need to make myself somatically comfortable so as not to be distracted by my own body tensions and in order to communicate the right message to the client. Otherwise, I will be passing my feelings of somatic tension and unease to the client when I touch him. And because one often fails to realize when and why one is in a mild state of somatic discomfort, part of the Feldenkrais training is devoted to teaching one how to discern such states and distinguish their causes.

Clearer awareness of one's somatic reactions can also improve one's behavior toward others in much wider social and political contexts. Much ethnic and racial hostility is not the product of logical thought but of deep prejudices that are somatically expressed or embodied in vague but disagreeable feelings that typically lie beneath the level of explicit consciousness. Such prejudices and feelings thus resist correction by mere discursive arguments for tolerance, which can be accepted on the rational level without changing the visceral grip of the prejudice. We often deny

[14] Feldenkrais Method deploys an educational rather than pathological model. Practitioners thus regard the people we treat as "students" rather than "patients," and we speak of our work as giving "lessons" rather than "therapy sessions." Functional Integration is only one of the two central modes of the Method, the other being Awareness Through Movement. The latter is best described in Feldenkrais's introductory text, *Awareness Through Movement* (New York: Harper and Row, 1972). A very detailed but difficult account of Functional Integration is provided in Yochanan Rywerant, *The Feldenkrais Method: Teaching by Handling* (New York: Harper and Row, 1983). For a comparative philosophical analysis of the Feldenkrais Method, the Alexander Technique, and bioenergetics, see chapter 8 of my *Performing Live* (Ithaca, NY: Cornell University Press, 2000).

that we have such prejudices because we do not realize that we feel them, and the first step to controlling or expunging them is to develop the somatic awareness to recognize them in ourselves.[15]

Somatic disciplines can further be classified in terms of whether their major orientation is toward external appearance or inner experience. Representational somaesthetics (such as cosmetics) is concerned more with the body's exterior or surface forms, while experiential disciplines (such as yoga) aim more at making us "feel better" in both senses of that ambiguous phrase (which reflects the productive ambiguity of the aesthetic): to make the quality of our somatic experience more satisfyingly rich but also to make it more acutely perceptive. Cosmetic practices (from hairstyling to plastic surgery) exemplify the representational side of somaesthetics, while practices like Feldenkrais' "Awareness Through Movement" or mindfulness meditation are paradigmatic of the experiential mode.

The distinction between representational and experiential somaesthetics is one of dominant tendency rather than a rigid dichotomy. Most somatic practices have both representational and experiential dimensions (and rewards), because there is a basic complementarity of representation and experience, outer and inner. How we look influences how we feel, and vice versa. Practices like dieting or bodybuilding that are initially pursued for representational ends often produce inner feelings that are then sought for their own experiential sake. The dieter becomes an anorexic craving the inner feel of hunger; the bodybuilder becomes addicted to the experiential surge of "the pump." Moreover, somatic methods aimed at inner experience often employ representational means as cues to effect the body posture necessary for inducing the desired experience, whether by consulting one's image in a mirror, focusing one's gaze on a body part like the tip of the nose or the navel, or simply visualizing a body form in one's imagination. Conversely, representational practices such as bodybuilding use acute awareness of experiential clues (e.g., of optimal fatigue, body alignment, and full muscle extension) to serve its sculptural ends of external form, helping to distinguish, for example, the kind of pain that builds muscle from the pain that indicates injury.

Nonetheless, the representational/experiential distinction remains useful, particularly for refuting certain arguments that would condemn

---

[15] I elaborate this argument more fully in Chapter 4 of this book, which treats Wittgenstein's somatic philosophy.

somaesthetics as intrinsically superficial and devoid of the spiritual. Horkheimer and Adorno's famous critique of somatic cultivation provides a good example of such arguments. Any attempt "to bring about a renaissance of the body" must fail, they claim, because it implicitly reinforces our culture's "distinction . . . between the body and the spirit." As an object of care, the body will be representationally exteriorized as a mere physical thing ("the dead thing, the '*corpus*'") in contrast to the inner living spirit.[16] Attention to the body is thus always *alienated* attention to an external representation outside one's spiritual self. Moreover, as external representation, it is inescapably dominated and deployed by society's corrupt masters of the image – advertising and propaganda. "The idolizing of the vital phenomena from the 'blond beast' to the South Sea islanders inevitably leads to the 'sarong film' and the advertising posters for vitamin pills and skin creams which simply stand for the immanent aim of publicity: the new, great, beautiful, and noble type of man – the Führer and his storm troopers" (DoE, 233–234).

Enthusiasts of bodily beauty and bodily training are not merely superficial; they are more sinisterly linked to fascist exterminators, who treat the human body as a mere "physical substance" (DoE, 234), a malleable mechanical tool whose parts must be shaped to make it more effectively serve whatever power controls it. By such Nazi logic, if bodies are no longer in good repair, they should be melted down into soap or converted into some other useful thing like a lampshade.

> Those who extolled the body above all else, the gymnasts and scouts, always had the closest affinity with killing. . . . They see the body as a moving mechanism, with joints as its components and flesh to cushion the skeleton. They use the body and its parts as though they were already separated from it. . . . They measure others, without realizing it, with the gaze of a coffin maker [and so call them] tall, short, fat or heavy. . . . Language keeps pace with them. It has transformed a walk into motion and a meal into calories (DoE, 235).

Formulated more than fifty years ago, Horkheimer and Adorno's critique remains a powerful summary of today's major indictments against aestheticizing the body. By promoting seductive images of bodily beauty and excellence, somatic aesthetics stands accused as a tool of capitalist advertising and political repression. It alienates, reifies, and fragments the body, treating it as an external means and mechanism that is anatomized

---

[16] See Max Horkheimer and Theodor Adorno, *Dialectic of Enlightenment*, trans. John Cumming (New York: Continuum, 1986), 232, 233, hereafter DoE.

into separate areas of intensive labor for ostentatious measurable results and the sale of countless commodities marketed to achieve them. Hence, we find our preoccupation with body measurements and with special-ized "fitness" classes devoted to "abs," thighs, butts, and so forth; hence the billion-dollar cosmetics industry, with its specialized products for dif-ferent body parts. A somatic aesthetics, the argument continues, must therefore undermine individuality and freedom by urging conformity to standardized bodily measures and models as optimally instrumental or attractive. These models, moreover, reflect and reinforce oppressive social hierarchies (as, for example, the North American ideal of tall, lean, blond, blue-eyed bodies obviously serves the privilege of its dominant eth-nic groups).

Potent as such indictments may be, they all depend on construing somaesthetics as a theory that reduces the body to an external object – a mechanical instrument of atomized parts, measurable surfaces, and standardized norms of beauty. They ignore the body's subject-role as the living locus of beautiful, felt experience. But somaesthetics, in its *experien-tial* dimension, clearly refuses to exteriorize the body as an alienated thing distinct from the active spirit of human experience. Nor does it tend to impose a fixed set of standardized norms of external measurement (e.g., optimal pulse) to assess good somaesthetic experience.[17]

The blindness of culture critics to the somatics of experience is under-standable and still widespread. For the somaesthetics of representation remains far more salient and dominant in our culture, a culture largely built on the division of body from spirit and economically driven by the capitalism of conspicuous consumption that is fueled by the marketing of body images. But precisely for this reason, the field of somaesthetics, with its essential experiential dimension, needs more careful, reconstructive attention from philosophers.

The representational/experiential distinction is thus useful in defend-ing somaesthetics from charges that neglect its interior, experienced depth. However, just as this distinction should not be understood as a rigidly exclusive dichotomy, neither is it exhaustive. A third category of *performative* somaesthetics can be introduced for disciplines devoted pri-marily to bodily strength, skill, or health (such as martial arts, athletics,

---

[17] This is not to say that experiential somaesthetics can present no norms or ideals. The famed "runner's high," bodybuilder's "pump," and lover's orgasm might be seen as stan-dards of experiential success; and, if misconstrued as the sole measure of experiential value for their relevant practices, they can also wield an oppressive power that somaes-thetic critique needs to challenge.

and aerobics or calisthenics). To the extent that such performance-oriented disciplines aim either at external exhibition or at enhancing one's inner feelings of power, skill, and health, we might assimilate them into either the dominantly representational or experiential mode.

3. No matter how we classify the different methodologies of pragmatic somaesthetics, they need to be distinguished from their actual practice. I call this third branch *practical* somaesthetics. It is not a matter of producing texts, not even texts that offer pragmatic methods of somatic care; it is instead about actually pursuing such care through intelligently disciplined practice aimed at somatic self-improvement (whether in representational, experiential, or performative modes). Concerned not with saying but with *doing*, this practical dimension is the most neglected by academic body philosophers, whose commitment to the discursive *logos* typically ends in textualizing the body. For practical somaesthetics, the less said the better, *if* this means the more work actually done. But because, in philosophy, what goes without saying typically goes without doing, the concrete activity of somatic training must be named as the crucial practical dimension of somaesthetics, conceived as a comprehensive philosophical discipline concerned with self-knowledge and self-care.[18]

Foucault is exemplary for working in all three dimensions of somaesthetics. The analytic genealogist, who showed how "docile bodies" were systematically yet subtly, secretly shaped by seemingly innocent body disciplines and regimes of biopower so as to advance oppressive sociopolitical agendas and institutions, emerges also as the pragmatic methodologist proposing alternative body practices to overcome the repressive ideologies covertly entrenched in our docile bodies. Foremost among these alternatives were practices of consensual homosexual sadomasochism (S/M), whose experiences, he argued, challenged not only the hierarchy of the head but also the privileging of genital sexuality, which in

---

[18] For further elaboration of somaesthetics, see my *Performing Live*, ch. 7–8, and "Thinking Through the Body, Educating for the Humanities: A Plea for Somaesthetics," *Journal of Aesthetic Education*, 40, no. 1 (2006): 1–21. For critical discussions and interpretive applications of somaesthetics, see the essays of Martin Jay, Gustavo Guerra, Kathleen Higgins, Casey Haskins, and my response in *Journal of Aesthetic Education* 36, no. 4 (2002): 55–115. See also the articles by Thomas Leddy, Antonia Soulez, and Paul C. Taylor, and my response in *Journal of Speculative Philosophy*, 16, no. 1 (2002): 1–38; Gernot Böhme, "Somästhetik – sanft oder mit Gewalt?" *Deutsche Zeitschrift für Philosophie*, 50 (2002): 797–800; J. J. Abrams, "Pragmatism, Artificial Intelligence, and Posthuman Bioethics: Shusterman, Rorty, Foucault," *Human Studies*, 27 (2004): 241–258; and Eric Mullis, "Performative Somaesthetics," *Journal of Aesthetic Education*, 40, no.4 (2006): 104–117.

turn privileges heterosexuality. Foucault also repeatedly advocated strong "drugs, which can produce very intense pleasure," insisting that they "must become a part of our culture" (FL, 384; cf. 378). And boldly practicing what he preached, Foucault tested his chosen methods through practical somasthetics by experimenting on his own flesh and with other live bodies.

Any criticism of these methods should not ignore the particular value of drugs and S/M for certain projects of self-care with which Foucault was personally most concerned: projects of radical innovation, gay liberation, and his own extremely problematic quest for pleasure. However, their apparent indispensability for Foucault neither entails the exemplary value of these methods for others nor precludes their having noxious effects if widely practiced in society. The proverb "different strokes for different folks" affirms a vernacular wisdom appropriate for more than S/M disciples. To the extent that each particular self is the unique product of countless contingencies and different contextual factors, we should expect and respect a certain diversity of somaesthetic methods and goals for self-cultivation. But since our embodied selves share significant commonalities of biological makeup and societal conditioning, there should be grounds for some generalizations about the values and risks of different somatic methods. How could philosophy or science (or even practical life) be possible without such generalization?

IV

Concentrating on the methods and aims of Foucault's pragmatic somaesthetics, this chapter cannot give adequate attention either to his fascinating genealogical studies in analytic somaesthetics or to the enticingly controversial details of his actual bodily practices. Our critical study of Foucault's pragmatic program will go, however, beyond the particular problems of his specific recommended methods, extending to broader issues concerning his aims of pleasure and aesthetic self-fashioning and leading to even more general worries about the value of somaesthetics as an interpretation of philosophical self-care. The arguments of this chapter could be gravely misunderstood if three important points are not kept clearly in mind.

First, critique of a particular program or method of pragmatic somaesthetics does not imply a refutation or rejection of the validity and value of this field per se, which indeed is constituted as a complex, nuanced field of comparative critique of competing methods and goals. Conversely, to affirm the value of pragmatic somaesthetics is not to advocate that all the diverse methods that this field covers are in fact valuable and should be adopted for practice. Indeed, since some methods are clearly incompatible with each other, we could not consistently endorse all of them. Such complexity, which is shared by philosophy itself, in no way involves a vitiating contradiction. We can certainly affirm the value of philosophy without affirming the truth and value of all of its theories, just as the condemnatory critique of a particular theory or group of theories in philosophy does not entail a rejection of philosophy per se, but rather constitutes an affirmation of philosophy as critique.

Second, the principal strategy of our study is an immanent critique of Foucault's pragmatic somaesthetics, not a simple repudiation of Foucault's general somaesthetic program because of mere distaste for his basic aims and the desire to advocate in their place radically different somatic and cultural values. Rather than moralizing about the problems of violent drugs and sadomasochistic sex (whose somatic, ethical, and social dangers I do not deny), our key arguments instead show how Foucault's recommended methods stand in concealed but fundamental conflict with his professed aims (such as the multiplication of somatic pleasures and forms of self-fashioning) and thus tend to undermine a fuller realization of these aims.

Third, our purpose is not to discredit Foucault's theories through ad hominem attacks that demonize his aims, methods, and personal practices as *peculiarly* perverse. Instead our arguments will suggest how Foucault's somaesthetic program, though transgressively unconventional, is nonetheless representative of distinctive trends in contemporary culture's approach to somatic experience that tend toward technologies of radicalization and violent sensationalism. Before criticizing the one-sided celebration of these tendencies in Foucault's pragmatic somaesthetics, we should underline the exemplary value of Foucault's other contributions to somaesthetics (such as his seminal theories of biopower, gender construction, and somatically based social domination). This is especially important because there is a regrettable tendency in recent Anglo-American discourse to scandalize and thus neutralize the power of Foucault's ideas by linking them to his early death from AIDS in 1984, as if this death represented a performative refutation of all his somatically related theories so that there should be no need for serious critical engagement with them. Such attitudes form part of a more general strategy to demonize yet trivialize a diversity of late-twentieth-century French theorists who are falsely lumped together under the rubric of "postmodernism" (even when those theorists resist association with that concept).

From such a lamentably Francophobic bias, Foucault's advocacy of drugs and S/M would be ridiculed and rejected as simply signifying a nihilistic French sophisticate's jaded taste for narcotic, sexual perversion. We must, however, emphasize that Foucault's declared aim is quite the contrary: to break our obsession with sex as the key to all pleasure, to liberate us from our culture's repressive fetishism of sex, which blinds us from realizing other somatic pleasures that could render life more beautiful and satisfying. Rather than fanatically focusing on the pleasures of sex and the mystery of its true nature (which unhappily brands socially deviant sexual expressions as abjectly unnatural), we need to advocate more generally "the reality of the body and the intensity of its pleasures."[19] "We should be striving,", Foucault repeatedly insists, "toward a desexualization, to a general economy of pleasure that would not be sexually normed." Condemning what he called "the monarchy of sex," Foucault advocates "fabricating other forms of pleasure" through "polymorphic relationships with things, people, and bodies" for which the traditional "'sex' grid is a veritable prison."[20] Foucault explicitly recommends homosexual S/M *not* for its sexual kick but for its creative "desexualization of pleasure" by "inventing new possibilities of pleasure with strange parts of [the] body – through the eroticization of the body." S/M, he elaborates, is

a creative enterprise, which has as one of its main features what I call the desexualization of pleasure. The idea that bodily pleasure should always come from sexual pleasure [which] is the root of *all* our possible pleasure. I think *that's* something quite wrong. These practices are insisting that we can produce pleasures with very odd things, very strange parts of our bodies, in very unusual situations, and so on. ("Sex, Power, and Politics of Identity," FL, 384)

How, one may wonder, can the body and its pleasures be simultaneously desexualized and eroticized? The paradox is muted by recalling that the term for sex in French also denotes the genitals, so desexualizing somatic pleasure can simply mean undermining the primacy of genital gratification by eroticizing other body parts. Eros remains fully sexual but no longer focused on *le sexe*. This displacing of "genital-centrism" is

[19] Michel Foucault, "Introduction," in *Herculine Barbin: Being the Recently Discovered Memoirs of a Nineteenth Century Hermaphrodite*, trans. Richard McDougall (New York: Pantheon, 1980), vii.
[20] Michel Foucault, "Power Affects the Body" and "The End of the Monarchy of Sex" in FL, 212, 214, 218–219.

dr. home titles no for this move

clearly one of Foucault's major aims, a point where he compellingly critiques both de Sade and Wilhelm Reich. Can bodily erotics, however, also designate something not merely independent from *genital* sex, but altogether free from the grid of sexual desire, something to be understood and cultivated "under a general economy of pleasure"? This more radical form of desexualized eroticization would more fully serve Foucault's goal to make the body "infinitely more susceptible to pleasure," by developing its capacities for varieties of somatic pleasure that transcend the sexual.[21]

Despite the possible creative import of its transgressions, S/M remains dominated by sex and hence overly confined in its palette of pleasures. Foucault's own advocatory accounts betray these limits. In "Sexual Choice, Sexual Act," gay S/M is praised because "all the energy and imagination, which in the heterosexual relationship were channeled into courtship, now become devoted to *intensifying* the act of sex itself. A whole new art of sexual practice develops which tries to explore all the internal possibilities of sexual conduct." Likening the gay leather scenes in San Francisco and New York to "laboratories of sexual experimentation," Foucault claims such experimentation is strictly controlled by consensual codes, as in the medieval chivalric courts "where strict rules of proprietary courtship were defined." Experimentation is necessary, explains Foucault, "because the sexual act has become so easy and available . . . that it runs the risk of quickly becoming boring, so that every effort has to be made to innovate and create variations that will enhance the pleasure of the act." "This mixture of rules and openness," Foucault concludes, "has the effect of intensifying sexual relations by introducing a perpetual novelty, a perpetual tension and a perpetual uncertainty which the simple consummation of the act lacks. The idea is also to make use of every part of the body as a sexual instrument" (FL, 330–331).

This is hardly a promising recipe for breaking free of the sexual grid toward a polymorphism of pleasure that Foucault claims to be seeking. All somatic imagination is instead narrowly focused on intensifying "the sexual act" and reducing every segment of the soma to a "sexual instrument." No matter how transgressive and experimental, Foucault's vision of S/M unwittingly reinforces the homogenizing normalization of pleasure as sexual and structured by "the act" (however deviantly consummated). Its very tools and icons of bondage (chains, ropes, whips, dungeons, etc.) ironically convey S/M's captivity to the *sexual* norm of pleasure and its eroticizing affirmation of painful enslavement. The monotony of these

[21] See "Friendship as a Way of Life," FL, 310.

old-fashioned images of discipline and the creative poverty of newer ones like Nazi "boots, caps, and eagles" do not speak well for S/M's imaginative daring, a problem Foucault himself admits with some dismay, for such imaginative weakness betrays its deficiency for creative self-fashioning.[22]

His one-sided advocacy of homosexual S/M, moreover, suggests the severe limits of a narrowly masculinist sexuality focused on violence, as if there could not also be equally creative and pleasurable erotics expressing differently gendered subjectivities and desires and deploying gentler methods of sexual contact.[23] What model of erotic, ethical, and social self-fashioning is promoted by zealous immersion in a sexual theater wholly devoted to celebrating violence, domination, and subjugation as the best source of pleasure? What exemplar of one's relation to others is promoted by S/M's fist-fucking? The polyvalent power of eros is reduced to an erotics of dominational power that seems to leave no place for the somatics of loving tenderness that surely plays (along with more violent movements) a worthy role in erotic culture both East and West.[24]

---

[22] Foucault complains: "The problem raised is why we imagine today to have access to certain erotic phantasms through Nazism. Why these boots, caps, and eagles that are found to be so infatuating, particularly in the United States? ... Is the only vocabulary that we possess to rewrite this great pleasure of the body in explosion this sad tale of a recent political apocalypse? Are we unable to think the intensity of the present except as the end of the world in a concentration camp? You see how poor our treasure of images really is!" ("Sade: Sergeant of Sex," FL, 188–189). Insider studies of S/M, moreover, insist that innovational surprise and daring are narrowly constrained by elaborate codes and conventions that govern the so-called theatrical "scripting" of the encounter and are aimed more at guaranteeing safety and satisfying expectations than at providing the real shock of the new. See, for example, G. W. Levi Kamel, "The Leather Career: On Becoming a Sadomasochist" and "Leathersex: Meaningful Aspects of Gay Sadomasochism," in Thomas S. Weinberg (ed.), *S&M: Studies in Dominance and Submission* (Amherst, NY: Prometheus Books, 1995), 51–60, 231–247.

[23] The implied, universalized masculine subject of Foucault's somatic philosophy is sometimes criticized by feminists for its gender blindness, while his identification of the sexual with violence surely reflects the masculinist erotics of de Sade and Georges Bataille. For Bataille, it is "the feeling of elemental violence which kindles every manifestation of eroticism. In essence, the domain of eroticism is the domain of violence, of violation. ... What does physical eroticism signify if not a violation of the very being of its practitioners? – a violation bordering on death, bordering on murder? ... The whole business of eroticism is to destroy the self-contained character of the participators as they are in their normal lives," with sexual violence serving to break through such subjectivities so as to transform them. The presumption seems to be that self-containment and interpersonal barriers cannot be overcome through other, gentler ways. Georges Bataille, *Eroticism*, trans. Mary Dalwood (London: Penguin, 2001), 16–17.

[24] Foucault makes commendatory references to the ancient Asian *ars erotica* as focused on pleasure in contrast to Western *scientia sexualis* dominated by truth and the medical model. See Michel Foucault, *History of Sexuality*, trans. Robert Hurley, vol. 1 (New York:

Noting these limits in S/M is not to grant exclusive privilege to so-called standard practices of lovemaking – straight or gay; for all such practices share with Foucault's version of S/M precisely the same limiting sexual frame. My principal point here is instead to underline the importance of cultivating somatic pleasures that altogether escape the sexual frame and thus more widely multiply our palette of delight. Such asexual pleasures, which more democratically provide joy also to celibates, include more enjoyable modes of breathing, sitting, lying, stretching, walking, eating, as well as the enjoyment of more specific modes of exercise and disciplines of heightened bodily awareness. These asexual pleasures are not inconsistent with sexual delight. Indeed, through both the variety that such pleasures introduce and the somaesthetic techniques of self-mastery through which they are pursued, they can even intensify the sexual pleasures from which they distinguish themselves.

If confined both to the sexual grid and to a very conventional (albeit transgressive and varied) repertoire of scripted practices, how could homosexual S/M win Foucault's ardent endorsement as the somaesthetic key to creating a radically new (even "unforseeable") way of life and self-stylized ethical subject? First, S/M's distinctively cultural character – with its challenge to the natural conception of sex and its theatrical playing of reversible roles – suggests that our erotic pleasures are socially constructed. Moreover, it inculcates two crucial Foucauldian messages: that our selves are not fixed ontological identities (naturally defined by a physically determined and determinate sex in terms of one's sexual organs) but are instead socially constructed roles that we play with respect to others; and, therefore, that we can to some extent refashion ourselves by deliberately adopting different role-playing performances. But perhaps Foucault's strongest reason for advocating S/M was the lived, intense hedonic power of his actual experience. What does it matter if

Pantheon, 1980), 57–71; and his "On the Genealogy of Ethics: An Overview of Work in Progress" first published in English in Hubert Dreyfus and Paul Rabinow, eds., *Michel Foucault: Beyond Structuralism and Hermeneutics* (Chicago: University of Chicago Press, 1983), but revised by Foucault in a more complete French version published in his *Dits et Écrits*, vol. 2: 1976–1988 (Paris: Gallimard, 2001), 1428–1450. Unfortunately, his brief remarks on these erotic arts (which are extremely remote from gay S/M) suggest that his understanding of them was rather limited, for he even seems to misconstrue the main points of the scholarly source on which he bases his remarks, Robert van Gulik's *Sexual Life in Ancient China: A Preliminary Survey of Chinese Sex and Society from ca. 1500 B.C. till 1644 A.D.* (Leiden: Brill, 1974). I examine the aesthetics of Asian *ars erotica* (and explain Foucault's misinterpretation of them), in "Asian *Ars Erotica* and the Question of Sexual Aesthetics," *Journal of Aesthetics and Art Criticism*, 65, no.1 (2007), 55–68.

the means are conventional or even banal, if the results are so intense and pleasurable?

Here, we reach a second objection to Foucault's pragmatic somaesthetics. By championing only the most intense delights, which he identifies with strong drugs and sex, Foucault once again starkly reduces our range of pleasures, thus confounding his explicit aim of rendering us "infinitely more susceptible to pleasure" through a greater deployment of its multiple somatic modalities. Revealing a basic anhedonia ("pleasure is a very difficult behavior . . . and I always have the feeling that I do not feel the pleasure, the complete total pleasure"), Foucault rejects what he calls "those middle range of pleasures that make up everyday life" (dismissively denoted by the conventional American "club sandwich," "coke," and "ice cream" or even a "glass . . . of good wine"). "A pleasure must be something incredibly intense," he avows, or it is "nothing for me" ("An Ethics of Pleasure," FL, 378). True pleasure is therefore narrowly identified with overpowering limit-experiences and thus "related to death," the ultimate limit-experience, which so fascinated Foucault that he thought long and seriously about suicide (and even, more than once, attempted it).[25] "The kind of pleasure I would consider as *the* real pleasure," Foucault affirms, "would be so deep, so intense, so overwhelming that I couldn't survive it. I would die . . . [and] some drugs are really important for me because they are the mediation to those incredibly intense joys that I am looking for and that I am not able to experience, to afford by myself" (FL, 378).

Because of his avowed "real difficulty in experiencing pleasure," Foucault apparently needs to be overwhelmed by sensorial intensity to enjoy it. We should not dismiss this anhedonia and need for extreme intensity as merely Foucault's personal problem, and he indeed claims "I am not the only one like that" (FL, 378). It instead reflects more general and troubling trends with respect to our culture's somatic consciousness. First is

[25] In his *plaidoyer* for cultivating the pleasure of suicide, Foucault describes it as "a fathomless pleasure whose patient and relentless preparation will enlighten all of your life" (FL, 296). On Foucault's suicide attempts as a student, see Didier Eribon, *Michel Foucault* (Cambridge, MA: Harvard University Press, 1991), 26–27. Foucault's close friend Paul Veyne testifies to Foucault's personal fascination with suicide in his later years, even regarding his AIDS-related death as a form of suicide, though this drastic, speculative conclusion is surely hard to justify. See Paul Veyne, "The Final Foucault and his Ethics," *Critical Inquiry*, 20 (1993): 1–9. If Foucault's advocacy of suicide as pleasure remains rather iconoclastic, his emphasis on the close connection between ecstatic self-transcendence and the passion of bodily death certainly resonates with familiar images of joyous religious martyrdom.

the pervasive devastating dichotomy drawn between the allegedly meaningless bodily pleasures of everyday life (unimaginatively identified with
food and drink) and those truly significant somatic pleasures defined by
their violent intensity and identified with transgressive drugs and sex.[26]
But everyday somatic pleasures can also include breathing, stretching,
and walking; and these can even be developed to produce experiences
of great power and exaltation, as we see in the familiar yoga methods
of *pranayama* and *asana* or in Buddhist disciplines of meditative sitting,
walking, and dancing.[27] Conversely, the experience of strong drugs and
heavy sex can become routinized and meaningless. The psychology of
sensory perception means that intensification of pleasure cannot simply be achieved by intensity of sensation. Sensory appreciation is typically
dulled when blasted with extreme sensations. The most intensely enjoyed
music is not the loudest. A gentle grazing touch can provide more potent
pleasure than a thunderous thrust.

Pleasure has a complicated logic; ascetics know how to get it by rejecting
it. Yogis find its highest intensities not from the sensory explosions of narcotic orgasms but rather from an emptiness that reveals its own empowering intensity and fullness. In proposing an "ethics of pleasure," doesn't
Foucault need a more careful "logic" and "logistic" of its central concept,
a more refined and delicate appreciation of the diversities and subtleties
of pleasure, including its more tender, gentle, and mild varieties? Pierre
Hadot has criticized Foucault for hedonistically misreading the ancients
by confusing the sensual pleasure of *voluptas* with the more spiritual, religious notion of joy (*gaudium*).[28] Helpful as this distinction may be, it
remains too simple. For there is also delight, satisfaction, gratification,
gladness, contentment, pleasantness, amusement, merriment, elation,
bliss, rapture, exultation, exhilaration, enjoyment, diversion, entertainment, titillation, fun, and so forth. Shouldn't we more carefully recognize the many different varieties of experience typically grouped under

[26] Foucault's blind rejection of middle-range pleasures is complemented by a parallel failure
to appreciate that, in contemporary culture as well as in ancient Greece, to make one's
life a work of art does not require a life of radical, transgressive novelty and uniqueness.
For critique of this blindness, which apparently comes from implicitly identifying art with
the intensity, difficulty, and originality of avant-garde masterpieces (and which stands in
sharp contrast to Foucault's acknowledgment of more moderate artful living in ancient
times), see my *Practicing Philosophy*, ch. 1.

[27] For discussion of these Japanese disciplines that are less familiar to us than yoga and *zazen*
(seated meditation), see Yuasa, *The Body, Self-Cultivation, and Ki-Energy*, 11–14, 20–36.

[28] Pierre Hadot, "Reflections on the Idea of the 'Cultivation of the Self'", in *Philosophy as a
Way of Life*, 207.

pleasure so as to give each its due appreciation and more fully derive
from each its proper value? If this seems too tedious a task to pursue in
the spirit of hedonism, we must at least recognize (more than Foucault)
that the intensification of pleasure neither requires a one-sided diet of
sensational limit-experiences nor, in fact, is well served by such a regimen.

If pleasure is so hard for Foucault, both in the sense of difficult to
achieve and as narrowly directed toward the hardest, most violent intensities exemplified by S/M and strong drugs, it is tempting to see these two
forms of hardness as causally connected. Anhedonia may both generate
and result from an ever-escalating demand for stronger sensations. If dissatisfaction with ordinary pleasures spurs the demand for more intense
stimulation, then meeting that demand raises the threshold of what can
be felt as satisfying, thus condemning too much of everyday experience
to joyless tedium. Anhedonia's link to drug abuse (and suicide) is by now
well documented, and the precise neural mechanisms of this causal nexus
are currently being explored.[29]

The persistent demand for extreme intensities threatens not merely to
reduce the range of our felt pleasures but even to dull our affective acuity,
our very capacity to feel our bodies with real clarity, precision, and power.
For Foucault, vivid somatic consciousness does not arise unless the body is
somehow engaged in violent sensations; and without such consciousness
our bodies become the unwitting docile instruments of social oppression.
The extremism of limit-experiences thus becomes necessary for Foucault
not just to feel somatic pleasure but even to produce the only sort of
heightened body consciousness that can be felt and thus deployed to
cultivate and liberate the self. If this apparent necessity reflects the dulling
of Foucault's somatic consciousness through anhedonia and an abusive
overdose of stimulation, then less sensationalist and pleasure-challenged
subjects will find that a lowering of sensorial violence and intensity can
paradoxically lead to more attentive and acute somatic consciousness,
enabling feelings of more rewarding and even more intense pleasure.

This argument for sensorial moderation finds support from a classic principle of psychophysics embodied in the famous Weber-Fechner
law, which formulates a truth we also know from common experience:

[29] See, for example, L. Janiri et al., "Anhedonia and Substance-Related Symptoms in Detoxified Substance-Dependent Subjects: A Correlation Study," *Neuropsychobiology*, 52, no. 1
(2005): 37–44; and, for suicide, K. G. Paplos et al., "Suicide Intention, Depression and
Anhedonia among Suicide Attempters," *Annals of General Hospital Psychiatry*, 2 (2003,
suppl. 1): S10.

a smaller stimulus can be noticed more clearly and easily if the already preexisting stimulation experienced by the stimulated organ is small. Conversely, the threshold for noticing a sensation will be so much the larger, the greater the preexisting stimulation is. The light of a cigarette, for instance, while barely visible from a short distance in blazing sunlight can be seen from afar in the dark of night; sounds of windblown leaves that we hear in the silence of woods at midnight are inaudible in the city's noise of day. A strongly clenched fist will not be as sensitive to fine discriminations of touch and texture as a soft hand free from muscular strain.

Our culture's constant lust for ever greater intensities of somatic stimulation in the quest for happiness is thus a recipe for increasing dissatisfaction and difficulty in achieving pleasure, while our submission to such intensities dulls our somatic perception and consciousness. We cannot delight to the sound of our quietly beating hearts if we are hurtling forward in a noisy jet with loud music blaring in our earphones. Even the appreciation of loud music, an undeniable joy for many (myself included), is dulled by a one-sided diet of deafening volume, which ultimately vitiates the experienced power and meaning of thunderous sound. The value of mind-altering drugs is likewise vitiated by disproportionate use.[30] Our culture's sensationalist extremism both reflects and reinforces a deep somatic discontent that relentlessly drives us, yet is felt only vaguely by our underdeveloped, insufficiently sensitive, and thus understandably unsatisfied body consciousness. Though Foucault's radical somaesthetic tastes will strike many as dreadfully deviant, his anhedonia and extremism clearly express a common trend of late-capitalist Western culture, whose unquestioned economic imperative of ever-increasing growth also promotes an unquestioned demand for constantly greater stimulation, ever more speed and information, ever stronger sensations and louder music. The result is a pathological yet all too common need for hyperstimulation in order to feel that one is really alive, a problem that is expressed not only in substance addiction but also in a host of other increasingly prevalent psychosomatic ills that range from violent actions of self-mortification (such as cutting) to the passive nightly torture of

[30] I should note that my views on somaesthetics have in fact been deployed to recommend using strong mind-altering drugs, though in moderation and in carefully controlled contexts, to promote insights in education. See Ken Tupper, "Entheogens and Education: Exploring the Potential of Psychoactives as Educational Tools," *Journal of Drug Education and Awareness*, 1, no. 2 (2003): 145–161.

insomnia.[31] Foucault's neglect of more tranquil methods of somaesthetic reflection for heightened body consciousness likewise reflects the general failure of twentieth-century philosophy to advocate and cultivate a heightened, explicit, somatic self-consciousness. This tradition of neglect or denial of somaesthetic reflection by even body-friendly philosophers will be traced in this book's subsequent chapters.

V

Our critique of Foucault's pragmatic somaesthetics has so far aimed to redeem its appreciation of somatic pleasure by refining its hedonism to transcend his limiting fixations on sexuality, transgression, and sensational intensity. But is there not a deeper problem in its very concern with pleasure of whatever form? Should a pleasure-respecting pragmatic somaesthetics not be condemned as a trivial narcissistic hedonism in contrast to analytic somaesthetics' noble aim of descriptive truth (whether genealogical, sociological, or ontological)? Moreover, does not such concern with somatic pleasure contradict the very idea of strict discipline or *askesis* that is so central to classical ethical notions of care of the self?[32] Is there not a fundamental opposition between an aesthetics of pleasure and the ascetics of ethical self-cultivation that implies an essential regard for others rather than self-indulgence in gratifying one's pleasures.

Since my aesthetic theory has sometimes been criticized as hedonistic, the critique of pleasure is very important to me, though far too complex to treat adequately here.[33] Let me merely make the following brief points.

---

[31] One young cutter expressed the problem as follows: "How do I know I exist? At least I know I exist when I cut." See J. L. Whitlock et al., "The Virtual Cutting Edge: The Internet and Adolescent Self-Injury," *Developmental Psychology*, 42 (2006), 407–417.

[32] Pierre Hadot levels this critique at Foucault's "aesthetics of existence," along with the related charge that the very idea of *aesthetic* self-fashioning involves an adding of artificiality that was foreign to the classical notion of self-cultivation through *askesis* (which involved reduction to the essentials rather than adding beautifying ornament). See Pierre Hadot, "Reflections on the Idea of Self-Cultivation," in *Philosophy as a Way of Life*, 207–213, and, in the same book, "Spiritual Exercises," especially 100–102. In *Practicing Philosophy*, ch. 1, I defend an aesthetic version of self-cultivation and respond to Hadot's critique of this notion. But I also argue more generally (as I already did in *Pragmatist Aesthetics* [Oxford: Blackwell, 1992] 246–255) that there is no necessary tension between the ascetic and the aesthetic, and that aesthetic self-construction can take the form of an ascetic reduction to bare essentials, as we see in the aesthetics of minimalism, or in the very model of sculptural reduction that Hadot cites from Plotinus to make his case (*Philosophy as a Way of Life*, 100).

[33] For critique of my alleged hedonism, see Rainer Rochlitz, "Les esthétiques hédonistes," *Critique*, 540 (May 1992): 353–373; Alexander Nehamas, "Richard Shusterman on

1. First, even if most pleasures, taken individually, were superficial and meaningless, pleasure itself plays a deeply important role in the direction of life. Philosophers therefore often prefer to define it not in terms of distinctly conscious sensations but in motivational terms. Not all forms of pleasure or enjoyment display a specific conscious quality, but they all have a prima facie motivational import. *Ceteris paribus,* it makes no sense to say that one greatly enjoys doing something but has absolutely no reason for doing it. At the evolutionary and psychological levels, pleasure advances life not only by guiding us to what we biologically need (long before and much more powerfully than deliberative reason can) but also by offering the promise that life is worth living. As Aristotle praises pleasure for strengthening our activity, so Spinoza (far from a radical voluptuary) later defines it as "the transition of man from a less to a greater perfection," "the greater the pleasure whereby we are affected, the greater the perfection to which we pass."[34] Moreover, pleasure's positive emotional surge encouragingly opens us to new experiences and to other people.

2. Partly for this reason, somaesthetics pleasures should not be condemned as necessarily entailing a retreat into selfish privacy. Feeling *bien dans sa peau* can make us more comfortably open in dealing with others; and somaesthetics' representational dimension is centrally concerned with making one's body attractive to others. Though this may turn into the narcissism of pleasing others simply to please one's pride of self (a problem that some see epitomized by the vain posing of the bodybuilder), such distorting temptations of pride are present in even the most antihedonic, body-scorning ethical forms.

3. We must also reject the dogma that the body is irremediably too private, subjective, and individualistic in its pleasures to form the substance

Pleasure and Aesthetic Experience," *Journal of Aesthetics and Art Criticism,* 56 (1998): 49–51; and Wolfgang Welsch, "Rettung durch Halbierung?: Zu Richard Shustermans Rehabilitierung ästhetischer Erfahrung," *Deutsche Zeitschrift für Philosophie,* 47 (1999): 11–26. I reply to their critique in "Interpretation, Pleasure, and Value in Aesthetic Experience," *Journal of Aesthetics and Art Criticism,* 56 (1998): 51–53; and "Provokation und Erinnerung: Zu Freude, Sinn und Wert in ästhetischer Erfahrung," *Deutsche Zeitschrift für Philosophie,* 47 (1999): 127–137. I never claim that pleasure is the only or highest value in art and aesthetic experience. For more on the varieties and values of pleasure but also on other values in aesthetic experience, see my "Entertainment: A Question for Aesthetics," *British Journal of Aesthetics,* 43 (2003): 289–307; and "Aesthetic Experience: From Analysis to Eros, *Journal of Aesthetics and Art Criticism,* 64 (2006), 217–229.

34 See Benedict de Spinoza, *The Ethics,* in *Works of Spinoza,* trans. R. H. M. Elwes (New York: Dover, 1955), 174.

of ethics and politics. We share our bodies and somatic pleasures as much as we share our minds, and they surely appear as public as our thoughts. Pleasure is misconstrued as intrinsically private by being misidentified as merely an inner bodily sensation to which the individual has unique access. Most pleasure or enjoyment does not have the character of a specific, narrowly localized body feeling (unlike a toothache or stubbed toe). The pleasure of playing tennis cannot be identified in one's running feet, beating heart, or sweating racket hand. Somatic enjoyments like tennis cannot be mere sensation for two other reasons. The stronger a sensation the more attention it claims for itself and the more it distracts from concentration on other things. If enjoying tennis were only the having of strong sensations, the more we enjoyed it, the harder it would be to concentrate on the game, but clearly the opposite is true. Second, if pleasure were merely blind sensation, we might in principle enjoy the pleasure of tennis without any connection to the actual or imagined playing of the game.

Such objections indicate a more general point. Pleasure, even when identified with pleasurable feelings, cannot be simply identified with blind sensation because the very enjoyment of sensation depends on the context or activity that shapes its meaning. The glass of (even mediocre) wine that Foucault condemns to everyday banality can be the site of intense pleasure, even spiritual joy, when framed in the proper sacred context. Such examples (just like S/M's hedonic transfiguration of pain) testify to pleasure's semantic and cognitive dimensions that defy its reduction to mere sensationalism. As philosophy has long insisted, we also take pleasure in knowing, and this pleasure inspires us to learn more.

4. Even if most pleasures seem trivial, some experiences of delight are so powerful that they deeply mark us, transforming our desires and thus redirecting our way of life. Deep aesthetic experience and mystical religious experience share this power, and in many cultures they are intimately linked: the poet and prophet likewise inspired and inspiring through exaltedly altered mental states.[35] The overwhelming spirituality of such experience is often expressed and heightened by a deeply somatic deliciousness that Saint Teresa describes as "penetrating to the marrow of the bones," enthralling and transfiguring us.[36] The terms "rapture" and "ecstasy" convey this idea of being seized and transported outside

---

[35] See, for example, the strong parallels traditionally drawn between the experience of *waka* poetry, Nō theatre, and Buddhist *satori*, as summarized in Yuasa, *The Body, Self-Cultivation, and Ki-Energy,* 21–28.

[36] Saint Teresa, *The Interior Castle,* cited in William James, *The Varieties of Religious Experience* (New York: Penguin, 1982), 412.

ourselves by pleasure so intense that it sometimes seems almost painful to endure. This is not the easy pleasure of self-gratification but the terrifying thrill of self-surrender in the quest for self-transformation. Seized by this ravishing delight, some have felt close to dying from its electrifying power (and studies of mystical experience show in fact that heartbeat, breath, and circulation are virtually arrested).[37] Yet these heart-stopping ecstasies are also celebrated for providing somatic empowerment and spiritual redirection. The aim is not sensual delectation per se, but the self-transformation that intense pleasure can induce, as in the Sufi mystic Al-Ghazzali's formula of "transport, ecstasy, and the transformation of the soul."[38] Though typically religious, these climactic experiences of transcendent joy and spiritual transfiguration need not require a conventional theological faith.

The highest forms of pragmatic somaesthetics combine such delights of self-transformational self-surrender with strict disciplines of somatic self-control (of posture, breathing, ritualized movement, etc.). Such disciplines not only prepare and structure ecstatic experience but they also provide a controlled field where the inspiring energy of peak experience can be deployed and preserved in systematic practices that promote the re-achievement of these peaks in healthy contexts. This ensures that soaring self-surrender can fall back on a safety net of disciplined self-mastery in preparation for a further leap. Beneath the breathless rapture of *samadhi* rests the yogi's years of disciplined breath control. Such somaesthetic discipline also provides its own pleasures of self-governance, while its cognitive and ethical benefits – in training the senses, will, and character – further transcend the values typically identified with hedonism.

VI

These arguments for pleasure should also show that the aesthetic aims of pragmatic somaesthetics are not confined to the narrow pursuit of pleasure (however valuable such pleasure may be). Somaesthetics connotes both the cognitive sharpening of our aesthesis or sensory perception *and* the artful reshaping of our somatic form and functioning, not simply to make us stronger and more perceptive for our own sensual satisfaction but also to render us more sensitive to the needs of others and more capable of responding to them with effectively willed action. In the context

[37] See William James, *The Varieties of Religious Experience*, 412; Yuasa, *The Body, Self-Cultivation, and Ki-Energy*, 59–60.
[38] Cited in James, *The Varieties of Religious Experience*, 403.

of such broader goals, somaesthetics should not be seen as self-indulgent luxury. Higher somaesthetic forms therefore make pleasure the essential by-product of an ascetic, yet aesthetic, quest for something better than one's current self, a quest pursued by learning and mastering one's soma and refining it into a vessel of experienced beauty so that one can attain still greater powers and joys potentially within us – a higher self, perhaps even a divine spirit or Oversoul. Such somaesthetic discipline (evident in yoga and Zen meditation but also in Western practices such as the Feldenkrais Method and the Alexander Technique) involves, of course, a significant degree of intellectual *askesis* as well.

Rejecting the mind/body dualism (since the very phenomenon of sense perception defies it), these practices aim at the holistic transformation of the subject, in which the dimensions of aesthetic, moral, and spiritual improvement are so intimately intertwined that they cannot effectively be separated. Thus hatha yoga's state of *Ghata Avasthâ* is simultaneously described as one where "the Yogi's posture becomes firm, and he becomes wise like a god ... indicated by [the] highest pleasure experienced," involving the acute perception of a subtle drumlike sound of divine energy "in the throat."[39]

Although yoga is surely remote from Foucault's disciplinary program of S/M, could his devoted quest for the most intense somatic pleasures still be understood in terms of a spiritually transformative *askesis*, however dangerously misguided? He seems to see it that way, and he certainly appreciates the spiritual dimension of the somatic. Asserting already in *Discipline and Punish* that the soul in fact "has a reality" as "produced permanently around, on, within the body by the functioning of ... power," he goes on to highlight the role of somatic *askesis* (along with technologies of self-writing) in his later study of Greco-Roman and ancient Christian

---

[39] Svatmarama Swami, *The Hatha Yoga Pradapika*, trans. Pancham Sinh (Allahabad, India: Lahif Mohan Basu, 1915), 57. Similarly, it is alleged that in *Parichaya Avasthâ*, an "ecstasy is spontaneously produced which is devoid of evils, pains, old age, disease, hunger, and sleep." In such conditions of *samadhi*, the yogi is even said to conquer death. But paradoxically, precisely in their struggle to overcome life's painful somatic limitations, somaesthetic practices like yoga usefully underline the body's inescapable mortality, teaching us the wisdom of humility. Only a puerile somaesthetics would forget that embodiment implies ineliminable finitude and weakness. Philosophy's neglect of the body can partly be explained as a proud and wishful denial of our mortal limits. But bodily finitude does not entail the futility of working on our somatic selves; no more than our failure to know everything discredits the attempt to achieve greater knowledge. Somatic self-consciousness, rather than a denial of our mortality and limitation, can provide a clearer awareness of our finitude and, as we shall see below, a better preparation for aging and death.

spiritual care of the self.[40] If Foucault's own pragmatic somaesthetics of pleasure has a transformative spiritual dimension,[41] the power of its spirituality seems diminished or put in question not merely by his excessive concentration on the sensationalist pleasures of strong drugs and sexual violence, but also by his choosing Charles Baudelaire's model of dandyism to embody his own ideal of transformative somaesthetic *askesis*.[42]

Nevertheless, should we not recognize that consciousness-altering drugs and intensified sexuality play a meaningful role in many religious traditions and that expressions of sadomasochism are surely not foreign to the Catholic spiritual sensibilities that have shaped our own culture? Consider, for example, the eroticized images of the crucifixion's tortured, suffering passion of fatal bondage (overseen by an omnipotent God the Father) or the many saintly mortifications of the flesh and inquisitional trials of faith, or the frequent expression of religious love in terms of joyfully yearning, ravished domination. "Batter my heart, three-personed God," urges John Donne in "Holy Sonnet 14," continuing this prayer of sacred ardor by heightening its erotic violence: "o'erthrow me, and bend/ Your force, to break, blow, burn, and make me new/ ... Yet dearly I love you, and would be loved fain,/ ... Take me to you, imprison me, for I/ Except you enthrall me, never shall be free,/ Nor ever chaste, except you ravish me." Here again, we see how Foucault's S/M program deserves our careful critical attention not so much as a perverse transgression of our culture's values but as an explicit, intensified expression of deeply problematic tendencies that historically subtend those values and the practices they generate, even in our spiritual and religious experience.

In deploying Baudelarian dandyism as the modern paradigm of self-transformative aesthetic discipline, Foucault affirms "the philosophical ethos" implied in its respect for "the ephemeral," its strenuous "will 'to heroize' the present" moment and capture "the swift joys of the *depraved animal*." But he especially celebrates its demanding "doctrine of elegance," the transfiguring "asceticism of the dandy who makes of his body,

---

[40] Michel Foucault, *Discipline and Punish*, trans. Alan Sheridan (New York: Vintage, 1979), 29.

[41] Jeremy Carrette, *Foucault and Religion: Spiritual Corporality and Political Spirituality* (London: Routledge, 2000), makes an extended case for an insufficiently recognized "spiritual corporality" in Foucault's writings, explaining it (through links to Sade, Nietzsche, Klossowski, Bataille, and others) in terms of the body taking the central position in human life after our culture's recognition of the death of God. Bataille, of course, insists that "all eroticism has a sacramental character" (*Eroticism*, 15–16).

[42] Michel Foucault, "What Is Enlightenment?" *The Essential Works of Michel Foucault*, trans. Robert Hurley (New York: New Press, 1997), 1:303–319.

his behavior, his feelings and passions, his very existence, a work of art."[43] Since the dandy's aesthetic "cult of the self," in Baudelaire's account, is focused "above all else" on the "distinction" of "elegance and originality" and linked with an intense appreciation of "the lofty spiritual significance of the toilet" ("in praise of cosmetics") and "the special beauty of evil" as "pure art," Foucault's exaltation of this exemplar renders the whole idea of spiritual self-transformation through somaesthetic *askesis* far more suspect and vulnerable to Pierre Hadot's charge that such aestheticism only amounts to superficial, artificial self-posturing rather than the earnest sort of deep spiritual transformation we expect of the ethical ideal of self-care.[44] Somaesthetic self-fashioning, however, can find a far more convincing exemplar of ethical-spiritual transformation in the divinely inspired self-discipline of Socrates, whose somaesthetic power (honed through persistent exercise and dance training) could cast a seductive spell, despite his old age and ugly facial features, thus enabling him to argue he was more beautiful than the famously handsome Critobulus in Xenophon's *Symposium* (2.8–2.19, 5.1–5.10). Equally powerful examples of spiritually uplifting somaesthetic discipline can be found in the Confucian tradition, whose emphasis on art, ritual, and attractive somatic demeanor for instilling greater spiritual harmony in both personal character and social life is so prominent that the Confucians were sometimes even criticized as aesthetes.[45]

If such ancient examples prove that aesthetic concerns are not essentially opposed to ethical and spiritual *askesis* (which has its own austere beauty), we should also recall how, in modern times, art has often supplanted traditional religion as the site of transcendent spirituality. Even Foucault's model of aesthetic self-transformation is not without its

---

[43] Ibid., 310–312.

[44] Charles Baudelaire, *The Painter of Modern Life and Other Essays*, trans. Jonathan Mayne (London: Phaidon, 1964), 1–40, quotations from 27, 28, 31, 32, 38. Baudelaire admits that the dandy is "a weird kind of spiritualist," whose "excessive love of visible, tangible things ... [involves] a certain repugnance for the things that form the impalpable kingdom of the metaphysician," and makes it hard to "bestow upon him the title of philosopher" (9, 28). Hadot critiques Foucault's model of self-cultivation as "a new form of Dandyism, late twentieth-century style," that is "*too* aesthetic" to be a good "ethical model," see *Philosophy as a Way of Life*, 211.

[45] Mozi, for instance, expressed such criticism. See *The Ethical and Political Works of Motse*, trans. W. P. Mei (London: Probsthain, 1929). For a more detailed discussion of the somaesthetics of Confucianism and its relation to ethical and spiritual *askesis*, see my, "Pragmatism and East-Asian Thought," in *The Range of Pragmatism and the Limits of Philosophy*, ed. Richard Shusterman (Oxford: Blackwell, 2004), 13–42.

suggestion of a religious moment. In the very interview where he advocates a sexual ethics of intense pleasure, Foucault equally insists that the aesthetic quest for self-transformation holds the promise of salvation but demands a "work like a dog" discipline of intellectual effort. "For me intellectual work is related to what you could call aestheticism, meaning transforming yourself . . . I know that knowledge can transform us . . . And maybe I will be saved. Or maybe I'll die but I think that is the same anyway for me. (Laughs)." This ambiguous laughter in equating salvation and death (which could express black humor, or irony toward Christian salvation through death, or even embarrassment about his fascination with death or about his very use of the religiously charged notion of salvation) cannot conceal that Foucault is very serious about the aesthetic dimension of self-transformation. For he goes on to insist: "This transformation of one's self by one's own knowledge is, I think, something rather close to the aesthetic experience. Why should a painter work if he is not transformed by his own painting?" (FL, 379).

But why, to continue this line of argument, should one work so hard, if the aesthetic transformation is merely perfunctory and superficial: a line of mascara, the shallow shimmer-shine of tinted hair? Modernity's sad irony is that art has inherited religion's spiritual authority, while being compartmentalized from the serious business of life. Aestheticism must seem amoral and superficial when art is falsely relegated from ethical praxis and instead confined to the realm of mere *Schein* (i.e., appearance, illusion). Challenging this false dichotomy between art and ethics, pragmatism seeks to synthesize the beautiful and the good. While recognizing (with Montaigne) that our greatest artworks are ourselves (inextricably bound up with and shaped by others), it also brings ethical considerations into the project of aesthetic self-fashioning and the judgment of such art. If pragmatism can claim Foucault as a partial though problematic ally, it finds its best nineteenth-century exemplars neither in Baudelaire nor in Nietzsche but in America's Emerson and Thoreau, past prophets of the somaesthetics that I advocate. Let me close this chapter by quoting them.

"Every man," says Thoreau, "is the builder of a temple, called his body to the god he worships, after a style purely his own, nor can he get off by hammering marble instead. We are all sculptors and painters, and our material is our own flesh and blood and bones. Any nobleness begins to refine a man's features, any meanness or sensuality to imbrute them." "Art," Emerson claims, "is the need to create; but in its essence, immense and universal, it is impatient of working with lame or tied hands, and of making cripples and monsters, such as all pictures and statues are. "Nothing less than the creation of man and nature is its end."[46]

In the American culture that Emerson and Thoreau helped shape and that globalization has consequently thrust upon all the world's cultures, how are we to create and care for our embodied selves today? With drugs and dieting, steroids and silicone implants, with prick rings and leather masks and fist-fucking in dungeons, with aerobics and triathlons, with dance and *pranayama*, or with new technologies of genetic and neural engineering? Foucault may not give us the best answers to such questions, but his somaesthetics confronts us (even affronts us) with the crucial issue: conceived as an art of living, philosophy should attend more closely to cultivating the sentient body through which we live. Such cultivation not only involves refining the body and its unconscious motor programs; it also means enhancing somatic sentience through heightened, reflective body consciousness. Foucault errs in presuming that such consciousness is best heightened through maximized intensity of stimulation, whose violence ultimately will only dull our sensibility and deaden our pleasure.

[46] Henry David Thoreau, *Walden*, in *The Portable Thoreau*, ed. Carl Bode (New York: Viking, 1964), 468; and Ralph Waldo Emerson, "Art," in *Ralph Waldo Emerson*, ed. Richard Poirier (Oxford: Oxford University Press, 1990), 192.

2

The Silent, Limping Body of Philosophy

Somatic Attention Deficit in Merleau-Ponty

[handwritten marginalia: see also his statement for PoP pp. 37.6-77, on p. 98 N-how]

I

In the field of Western philosophy, Maurice Merleau-Ponty is something like the patron saint of the body. Though La Mettrie, Diderot, Nietzsche, and Foucault have also passionately championed the bodily dimension of human experience, none can match the bulk of rigorous, systematic, and persistent argument that Merleau-Ponty provides to prove the body's primacy in human experience and meaning. With tireless eloquence that almost seems to conquer by its massive unrelenting flow, he insists that the body is not only the crucial source of all perception and action but also the core of our expressive capability and thus the ground of all language and meaning.

Paradoxically, while celebrating the body's role in expression, Merleau-Ponty typically characterizes it in terms of silence. The body, he writes in *Phenomenology of Perception*, constitutes "the tacit *cogito*," "the silent *cogito*," the "unspoken *cogito*."[1] As our "primary subjectivity," it is "the consciousness which conditions language," but itself remains a "silent consciousness" with an "inarticulate grasp upon the world" (PoP, 402–404). Forming "the background of silence" that is necessary for language to emerge, the body, as gesture, is also already "a tacit language" and the ground of all expression: "every human use of the body is already *primordial expression*"

[1] I shall be citing from the works of Merleau-Ponty using the following editions and abbreviations: *Phénoménologie de la perception* (Paris: Gallimard, 1945), hereafter Pdp; English translation: *Phenomenology of Perception*, trans. Colin Smith (London: Routledge, 1962), hereafter PoP; *In Praise of Philosophy and Other Essays*, trans. John Wild, James Edie and John O'Neill (Evanston, IL: Northwestern University Press, 1970), hereafter IPP; *Signs*, trans. Richard C. McCleary (Evanston, IL: Northwestern University Press, 1964), hereafter S; *The Visible and the Invisible*, trans. Alphonso Lingis (Evanston, IL: Northwestern University Press, 1968), hereafter VI.

(S, 46–47, 67). There is a further paradox. Though surpassing other philosophers in emphasizing the body's expressive role, Merleau-Ponty hardly wants to listen to what the body seems to say about itself in terms of its self-conscious sensations, such as explicit kinaesthetic or proprioceptive feelings. The role of such feelings gets little attention in his texts, and they tend to be sharply criticized when they are discussed.[2] They are targets in Merleau-Ponty's general critique of representations of bodily experience, along with other "thematized" somatic perceptions. Our body, he insists, wonderfully guides us, but "only on condition that we stop analyzing it" and its feelings in reflective consciousness, only "on the condition that I do not reflect expressly on it" (S, 78, 89).

This chapter will explore the reasons for Merleau-Ponty's insistence on somatic silence and resistance to explicitly conscious body feelings by showing how they emerge from and illustrate his specific goals for a phenomenology of embodiment and a revaluation of our basic spontaneous perception that has been the target of philosophical denigration since ancient times. Some of these reasons are not very clearly articulated in his writings, perhaps because they were so closely tied to his basic philosophical vision that he simply presumed them. He may have not really seen them clearly by seeing through them, just as we see through eyeglasses without seeing them clearly (and the clearer we see through them, the less clearly they are seen). I will do my best to explain Merleau-Ponty's resistance to thematized somatic consciousness or somaesthetic reflection. But I will not be able to justify it. For this attitude is precisely one of the features of his somatic theory that I find most problematic, not only as a pragmatist philosopher, but as a somatic educator.

Merleau-Ponty's attitude derives both from his specific goals in somatic phenomenology and his general conception of philosophy. Just as he paradoxically describes the body's expressiveness in terms of silence, so in his lecture "In Praise of Philosophy" (his project-defining, *leçon inaugurale* at the Collège de France), he stunningly describes philosophy as "limping" and yet goes on to celebrate it precisely in terms of this crippling metaphor: "the limping of philosophy is its virtue" (IPP, 58, 61).

[2] William James, John Dewey, and Ludwig Wittgenstein all give more attention to such explicit, thematized somatic feelings. Chapter 5 shows how introspective attention to bodily feelings plays a central role in James's explanations of the self, the emotions, and the will, while Chapter 4 explains why Wittgenstein rejects the use of these feelings to explain such concepts, though allowing other philosophical uses for bodily feelings. Dewey's advocacy of careful attention to somatic feelings (inspired by his study of F. M. Alexander's Technique of heightened reflective somatic awareness and self-use) will be discussed in Chapter 6.

Why should a brilliant body philosopher like Merleau-Ponty use such a metaphor of somatic disempowerment to characterize his philosophical project? While exploring his reasons, this chapter will contrast his philosophical vision with a more practical, reconstructive pragmatist approach to somatic philosophy. This approach advocates more attention to explicit somatic consciousness or somaesthetic reflection in trying to achieve not only a theoretical rehabilitation of the body as a central concept for philosophy but also a more practical, therapeutic rehabilitation of the lived body as part of a philosophical life of greater mindfulness.

II

The key to Merleau-Ponty's strategy is to transform our recognition of the body's weakness into an analysis of its essential, indispensable strength. The pervasive experience of bodily weakness may be philosophy's deepest reason for rejecting the body, for refusing to accept it as defining human identity. Overwhelming in death, somatic impotence is also daily proven in illness, disability, injury, pain, fatigue, and the withering of strength that old age brings. For philosophy, bodily weakness also means cognitive deficiency. As the body's imperfect senses can distort the truth, so its desires distract the mind from the pursuit of knowledge. The body, moreover, is not a clear object of knowledge. One cannot directly see one's outer bodily surface in its totality, and the body is especially mysterious because its inner workings are always in some way hidden from the subject's view. One cannot directly scan it in the way we often assume we can examine and know our minds through immediate introspection. Regarding the body as at best a mere servant or instrument of the mind, philosophy has often portrayed it as a torturous prison of deception, temptation, and pain.

One strategy for defending the body against these familiar attacks from the dominant Platonic-Christian-Cartesian tradition is to challenge them in the way Nietzsche did. Radically inverting the conventional valuations of mind and body, he argued that we can know our bodies better than our minds, that the body can be more powerful than the mind, and that toughening the body can make the mind stronger. Concluding this logic of reversal, Nietzsche insisted that the mind is essentially the instrument of the body, even though it too often is misused (especially by philosophers) as the body's deceptive, torturing prison.[3]

---

[3] For more detailed discussion of this Nietzschean strategy, see my *Performing Live* (Ithaca, NY: Cornell University Press, 2000), ch. 7.

Though appealingly ingenious, this bold strategy leaves most of us unconvinced. The problem is not simply that its radical transvaluation of body over mind goes too much against the grain of philosophy's intellectualist tradition. Nor is it merely that the reversal seems to reinforce the old rigid dualism of mind and body. Somatic deficiency is, unfortunately, such a pervasive part of experience that Nietzsche's inversion of the mind/body hierarchy seems too much like wishful thinking (particularly when we recall his own pathetic bodily weakness). Of course, we should realize that our minds are often impotent to explain discursively what our bodies succeed in performing, and that our minds often fatigue and strike work while our bodies unconsciously continue to function. But despite such recognition of mental deficiencies, the range of what we can do or imagine with the power of our minds still seems far superior to what our bodies can actually perform.

In contrast to Nietzsche's hyperbolic somaticism, Merleau-Ponty's argument for the body's philosophical centrality and value is more shrewdly cautious. He embraces the body's essential weaknesses, but then shows how these dimensions of ontological and epistemological limitation are a necessary part and parcel of our positive human capacities for having perspectives on objects and for having a world. These limits thus provide the essential focusing frame for all our perception, action, language, and understanding. The limitation the body has in inhabiting a particular place is precisely what gives us an angle of perception or perspective from which objects can be grasped, while the fact that we can change our bodily place allows us to perceive objects from different perspectives and thus constitute them as objective things. Similarly, although the body is deficient in not being able to observe itself wholly and directly (since, for example, the eyes are fixed forward in one's head, which they therefore can never directly see), this limitation is part and parcel of the body's permanent, privileged position as the defining pivot and ground orientation of observation. Moreover, the apparent limitation that bodily perceptions are vague, corrigible, or ambiguous is reinterpreted as usefully true to a world of experience that is itself ambiguous, vague, and in flux. This logic of uncovering the strengths entailed in bodily weakness is also captured in Merleau-Ponty's later notion of "the flesh" (VI, 135–155). If the body shares the corruptibility of material things and can be characterized as "flesh" (the traditional pejorative for bodily weakness in Saint Paul and Augustine), this negative notion of flesh is transformed to praise and explain the body's special capacity to grasp and commune with the world of sensible things, since its flesh is itself sensible as well as sensing.

Shusterman 's Buddism + Cosmic Bass
the Boot

Before I go further into how Merleau-Ponty's strategy of rehabilitating the body leads him to neglect or resist the role of explicitly conscious somatic sensations, let me make some introductory remarks about such sensations and their use. These are conscious, explicit, experiential perceptions of our body: they include distinct feelings, observations, visualizations, and other mental representations of our body and its parts, surfaces, and interiors. Their explicit or represented character distinguishes them clearly from the kind of primary consciousness that Merleau-Ponty advocates. Though these explicit perceptions include the more sensual feelings of hunger, pleasure, and pain, the term "sensation" is meant to be broad enough to cover perceptions of bodily states that are more distinctively cognitive and do not have a very strong affective character. Intellectual focusing or attentive awareness of the feel, movement, orientation, or state of tension of some part of our body would count as a conscious body sensation even when it lacks a significant emotional quality or direct input from the body's external sense organs. Conscious body sensations are therefore not at all opposed to thought, but instead are understood as including conscious, experiential body-focused thoughts and representations.

Among these explicitly conscious bodily sensations, we can distinguish between those dominated by our more external or distance senses (like seeing, hearing, etc.) and those more dependent on more internal bodily senses such as proprioception or kinaesthetic feelings. I can consciously sense the position of my hand by looking at it and noting its orientation, but I can also close my eyes and try to sense its position by proprioceptively feeling its relation to my other body parts, to the force of gravity, to other objects in my field of experience. Such explicit proprioceptive perceptions can be regarded as somaesthetic perceptions par excellence, because they are not only somaesthetic by invoking mindful aesthesis or discriminating, thematized perception, but also by relying essentially on the somaesthetic sensory system rather than our teleceptors.

By instructing us about the condition of our bodies, both these kinds of mindfully conscious somatic perceptions can help us to perform better. A slumping batter, by looking at his feet and hands could discover that his stance has become too wide or that he is choking up too far on the bat. A dancer can glance at her feet to see that they are not properly turned out. But besides these external perceptions, most people have developed enough internal somatic awareness to know (at least roughly) where their limbs are located. And through systematic practice of somaesthetic awareness this proprioceptive consciousness can be significantly improved to provide a sharper and fuller picture of our body shape, volume, density, and alignment without using our external senses. These two varieties of explicitly conscious or mindful sensations constitute only a relatively small portion of our bodily understandings and perceptions, which exhibit at least four levels of consciousness.

First, there are primitive modes of grasping that I am not really consciously aware of at all but that Merleau-Ponty seems to recognize as belonging to our most basic "corporeal intentionality" (S, 89). When Merleau-Ponty says "that my body is always perceived by me" (PoP, 91), he surely must realize that we are sometimes not consciously aware of our bodies. This is not simply when we are concentrating our consciousness on other things, but because we are sometimes simply unconscious *tout court* as in deep, dreamless sleep. Yet, even in such sleep, can we not discern a primitive bodily perception of an unconscious variety that recalls Merleau-Ponty's notion of basic "motor intentionality" or "motility as basic intentionality" (PoP, 137–138)? Consider our breathing while we sleep. If a pillow or some other object comes to block our breathing, we will typically turn our heads or push the object away while continuing to sleep, thus unconsciously adjusting our behavior in terms of what is unconsciously grasped.[4] Even if this lack of consciousness might make us shrink from applying the term "perception" here, there is no doubt that such behavior displays purposive understanding and intelligent intentional action.

A more conscious level of bodily perception could be characterized as conscious perception without explicit awareness. In such cases, I am conscious and perceive something, but I do not perceive it as a distinct object of awareness and do not posit, thematize, or predicate it as a specific object of consciousness. My awareness of it is at most a marginal or recessive awareness. If my attention is then explicitly directed to what is perceived, I could in turn perceive it with explicit awareness as a determinate, specific, predicative object. But the introduction of such focused attention and explicit awareness would mean going beyond this basic

---

[4] When defining consciousness as simply "being towards-the-thing through the intermediary of the body" in a relationship not of "I think that" but of "I can" (PoP, 137, 138–139), Merleau-Ponty would seem to imply that purposeful action in sleep should be construed as the action of consciousness. One might then wonder to what extent we can ever speak of unconscious human life, let alone unconscious human acts or intentions. But Merleau-Ponty sometimes speaks of consciousness as if it demanded a further "constituting" function: "To be conscious is to constitute, so that I cannot be conscious of another person, since that would involve constituting him as constituting" (S, 93).

level of consciousness, which Merleau-Ponty celebrates as "primary consciousness," describing it as "the unreflective life of consciousness" and "ante-predicative life of consciousness" (PoP, xv–xvi).

Consider two examples of this basic consciousness. Typically, in walking through an open door, I am not explicitly aware of the precise borders of its frame and its relation to my body dimensions and posture, though the fact that I perceive these spatial relations is shown by the fact that I smoothly navigate the opening, even if it is a completely new door and the passage is not very wide. Similarly, I can perceive in some vague marginal sense that I am breathing (in the sense of not feeling any suffocation or breathing impediment) without being explicitly aware of my breathing and its rhythm, style, or quality. In a state of excitement I may experience shortness of breath without my being distinctly aware that it is shortness of breath I am experiencing. Such shortness of breath is here *not* represented to consciousness as an explicit object of awareness or what Merleau-Ponty sometimes calls a thematized object or representation.

But perception can be raised to a third level in which we are consciously and explicitly aware of what we perceive, whether such perception is of external objects or of our own bodies and somatic sensations. Just as we can observe the door opening as a distinct object of perception, so we can consciously perceive (both visually and *proprioceptively*) whether our stance is wide or narrow and whether our arms are extended or close to our torso. We can likewise explicitly recognize that our breath is short or that our fists are clenched; we can even be mindfully aware of the distinct feelings of such breathing or clenching. At this level, which Merleau-Ponty regards as the level of mental representations, we can already speak of explicitly conscious somatic perception or somaesthetic observation.[5]

I would add a fourth layer of still greater consciousness in perception, a level that is very important in many somatic disciplines of body-mind attunement. Here we are not only conscious of what we perceive as an explicit object of awareness but we are also mindfully conscious of this focused consciousness as we monitor our awareness of the object of our awareness through its representation in our consciousness. If the third

[5] This level of explicit proprioceptive body consciousness is recognized by various somatic theorists. See, for example, Brian O'Shaughnessy, "Proprioception and the Body Image," in J. L. Bermúdez et al. *The Body and the Self* (Cambridge, MA: MIT Press, 1995), 175–203; and Jonathan Cole and Barbara Montero, "Affective Proprioception," in *Janus-Head*, 9 (2007), 299–317, which deploys my somaesthetic distinction between pleasure from external representations and that from inner experience such as proprioceptive feelings.

level can be characterized as conscious somatic perception with explicit awareness (or, more concisely, somaesthetic perception), then the fourth and more reflective level could be called self-conscious or reflective somatic perception with explicit awareness (or, more simply, somaesthetic self-consciousness or reflection). On this level, we will be aware not simply that our breath is short or even precisely *how* we are breathing (say, rapidly and shallowly from the throat or in stifled snorts through the nose, rather than deeply from the diaphragm); we will also be aware of *how* our self-consciousness of breathing influences our ongoing breathing and attentive awareness and related feelings. We will be focused on our self-awareness of how our fists are clenched not only in terms of specific attention to explicit feelings of tightness and orientation of thumb and fingers in the clenching but further to the feelings of that mindful attention itself and the ways such somatic self-consciousness influences our experience of fist-clenching and other experiences.

Merleau-Ponty's philosophy poses a challenge to the value of these two higher (or representational) levels of conscious somatic perception. It does so not merely by celebrating the primacy and sufficiency of unreflective "primary consciousness" but also by specific arguments against body observation and the use of kinaesthetic sensations and body representations. An adequate defense of somaesthetic mindfulness must do justice to the details of this challenge.

III

One principal aim in Merleau-Ponty's phenomenology is to restore our robust contact with the "things themselves" and "our world of actual experience" as they "are first given to us" (PoP, ix, 57). This means renewing our connection with perceptions and experience that precede knowledge and reflection, "to return to that world which precedes knowledge, of which knowledge always *speaks*" (PoP, ix). Phenomenology is therefore "a philosophy for which the world is always 'already there' before reflection begins – as an inalienable presence; and all its efforts are concentrated upon re-achieving a direct and primitive contact with the world, and endowing that contact with a philosophical status" (PoP, vii).

Philosophy is perforce a reflective act, but phenomenology's "radical reflection amounts to a consciousness of its own dependence on an unreflective life which is its initial situation, unchanging, given once and for all." "It tries to give a direct description of our experience as it is" in our basic prereflective state, pursuing "the ambition to make reflection emulate the unreflective life of consciousness." Such philosophy "is not the reflection of a pre-existing truth," but rather an effort "of describing our perception of the world as that upon which our idea of truth is forever based"; it aims at "relearning to look at the world" with this direct, prereflective perception and to act in it accordingly (PoP, vii, xiv, xvi, xx). Such primary perception and prereflective consciousness are embodied in an operative intentionality that is characterized by immediacy and spontaneity (S, 89–94). "Thus the proper function of a phenomenological philosophy ... [would] be to establish itself in the order of instructive spontaneity" (S, 97); and this basic, embodied spontaneity constitutes a worldly wisdom and competence that all people share. Merleau-Ponty therefore concludes that the special knowledge of the philosopher "is only a way of putting into words what every man knows well ... These mysteries are in each one of us as in him. What does he say of the relation between the soul and the body, except what is known by all men who make their souls and bodies, their good and their evil, go together in one piece" (IPP, 63)?

Three crucial themes resound in such passages. First, Merleau-Ponty affirms the existence and restoration of a primordial perception or experience of the world that lies below the level of reflective or thematized consciousness and beneath all language and concepts, but that is nevertheless perfectly efficacious for our fundamental needs and also provides the basic ground for higher reflection. This nondiscursive level of intentionality is hailed as the "silent consciousness" of "primary subjectivity" and "primordial expression." Second, he urges the recognition and recovery of *spontaneity* that is characteristic of such primordial perception and expression. Third is the assumption that philosophy should concentrate on conditions of human existence that are ontologically given as basic, universal, and permanent. Hence, its study of perception and the body-mind relationship should be in terms of what is "unchanging, given once and for all" and "known by all men" (and presumably all women) or at least all men and women deemed normal.[6]

Even the first theme alone would discourage Merleau-Ponty from sympathetic attention to explicitly conscious bodily sensations. Not only do

[6] Merleau-Ponty's notion of a primordial, universal bodily experience that is ungendered has been criticized for generating an account of embodied existence that in fact is androcentric rather than neutral. See, for instance, Judith Butler, "Sexual Ideology and Phenomenological Description: A Feminist Critique of Merleau-Ponty's Phenomenology of Perception," in *The Thinking Muse: Feminism and Modern French Philosophy*, ed. Jeffner Allen and Iris Marion Young (Bloomington: Indiana University Press, 1989), 85–100.

those sensations go beyond what he wishes to affirm as prereflective consciousness but they are typically used by scientific and philosophical thought to usurp the explanatory role and neglect the existence of the primary perception or consciousness that Merleau-Ponty so ardently advocates. This primordial consciousness has been forgotten, he argues, because reflective thought assumed such consciousness was inadequate to perform the everyday tasks of perception, action, and speech; so it instead explained our everyday behavior as relying on "representations," whether they were the neural representations of mechanistic physiology or the psychic representations of intellectualist philosophy and psychology. Merleau-Ponty's arguments are therefore devoted to showing that the representational explanations offered by science and philosophy are neither necessary nor accurate accounts of how we perceive, act, and express ourselves in normal everyday behavior (and also in more abnormal cases like "abstract movement" and "phantom limb" experience).

His excellent criticisms of the different representational explanations are too many and detailed to rehearse here, but they share a core strategy of argument. Representational explanations are shown to misconstrue the basic experience or behavior they seek to explain by describing it from the start in terms of their own products of reflective analysis. Further, such explanations are shown to be inadequate because they rely (in some implicit but crucial way) on some aspect of experience that they do not actually explain but that can be explained by primordial perception. For instance, in order to account for my successful passing through the threshold of an open door, a representational explanation would describe and explicate my experience in terms of my visual representations of the open space, the surrounding door frame, and of my conscious kinaesthetic sensations of my body's width and orientation of movement. But normally I do not have any such conscious representations when passing through a door. These representations, Merleau-Ponty argues (much like William James and John Dewey did earlier), are reflective, theoretical explanatory notions that are falsely read back or imposed onto original experience.[7] Moreover, even if I did have these different visual and kinaesthetic explanatory representations, they cannot themselves explain my experience because they cannot explain how they are properly sorted

---

[7] Dewey described this as "*the* philosophic fallacy," while James called it "the psychologist's fallacy." See John Dewey, *Experience and Nature* (Carbondale: Southern Illinois University Press 1988), 34; and William James, *The Principles of Psychology*, 1890 (Cambridge, MA: Harvard University Press, 1981), 195, 268.

out from other, irrelevant representations and synthesized together in successful perception and action. Instead, claims Merleau-Ponty, it is our basic unreflective intentionality that silently and spontaneously organizes our world of perception without the need of distinct perceptual representations and without any explicitly conscious deliberation.

Though this basic level of intentionality is ubiquitous, its very pervasiveness and unobtrusive silence conceal its prevailing presence. In the same way, its elemental, common, and spontaneous character obscures its extraordinary effectiveness. To highlight the astounding powers of this unreflective level of perception, action, and speech, Merleau-Ponty describes it in terms of the marvelous, miraculous, and even the magical. The "body as spontaneous expression" is like the unknowing "marvel of a style" in artistic genius (S, 65, 66).

> As the artist makes his style radiate into the very fibers of the material he is working on, I move my body without even knowing which muscles and nerve paths should intervene, nor where I must look for the instruments of that action. I want to go over there, and here I am, without having entered into the inhuman secret of the bodily mechanism or having adjusted that mechanism to the givens of the problem...I look at the goal, I am drawn by it, and the bodily apparatus does what must be done in order for me to be there. For me, everything happens in the human world of perception and gesture, but my "geographical" or "physical" body submits to the demands of this little drama, which does not cease to arouse a thousand natural marvels in it. Just my glance toward the goal already has its own miracles (S, 66).

If representations of body parts and processes are negatively described as mechanistically inhuman, the unreflective use of the body is not only linked to the human and the artistic but also suggests – through its miraculous marvels – the divine. In a section of *Phenomenology of Perception* where Merleau-Ponty is criticizing the use of kinaesthetic sensations, he likewise insists on the miraculous nature of bodily intentionality, describing its immediate, intuitive efficacy as "magical." There is no need to think of what I am doing or where I am in space, I just move my body "directly" and spontaneously achieve the intended result, even without consciously representing my intention. "The relations between my decision and my body are, in movement, magic ones" (PoP, 94).

Why should a secular philosopher hail our ordinary body intentionality in terms of miracle and magic? True, our mundane bodily competence can, from certain perspectives, provoke genuine wonder. But emphasizing the miraculous or magical also serves other functions in

Merleau-Ponty's somatic agenda. To celebrate the primal *mystery* of spontaneous body proficiency is a strong antidote against the urge to explain
our bodily perception and action through representational means, precisely the kind of explanation that has always obscured the basic somatic
intentionality Merleau-Ponty rightly regards as primary. Moreover, celebration of the body's miraculous mystery deftly serves Merleau-Ponty's
project of foregrounding the body's value while explaining it as silent,
structuring, concealed background. "Bodily space...is the darkness
needed in the theatre to show up the performance, the background
of somnolence or reserve of vague power against which the gesture and
its aim stand out." More generally, "one's own body is the third term,
always tacitly understood, in the figure-background structure, and every
figure stands out against the double horizon of external and bodily space"
(PoP, 100–101). The body is also mysterious as a locus of "impersonal"
existence, beneath and hidden from normal selfhood. It is "the place
where life hides away" from the world, where I retreat from my interest in
observing or acting in the world, "lose myself in some pleasure or pain,
and shut myself up in this anonymous life which subtends my personal
one. But precisely because my body can shut itself off from the world, it
is also what opens me out upon the world and places me in a situation
there" (PoP, 164–165).

   Merleau-Ponty may also have a more personal reason for advocating
the hidden mystery of the body: a deep respect of its need for some privacy
to compensate for its function in giving us a world by exposing us to it, by
being not only sentient but part of the sensible flesh of the world. Some
of his remarks express a strong sense of corporeal modesty. "Usually man
does not show his body, and, when he does, it is either nervously or with
an intention to fascinate" (PoP, 166). And when Merleau-Ponty wants
to exemplify "those extreme situations" in which one becomes aware of
one's basic bodily intentionality, when one grasps that "tacit *cogito*, the
presence of oneself to oneself...because it is under threat," the threatening situations that he gives are "the dread of death or of another's gaze
upon me" (PoP, 404).

   Merleau-Ponty's notion of bodily intentionality defies philosophical
tradition by granting the body a kind of subjectivity instead of treating it
as mere object or mechanism. But he is still more radical in extending
the range of unreflective somatic subjectivity far beyond our basic bodily
movements and sense perceptions to the higher operations of speech
and thought that constitute philosophy's cherished realm of *logos*. Here

language, logos

again, the efficacy of spontaneous body intentionality replaces conscious representations as the explanation of our behavior:

> thought, in the speaking subject, is not a representation...The orator does not think before speaking, nor even while speaking; his speech is his thought...What we have said earlier about the "representation of movement" must be repeated concerning the verbal image: I do not need to visualize external space and my own body in order to move one within the other. It is enough that they exist for me, and that they form a certain field of action spread around me. In the same way I do not need to visualize the word in order to know and pronounce it. It is enough that I possess its articulatory and acoustic style as one of the modulations, one of the possible uses of my body. I reach back for the word as my hand reaches toward the part of my body which is being pricked; the word has a certain location in my linguistic world, and is part of my equipment. (PoP, 180)

In short, just as "my corporeal intending of the object of my surroundings is implicit and presupposes no thematization or 'representation' of my body or milieu," so continues Merleau-Ponty, "Signification arouses speech as the world arouses my body – by a mute presence which awakens my intentions without deploying itself before them.... The reason why the thematization of the signified does not precede speech is that it is the result of it" (S, 89–90).

The marvelous mystery of this silent, yet spontaneously flowing somatic power of expression is likewise highlighted:

> like the functioning of the body, that of words or paintings remains obscure to me. The words, lines, and colors which express me...are torn from me by what I want to say as my gestures are by what I want to do...[with] a spontaneity which will not tolerate any commands, not even those which I would like to give to myself. (S, 75)

The mysterious efficacy of our spontaneous intentionality is surely impressive. But it alone cannot explain all our ordinary powers of movement and perception, speech, and thought. I can jump in the water and spontaneously move my arms and legs, but I will not reach my goal unless I first learned how to swim. I can hear a song in Japanese and spontaneously try to sing along, but I will fail unless I have first learned enough words of that language. Many things we now spontaneously do (or understand) were once beyond our repertoire of unreflective performance. They had to be learned, as Merleau-Ponty realizes. But how? One way to explain at least part of this learning would be by the use of various kinds of representations (images, symbols, propositions, etc.) that our consciousness could focus on and deploy. But Merleau-Ponty seems too critical of representations to accept this option.

Instead, he explains this learning entirely in terms of the automatic acquisition of body habits through unreflective motor conditioning or somatic sedimentation. "The acquisition of a habit [including our habits of speech and thought] is indeed the grasping of a significance, but it is the motor grasping of a motor significance"; "it is the body which 'understands' in the acquisition of habit." There is no need for explicitly conscious thought "to get used to a hat, a car or a stick" or to master a keyboard; we simply "incorporate them into the bulk of our own body" through unreflective processes of motor sedimentation and our own spontaneous corporeal sense of self (PoP, 143–144). The lived body, for Merleau-Ponty, thus has two layers: beneath the spontaneous body of the moment, there is "the habit-body" of sedimentation (PoP, 82, 129–130).

Affirming the prevalence, importance, and intelligence of unreflective habit in our action, speech, and thought, I also share Merleau-Ponty's recognition of habit's somatic base. Both themes are central to the pragmatist tradition that inspires my work in somatic philosophy. But there are troubling limits to the efficacy of unreflective habits, even on the level of basic bodily actions. Unreflectively, we can acquire bad habits just as easily as good ones. (And this seems especially likely if we accept the Foucauldian premise that the institutions and technologies governing our lives through regimes of biopower inculcate habits of body and mind that aim to keep us in submission.) Once bad habits are acquired how do we correct them? We cannot simply rely on sedimented habit to correct them – since the sedimented habits are precisely what is wrong. Nor can we rely on the unreflective somatic spontaneity of the moment, for that is already tainted with the trace of the unwanted sedimentations and thus most likely to continue to misdirect us.[8]

This is why various disciplines of somatic training typically invoke representations and self-conscious body focusing in order to correct our

---

[8] Nor, I should add, can we rely on mere trial and error and the formation of new habits because that process would be too slow and haphazard and would tend to repeat the bad habit unless that habit was critically thematized into explicit consciousness for correction. F. M. Alexander stresses these points in arguing for the use of the representations of reflective consciousness to correct faulty somatic habits. See Alexander's *Man's Supreme Inheritance* (New York: Dutton, 1918), and *Constructive Conscious Control of the Individual* (New York: Dutton, 1923); *The Use of the Self* (New York: Dutton, 1932), and my discussion in Chapter 6.

Shust. wants to agree 4 MP but there are problems

faulty self-perception and use of our embodied selves. From ancient Asian practices of mindfulness to modern systems like Alexander Technique and Feldenkrais Method, explicit awareness and conscious control are key, as are the use of representations or visualizations. These disciplines do not aim to erase the crucial level of unreflective behavior by the (impossible) effort of making us explicitly conscious of all our perception and action. They instead seek to improve unreflective behavior that hinders our experience and performance. But in order to effect this improvement, the unreflective action or habit must be brought into conscious critical reflection (if only for a limited time) so that it can be grasped and worked on more precisely.[9] Besides these therapeutic goals, disciplines of somatic reflection also enhance our experience with the added richness, discoveries, and pleasures that heightened awareness can bring.[10]

In advocating the unreflective lived body and its motor schema in opposition to the conceptual representations of scientific explanation, Merleau-Ponty creates a polarization of "lived experience" versus abstract "representations" that neglects the deployment of a fruitful third option – what could be called "lived somaesthetic reflection," that is, concrete but representational and reflective body consciousness. This polarizing dichotomy is paralleled by another misleading binary contrast that pervades his account of behavior. On the one hand, he discusses the performance of "normal" people whose somatic sense and functioning he describes as totally smooth, spontaneous, and unproblematic. On the other hand is his contrasting category of the abnormally incapacitated – patients like Schneider (PoP, 103–107, 155–156) who exhibit pathological dysfunction and are usually suffering from serious neurological injury (such as brain lesions) or grave psychological trauma.[11]

[9] Advocates of somatic mindfulness vary with respect to the degree, duration, and range of domains to which critical mindful reflection should be applied. For some the ideal is to return as quickly as possible to unreflective spontaneity with a corrected habit that ensures effective performance, while others seem to argue that critically mindful somatic self-consciousness be maintained even in the performance itself. See, for example, Zeami's theory of Nō performance in his treatise "A Mirror Held to the Flower (*Kakyō*)," in *On the Art of the Nō Drama*, trans. J. Thomas Rimer and Yamazaki Masakazu (Princeton: Princeton University Press, 1984).

[10] See, for example, F. M. Alexander's books cited in note 8; and Moshe Feldenkrais, *Body and Mature Behavior* (London: Routledge and Kegan Paul 1949); *Awareness Through Movement* (New York: Harper and Row, 1972); *The Potent Self* (New York: HarperCollins, 1992).

[11] This dualistic tendency (and related neglect of the value of somatic self-consciousness) can still be detected in some of today's best somatic philosophy inspired by Merleau-Ponty.

This simple polarity obscures the fact that most of us so-called normal, fully functional people suffer from various incapacities and malfunctions that are mild in nature but that still impair performance. Such deficiencies relate not only to perceptions or actions we cannot perform (though we are anatomically equipped to do so) but also to what we do succeed in performing but could perform more successfully or with greater ease and grace. Merleau-Ponty implies that if we are not pathologically impaired like Schneider and other neurologically damaged individuals, then our unreflective body sense (or motor schema) is fully accurate and miraculously functional. For Merelau-Ponty, just as my spontaneous bodily movements seem "magical" in their precision and efficacy, so my immediate knowledge of my body and the orientation of its parts seems flawlessly complete. "I am in undivided possession of it, and I know where each of my limbs is through a body image (*schéma corporel*) in which all are included" (PoP, 98).

While sharing Merleau-Ponty's deep appreciation of our "normal" spontaneous bodily sense, I think we should also recognize that this sense is often painfully inaccurate and dysfunctional.[12] I may think I am keeping my head down when swinging a golf club, though an observer will easily see I do not. I may believe I am sitting straight when my back is rounded. If asked to bend at the ribs, many of us will really bend at the waist and think that we are complying with the instructions. In trying to stand tall by arching their backs in extension, people usually think they are lengthening their spines when they are in fact contracting them. Disciplines of somatic education deploy exercises of representational

Shaun Gallagher, for example, in defending the (vague and contested) distinction between "body schema" (functioning automatically and "prenoetically" beneath the level of consciousness) and "body image" (involving conscious perception and personal awareness) builds his case by contrasting between normal behavior of people who can simply rely on their unconscious body schema for successful performance without any need for improvement through "conscious reflexive attention" and pathological cases (such as deafferented patients) who require such attention because their motor schema have been impaired or destroyed. See Gallagher's instructive book, *How the Body Shapes the Mind* (Oxford: Oxford University Press, 2005), which I review in *Theory, Culture, and Society*, 24, no. 1 (2007): 152–156.

[12] As Alexander documents our "unreliable sensory appreciation" or "debauched kinaesthesia" with respect to how our bodies are oriented and used, so Moshe Feldenkrais argues that if the term "normal" should designate what should be the norm for healthy humans, then we should more accurately describe most people's somatic sense and use of themselves as "average" rather than normal. For a comparative account of the nature and philosophical import of Alexander Technique and Feldenkrais Method, see *Performing Live*, ch. 8. The cited phrases are from Alexander's *Constructive Conscious Control*, 148–149.

awareness to treat such problems of misperception and misuse of our bodies in the spontaneous and habitual behavior that Merleau-Ponty identifies as primal and celebrates as miraculously flawless in normal performance.

Though exaggerating our unreflective somatic proficiency, Merleau-Ponty cannot generally be condemned for overestimating the body's powers. For he highlights the body's distinctive weakness in other ways, including its grave cognitive limitations of self-observation. Indeed, his insistence on the miraculous efficacy of the spontaneous body (and on the consequent irrelevance of representational, reflective consciousness for enhancing our somatic performance) helps keep the body weaker than it could be by implying that there is no reason or way to improve its performance through the use of representations. Conversely, his compelling defense of bodily limitations as structurally essential to our human capacities could also discourage efforts to overcome entrenched somatic impediments, for fear that such efforts would ultimately weaken us by disturbing the fundamental structuring handicaps on which our powers in fact rely.

This suggests another reason Merleau-Ponty might resist the contribution of reflective somatic consciousness and its bodily representations. Disciplines of somaesthetic awareness are usually aimed not simply at *knowing* our bodily condition and habits but at *changing* them. Even awareness alone can (to some extent) change our somatic experience and relation to our bodies. Merleau-Ponty acknowledges this when he argues that reflective thinking cannot really capture our primordial unreflective experience because the representations of such thinking inevitably change our basic experience by introducing categories and conceptual distinctions that were not originally given there. He especially condemns the posited distinctions of representational explanations of experience (whether mechanistic or rationalistic) for generating "the dualism of consciousness and body" (PoP, 138), while blinding us to the unity of primordial perception.

However, the fact that representational explanations do not adequately explain our primordial perception does not imply they are not useful for other purposes, such as improving our habits. Change of habits can in turn change our spontaneous perceptions, whose unity and spontaneity will be restored once the new improved habit becomes entrenched. In short, we can affirm the unity and unreflective quality of primary perceptual experience while also endorsing reflective body consciousness that deploys representational thought for both the reconstruction of better primary experience and the intrinsic rewards of somaesthetic reflection.[13]

In modifying one's relation to one's body, disciplines of somatic mindfulness (like other forms of somatic training) also highlight differences between people. Different individuals often have very different styles of body use (and misuse). Moreover, what one learns through sustained training in somatic awareness is not simply "what every man knows well" through the immediate grasp of primordial perception and unthinking habit. Many of us do not know (and may never learn) what it is like to feel the location of each vertebra and rib proprioceptively without touching them with our hands. Nor does everyone recognize, when he or she is reaching out for something, precisely which part of his or her body (fingers, arm, shoulder, pelvis, or head) initiates the movement.

If philosophy's goal is simply to clarify and renew the universal and permanent in our embodied human condition by restoring our recognition of primordial experience and its ontological givens, then the whole project of improving one's somatic perception and functioning through self-conscious reflection will be dismissed as a philosophical irrelevancy. Worse, it will be seen as a threatening change and distraction from the originary level of perception that is celebrated as philosophy's ultimate ground, focus, and goal. Merleau-Ponty's commitment to a fixed, universal phenomenological ontology based on primordial perception thus provides further reason for dismissing the value of explicit somatic consciousness. Being more concerned with individual differences and contingencies, with future-looking change and reconstruction, with pluralities of practice that can be used by individuals and groups for improving on primary experience, pragmatism is more receptive to reflective somatic consciousness and its disciplinary uses for philosophy. William James made somatic introspection central to his research in philosophy of mind, while John Dewey went further by advocating reflective body consciousness to improve one's self-knowledge and self-use.

IV

Given his philosophical agenda, Merleau-Ponty has adequate motives for neglecting or even resisting reflective body consciousness. But do

---

[13] Dewey recognizes this by advocating the reflective "conscious control" of Alexander Technique, while continuing to urge the primary importance of unreflective, immediate experience. On the fruitful dialectic between reflective body consciousness and body spontaneity, see *Practicing Philosophy*, ch. 6 and Chapters 5 and 6 in this volume.

they constitute compelling arguments or should we instead conclude that Merleau-Ponty's project of body-centered phenomenology could be usefully supplemented by a greater recognition of the functions and value of reflective body consciousness? We can explore this question by recasting our discussion of Merleau-Ponty's motives into the following seven lines of argument.

1. If attention to reflective somatic consciousness and its bodily representations obscures the recognition of our more basic unreflective embodied perception and its primary importance, then reflective somatic consciousness should be resisted. This argument has a problematic ambiguity in its initial premise. Our reflective somatic consciousness does distract us for a time from unreflective perception (since attention to anything inevitably means a momentary obscuring of some other things). But somatic reflection need not always or permanently blind us to the unreflective, especially because such reflection is not (nor is meant to be) constantly sustained. The use of somatic reflection in most body disciplines is not meant to preclude unreflective perception and habit, but instead to improve them, by putting them into temporary focus so they can be retrained. If such body disciplines can affirm the primacy of unreflective behavior while also endorsing the need for conscious representations to monitor and correct it, then so can somatic philosophy. Besides, if we adopt Merleau-Ponty's claim that experience always depends on the complementarity of figure-ground contrast, we could then argue that any real appreciation of unreflective perception depends on its distinctive contrast from reflective consciousness, just as the latter clearly relies on the background of the former.

2. Merleau-Ponty rightly maintains that reflective consciousness and somatic representations are not only unnecessary but also ineffective for explaining our ordinary perception and behavior, which are usually unreflective. From that premise, one might infer that representational somatic awareness is a misleading irrelevancy. But this conclusion does not follow: first, because there is more to explain in human experience than our unproblematic unreflective perceptions and actions. Representational somatic consciousness can help us with respect to cases where spontaneous competencies break down and where unreflective habits are targeted for correction. Moreover, explanatory power is not the only criterion of value. Somaesthetic reflection and its representations can be useful not for explaining ordinary experience but for altering it and supplementing it.

3. This prompts a further argument. If the changes that somatic reflection introduces into experience are essentially undesirable, then, on

well maybe gee find so not see its

agpts of the damage this reflects somet co hence do

pragmatic grounds, it should be discouraged. Merleau-Ponty shows how reflection's representations form the core of both mechanistic and intellectualist accounts of behavior that promote mind/body dualism. Reflective somatic consciousness thus seems condemned for engendering a falsely fragmented view of experience, a view that eventually infects our experience itself and blinds us to the unreflective unity of primary perception.[14] But the misuse of representational somatic thinking in *some* explanatory contexts does not entail its global condemnation. Likewise, to affirm the value of representational somatic consciousness is not to deny the existence, value, or even primacy of the unreflective. Representational and reflective consciousness, I repeat, can serve alongside somatic spontaneity as a useful supplement and corrective.

4. Merleau-Ponty prizes the body's mystery and limitations as essential to its productive functioning. He repeatedly touts the miraculous way we perform our actions without any conscious reflection at all. Could he, then, argue pragmatically that reflective somatic consciousness should be resisted because it endangers such mystery and "effective" weakness? This argument rests on a confusion. The claim that we can do something effectively *without* explicit or representational consciousness does not imply that we cannot also do it *with* such consciousness and that such consciousness cannot improve our performance. In any case, plenty of mystery and limitation will always remain. Somaesthetic reflection could never claim to provide our bodies with total transparency or perfect power, since our mortality, frailty, and perspectival situatedness preclude this. But the fact that certain basic bodily limits can never be overcome is not a compelling argument against trying to expand, to some extent, our somatic powers through reflection and explicit conscious control.

5. Here we face a further argument. Reflection impairs our somatic performance by disrupting spontaneous action based on unreflective habit. Unreflective acts are quicker and easier than deliberatively executed behavior. Moreover, by not engaging explicit consciousness, such unreflective action enables better focusing of consciousness on the targets at which action is aimed. A well-trained batter can hit the ball better when he is not reflecting on the tension in his knees and wrists or imagining the pelvic movement in his swing. Not having to think of such things, he can better concentrate on seeing and reacting to the sinking fastball

[14] Merleau-Ponty complains that reflective thought "detaches subject and object from each other, and . . . gives us only the thought about the body, or the body as an idea, and not the experience of the body" (PoP, 198–99). But this is not true for disciplines of somaesthetic reflection that focus on the body as concretely experienced.

not too solid m reputation

he must hit. Somatic self-reflection would here prevent him from react-ing in time. Deliberative thinking can often ruin the spontaneous flow and efficacy of action. If we try to visualize each word as we speak, our speech will be slow and halting; we may even forget what we wanted to say. In sexual behavior, if one thinks too much about what is happening in one's own body while visualizing to oneself what must happen for things to go right, there is much more chance that something will go wrong. Such cases show that explicit somatic consciousness can sometimes be more of a problem than a solution. The conclusion, however, is not to reject such consciousness altogether, but rather to reflect more carefully on the ways it can be disciplined and deployed for the different contexts and ends in which it can indeed be helpful.[15] That there can sometimes be too much of a good thing is also true for somatic awareness.

6. Describing the body as "*la cachette de la vie*" ("the place where life hides away" in basic impersonal existence), Merleau-Ponty suggests yet another argument against somatic mindfulness.[16] Explicit concentration on body feelings entails a withdrawal from the outer world of action, and this change of focus impairs the quality of our perception and action in that world: "when I become absorbed in my body, my eyes present me with no more than the perceptible outer covering of things and of other people, things themselves take on unreality, behavior degenerates into the absurd." To "become absorbed in the experience of my body and in the solitude of sensations" is thus a disturbing danger from which we are barely protected by the fact that our sense organs and habits are always working to engage us in the outer world of life. Absorbed somatic reflection thus risks losing the world but also one's self, since the self is defined by our engagement with the world (PoP, 165).

Merleau-Ponty is right that an intense focus on somatic sensations can temporarily disorient our ordinary perspectives, disturbing our custom-ary involvement with the world and our ordinary sense of self. But it

---

[15] For a review (based on experimental studies) of the different ways and contexts in which explicit self-awareness can be advantageous and disadvantageous, see T. D. Wilson and E. W. Dunn, "Self-Knowledge: Its Limits, Value, and Potential for Improvement," *Annual Review of Psychology*, 55 (2004): 493–518. One apparent conclusion is that explicit aware-ness helps in learning stages but often tends to interfere later. A more recent study confirms that "aware subjects demonstrated a small but significant advantage in their ability to adapt their motor commands," see E. J. Hwang, M. A. Smith, and R. Shadmehr, "Dissociable Effects of the Implicit and Explicit Memory Systems on Learning Control of Reaching," *Experimental Brain Research*, 173, no. 3 (2006): 425–437, quotation on 425.

[16] The French expression is from Pdp, 192 and is rendered by the parenthetical quotation in English from PoP, 164.

is wrong to conclude that absorption in bodily feelings is essentially a primitive impersonal level of awareness, beneath the notions of both self and world, and thus confined to what he calls "the anonymous alertness of the senses" (PoP, 164). One can be *self-consciously* absorbed in one's bodily feelings; somatic self-consciousness involves a reflective awareness that one's self is experiencing the sensations on which one's attention is focused. Of course, this "turning in" of bodily consciousness on itself involves to some extent withdrawing attention from the outside world, though that world always makes its presence somehow felt. *A pure feeling of one's body alone is an abstraction. One cannot really feel oneself somatically without also feeling something of the external world.* If I lie down, close my eyes, and carefully try to feel just my body in itself, I will also feel the way it makes contact with the floor and sense the space between my limbs. (And if I do so with attentive somatic self-consciousness, I will likewise feel it is I who am lying on the floor and focusing on my bodily feelings.) In any case, if somaesthetics' deflection of attention to our bodily consciousness involves a temporary retreat from the world of action, this retreat can greatly advance our self-knowledge and self-use so that we will return to the world as more skillful observers and agents. It is the somatic logic of *reculer pour mieux sauter.*

Consider an example. If one wants to look over one's shoulder to see something behind one's back, most people will spontaneously lower their shoulder while turning their head. This seems logical but is (and should feel) skeletally wrong; dropping the shoulder constrains the rib and chest area and thus greatly limits the spine's range of rotation, which is what really enables us to see behind ourselves. By withdrawing our attention momentarily from the world behind us and by instead focusing attentively on the alignment of our body parts in rotating the head and spine, we can learn how to turn better and see more, creating a new habit that eventually will be unreflectively performed.

7. Merleau-Ponty's most radical argument against reflective somatic observation is that one simply cannot observe one's own body at all, because it is the permanent, invariant perspective through which we observe other things. Unlike ordinary objects, the body "defies exploration and is always presented to me from the same angle . . . To say that it is always near me, always there for me, is to say that it is never really in front of me, that I cannot array it before my eyes, that it remains marginal to all my perceptions, that it is *with* me." I cannot change my perspective with respect to my body as I can with external objects. "I observe external objects with my body, I handle them, examine them, walk round them,

but my body itself is a thing which I do not observe: in order to be able to do so, I should need the use of a second body" (PoP, 90–91). "I am always on the same side of my body; it presents itself to me in one invariable perspective" (VI, 148).

It is certainly true that we cannot observe our own lived bodies in exactly the same way we do external objects, since our bodies are precisely the tools through which we observe anything and since one cannot entirely array one's body before one's eyes (because our eyes themselves are part of the body). However, it does not follow from these points that we cannot observe our lived bodies in important ways. First, it is wrong to identify somatic observation narrowly with being "before my eyes." Though we cannot see our eyes without the use of a mirroring device, we can, with concentration, observe directly how they feel from the inside in terms of muscle tension, volume, and movement, even while we are using them to see. We can also observe our closed eyes by touching them from the outside with our hands. This shows, moreover, that our perspective on our bodies is not entirely fixed and invariant. We can examine them in terms of different sense modalities; and even if we use a single modality, we can scan the body from different angles and with different perspectives of focus. Lying on the floor with my eyes closed and relying only on proprioceptive sensing, I can scan my body from head to foot or vice versa, in terms of my alignment of limbs or my sense of body volume, or from the perspective of the pressure of my different body parts on the floor or of their distance from the floor. Of course, if we eschew somatic reflection, then we are far more likely to have an invariant perspective on our bodies – that of primitive, unfocused experience and unreflective habit, precisely the kind of primordial unthematized perception that Merleau-Ponty champions.

Merleau-Ponty's notion of bodily subjectivity might provide a last-ditch argument against the possibility of observing one's own lived body. In his critique of "double sensations" (PoP, 93), he insists that if our body is the observing subject of experience, then it cannot at the same time be the object of observation. Hence, we cannot really observe our perceiving bodies, just as we cannot use our left hand to feel our right hand (as an object) while the right hand is feeling an object. Even in his later "The Intertwining – The Chiasm," where Merleau-Ponty insists that the body's essential "reversibility" of being both sensing and sensed is crucial to our ability to grasp the world, he strongly cautions that this reversibility of being both observer and observed, while "always imminent," is "never realized in fact" through complete simultaneity or exact "coincidence."

One cannot at the very same time feel one's hand as touching and touched, one's voice speaking and heard (VI, 147–148). In short, one cannot simultaneously experience one's body as both subject and object. So if the lived body is always the observing subject, then it can never be observed as an object. Besides, as G. H. Mead claims, the observing "I" cannot directly grasp itself in immediate experience, since by the time it tries to catch itself, it has already become an objectified "me" for the grasping "I" of the next moment.

Such arguments can be met in different ways. First, given the essential vagueness of the notion of subjective simultaneity, we could argue that, practically speaking, one *can* simultaneously have experiences of touching and being touched, of feeling our voices from inside while hearing them from without, even if the prime focus of our attention may sometimes vacillate rapidly between the two perspectives within the very short duration of time we phenomenologically identify as the present and which, as James long ago recognized, is always a "specious present," involving memory of an immediate past.[17] Part of what seems to disrupt the experience of simultaneous perception of our bodies as both sensing and being sensed is simply the fact that the polarity of these perspectives is imposed on our experience by the binary framing of the thought experiment, a case where philosophy's reflection "prejudges what it will find" (VI, 130). Moreover, even if it is a fact that most experimental subjects cannot feel their bodies feeling, this may simply be due to their undeveloped capacities of somatic reflection and attentiveness.

Indeed, even if one cannot simultaneously experience one's own body as feeling and as felt, this does not entail that one can never observe it; just as the putative fact that one cannot simultaneously experience one's own mind as pure active thinking (i.e., a transcendental subject) and as something thought (i.e., an empirical subject) does not entail that we cannot observe our mental life. To treat the lived body as a subject does not require treating it *only* as a purely transcendental subject that cannot also be observed as an empirical one. To do so would vitiate the essential reversibility of the perceiving sentience and the perceived sensible that enables Merleau-Ponty to portray the body as the "flesh" that grounds our connection to the world. The "grammatical" distinction between the body as subject of experience and as object of experience is useful in reminding

---

[17] James, *The Principles of Psychology*, 573–575. On the vague notion of mental simultaneity and the intractable problems of determining "absolute timing" of consciousness, see Daniel Dennett, *Consciousness Explained* (Boston: Little, Brown, 1991), 136, 162–166.

a admits quite a lot

us that we can never reach a full transparency of our bodily intentionality. There will always be some dimensions of our bodily feelings that will be actively structuring the focus of our efforts of reflective somatic awareness and thus will not be themselves the object of that awareness or the focus of consciousness. There will also always be the possibility of introspective error through failure of memory or misinterpretation. Nor should we desire simultaneous reflexive consciousness of all our bodily feelings. But the pragmatic distinction between the perceiving "I" and the perceived "me" should not be erected into an insurmountable epistemological obstacle to observing the lived body within the realm provided by the specious present and short-term memory of the immediate past.[18]

Ultimately, we can also challenge Merleau-Ponty's argument against bodily self-observation by simply reminding ourselves that such observation (even if it is merely noticing our discomforts, pains, and pleasures) forms part of our ordinary experience. Only the introduction of abstract philosophical reflection could ever lead us to deny its possibility. If we take our pretheoretic common sense experience seriously, as Merleau-Ponty urges us to do, then we should reject the conclusion that we can never observe our own lived bodies, and we could therefore urge that his philosophical project be complemented by greater appreciation of reflective somatic consciousness.

V

Given the insufficiency of these reconstructed arguments, Merleau-Ponty's resistance to somatic mindfulness and reflection can be justified only in terms of his deeper philosophical aims and presumptions. Prominent here is his desire for philosophy to bring us back to a pure, primordial state of unified experience that has "not yet been 'worked over'" or splintered by "instruments [of] reflection" and thus can "offer us all at once, pell-mell, both 'subject' and 'object,' both existence and essence," both mind and body (VI, 130). Such yearning for a return to

---

[18] Mead himself wisely allows this. In making his famous "I/me" distinction, Mead did not conclude that the "I" was unobservable and absent from experience. Though "not directly given in experience" as an immediate datum, "it is in memory that the 'I' is constantly present in experience." That "the 'I' really appears experientially as a part of a [subsequent] 'me'" does not therefore mean we cannot observe ourselves as subjective agents but only that we need to do so by observing ourselves over time through the use of memory. See George Herbert Mead, *Mind, Self, and Society* (Chicago: University of Chicago Press, 1962), 174–176.

prereflective unity suggests dissatisfaction with the fragmentation that reflective consciousness and representational thinking have introduced into our experience as embodied subjects.

Philosophy can try to remedy this problem in two different ways. First, there is the therapy of theory. Philosophical reflection can be used to affirm the unity and adequacy of unreflective body behavior, to urge that we concentrate on this unreflective unity, while rejecting somatic reflection and representational somatic consciousness as intrinsically unnecessary and misleading. Here the very mystery of unreflective bodily actions is prized as an enabling cognitive weakness that proves superior to performances directed by representational reflection. But a second way to remedy dissatisfaction with our experience as embodied subjects moves beyond mere abstract theory by actively developing our powers of reflective somatic consciousness so that we can achieve a higher unity of experience on the reflective level and thus acquire better means to correct inadequacies of our unreflective bodily habits. Merleau-Ponty urges the first way; my pragmatist somatic theory urges the second, while recognizing the primacy of unreflective somatic experience and habit.

The first way – the way of pure intellect – reflects Merleau-Ponty's basic vision of philosophy as drawing its theoretical strength from its weakness of action. "The limping of philosophy is its virtue," he writes, in contrasting the philosopher with the man of action by contrasting "that which understands and that which chooses." "The philosopher of action is perhaps the farthest removed from action, for to speak of action with depth and rigor is to say that one does not desire to act" (IPP, 59–61). Should the philosopher of the body, then, be the farthest removed from her own lived body, because she is overwhelmingly absorbed in struggling with all her mind to analyze and champion the body's role?

This is an unfortunate conclusion. But it stubbornly asserts itself in the common complaint that most contemporary philosophy of the body seems to ignore or dissolve the actual active soma within a labyrinth of metaphysical, psychological, social, gender, and brain-science theories. Despite their valuable insights, such theories fall short of considering practical methods for individuals to improve their somatic consciousness and functioning. Merleau-Ponty's phenomenological approach exemplifies this problem by devoting intense theoretical reflection on the value of unreflective bodily subjectivity, but dismissing the use of somatic reflection to improve that subjectivity in perception and action. In contrast to men of action (and other varieties of "the serious man"), the philosopher, says Merleau-Ponty, is never fully engaged in a practical way in what he affirms. Even in the causes to which he is faithful, we find "in his assent [that] something massive and carnal is lacking. He is not altogether a real being" (IPP, 59, 60).

Lacking in Merleau-Ponty's superb advocacy of the body's philosophical importance is a robust sense of the real body as a site for practical disciplines of conscious reflection that aim at reconstructing somatic perception and performance to achieve more rewarding experience and action. Pragmatism offers a complementary philosophical perspective that is friendlier to full-bodied engagement in practical efforts of somatic awareness. It aims at generating better experience for the future rather than trying to recapture the lost perceptual unity of a primordial past, a "return to that world which precedes knowledge" (PoP, ix).

If it seems possible to combine this pragmatist reconstructive dimension of somatic theory with Merleau-Ponty's basic philosophical insights about the lived body and the primacy of unreflective perception, this is partly because Merleau-Ponty's philosophy has its own pragmatic flavor. Insisting that consciousness is primarily "not a matter of 'I think that' but of 'I can'"(PoP, 137), he also recognized that philosophy is more than impersonal theory but also a personal way of life. If he urged philosophy as the way to recover a lost primordial unity of unreflective experience, if he defined it as "the Utopia of possession at a distance" (perhaps the recapture of that unreflective past from the distance of present reflection), were there reasons in his life that helped determine this philosophical yearning (IPP, 58)? Was there also a personal yearning for a utopian past unity – primitive, spontaneous, and unreflective – and recoverable only by reflection from a distance, if at all?

We know very little of the private life of Merleau-Ponty, but there is certainly evidence that he had such a yearning for "this paradise lost." "One day in 1947, Merleau told me that he had never recovered from an incomparable childhood," writes his close friend Jean-Paul Sartre. "Everything had been too wonderful, too soon. The form of Nature which first enveloped him was the Mother Goddess, his own mother, whose eyes made him see what he saw . . . By her and through her, he lived this 'intersubjectivity of immanence' which he has often described and which causes us to discover our 'spontaneity' through another." With childhood gone, "one of his most constant characteristics was to seek everywhere for lost immanence." His mother, Sartre explains, was essential to this utopian "hope of reconquering" this sense of childhood spontaneity and "immediate accord" with things. "Through her, it was preserved – out of reach, but alive." When she died in 1952, Sartre recounts, Merleau-Ponty was devastated and essentially "became a recluse."[19] There remained the consolation of philosophy and the project of reclaiming, at least in theory, the cherished but vanishing values of spontaneity, immediacy, and immanence that belonged to his lost world of unreflective innocence and harmony.

[19] Jean-Paul Sartre, "Merleau Ponty," in *Situations*, trans. Benita Eisler (New York: Braziller, 1965), 228, 235, 243, 301–302.

3

Somatic Subjectivities and Somatic Subjugation

Simone de Beauvoir on Gender and Aging

I

If Merleau-Ponty is unconvincing in positing a fixed ground of primordial perception that, though embodied, is "unchanging, given once and for all," and shared or "known by all"; if he is wrong in elevating this ground into a universal normative ideal of spontaneity whose recovery should be somatic philosophy's prime aim, then let us turn to theorists more sensitive to the diversity of embodied perception and the historicity of somatic norms. Insisting that variant historical, social, and cultural factors differently mold our experience as embodied subjects, such thinkers further argue that a culture's dominant forms of discourse tend to obscure or demean divergent subjectivities so as to universalize the consciousness of socially privileged subjects as naturally normative and definitive for the entire human race. Should all somatic subjectivity be assimilated to the kind described by philosophers who typically generalize from their phenomenological experience as privileged adult males in the prime of life? A philosophical account of body consciousness must confront the question of difference.

Simone de Beauvoir ranks among the most original and influential theorists of difference. A longtime philosophical friend and collaborator of Merleau-Ponty, she effectively challenges the ahistorical universalism of his approach to embodiment by exploring the problems of bodily difference (in women and the elderly) and by exposing the ways that historically dominant hierarchies of power shape our somatic experience and define the norms of bodily being. To expose the subtle mechanisms through which differently embodied subjectivities are subjugated through their bodies, Beauvoir shows how the distinctive bodily differences of women and old people are perceived as negatively marked in terms of social power that reflects society's male dominance. Such social disempowerment is reciprocally reinforced by the perceived bodily weakness of women and the elderly, which seems to justify their subordinate status as natural and necessary. Fostered and inculcated by the prevailing institutions and ideologies of our culture, such somatic and social subordination is, moreover, incorporated in the bodily habits of these dominated subjects who thus unconsciously reinscribe their own sense of weakness and domination.

Could cultivation of greater somaesthetic powers and consciousness help in liberating such subjugated subjectivities, and how does Beauvoir regard the emancipatory potential of somaesthetic praxis? To explore such issues, this chapter examines Beauvoir's rich somatic philosophy, focusing especially on two major works, *The Second Sex* (1949) and the *The Coming of Age* (1970), which explore somatic difference and subjugation in the ubiquitous human categories of woman and the aged.[1] If the body "is the instrument of our grasp upon the world" and if "freedom will never be given ... [but] will always have to be won," then Beauvoir should clearly affirm somatic cultivation as crucial for enhancing our bodily instrument to help us win greater freedom.[2] However, her approach is more ambiguous, complex, and conflicted.

Its complexities can be made clearer by framing our discussion in terms of the branches of somaesthetics outlined in Chapter 1. Beauvoir's *practical somaesthetics* – her actual personal engagement in bodily practices and disciplines – will not be studied here. Though factors of somatic biography can help us understand a philosopher's discursive views on embodiment, highlighting biography would feed a dangerous trend in

---

[1] Simone de Beauvoir, *Le deuxième sexe* (Gallimard: Paris, 1949), and *La Vieillesse* (Gallimard: Paris, 1970). For the former, I quote from the English version, *The Second Sex*, trans. H. M. Parshley (New York: Vintage, 1989), hereafter SS. Parshley's text is an unfortunately abridged and often poorly translated rendering of the original, so I occasionally use my own translation. For a powerful critique of Parshley's abridgment and translation, see Margaret Simons, *Beauvoir and* The Second Sex (New York: Rowman & Littlefield, 1999). *La Vieillesse*, translated into English (by Patrick O'Brien), was published as *The Coming of Age* (New York: Putnam, 1972), hereafter CA.

[2] SS, 34; and Simone de Beauvoir, *The Ethics of Ambiguity*, trans. Bernard Frechtman (New York: Citadel Press, 1964), 119. The body's crucial role in freedom is especially clear when we conceive freedom not narrowly in terms of negative liberty from imposed social constraints but of positive ability to perform. An infant is free in the negative sense to walk, but he has no positive freedom to do so until he masters the relevant bodily competence. Bodily power or movement is perhaps the elemental root of our concept of freedom, as I argue in "Thinking Through the Body, Educating for the Humanites," *Journal of Aesthetic Education*, 40 (2006): 1–21.

Beauvoir studies of "reducing the [work] to the woman" and then trivializing or discrediting her philosophical arguments "as mere displacements of the personal."[3] Biographical studies and her own extensive memoirs show she enjoyed a dynamic bodily life and expressed her taste in clothes, cosmetics, and grooming. Fond of skiing, cycling, and tennis, she was an especially avid hiker, who had a love of food, a robustly ample experience of sexuality, and, more remarkably, an avowed passion for violence, which she also manifested through some childhood experiments in radical asceticism.[4]

Beauvoir's contributions to analytic somaesthetics – her studies of human embodiment and its particular expression in women (of different ages, cultures, and social positions) and in the elderly (of different societies, professions, and classes) – are too richly wide ranging for adequate analysis here. Extending from the metaphysics and biology of

[3] See Toril Moi, *Feminist Theory and Simone de Beauvoir* (Oxford: Blackwell, 1990), 27, 32. A similar danger exists in using Beauvoir's fiction to probe her somatic views. Her philosophical arguments on these matters could then be dismissed as essentially a continuation of her fictional musings and thus not be taken as serious philosophy, and she herself might then be trivialized as merely a writer rather than a "real" philosopher. The strategy of marginalizing Beauvoir's philosophy is unfortunately encouraged by her own preference to call herself a writer rather than assume the title of philosopher (apparently in deference to Sartre's philosophical stature). I agree with Margaret Simons, Debra Bergoffen, and many others in ranking Beauvoir as an important philosopher. See Simons, *Beauvoir and* The Second Sex, and Debra Bergoffen, *The Philosophy of Simone de Beauvoir: Gendered Phenomenologies, Erotic Generosities* (Albany: SUNY Press, 1997).

[4] "There is within me I know not what yearning – maybe a monstrous lust – ever present, for noise, fighting, savage violence, and above all for the gutter," writes Beauvoir, who identifies her passion for "violence" as extending back to her early childhood at age three. Simone de Beauvoir, *Memoirs of a Dutiful Daughter*, trans. James Kirkup (New York: Harper, 1974), 13, 307. One biographer relates that in adolescence Beauvoir expressed her religious devotion in violent terms by "locking herself in the bathroom where she mortified her flesh by scraping her thighs with a pumice stone or whipping herself with a gold necklace until she drew blood." See Claude Francis and Fernande Gontier, *Simone de Beauvoir: A Life, a Love Story*, trans. Lisa Nesselson (New York: St. Martin's Press, 1985), 42. Such negativity toward the flesh seems to reflect Beauvoir's mother's strong distaste for the physical that "pushed contempt of the body, for herself and for her daughters, to the point of uncleanliness" (ibid., 35). Beauvoir avows she was taught "never to look at [her] naked body" because "the body as a whole was vulgar and offensive," her mother never explaining the body's true functions but instead suggesting that "little babies came out of the anus" (*Memoirs of a Dutiful Daughter*, 58, 82, 87). For additional autobiographical material, see Simone de Beauvoir, *The Prime of Life*, trans. P. Green (London: Penguin, 1965); *Force of Circumstance*, trans. Richard Howard (London: Penguin, 1968); *All Said and Done*, trans. Patrick O'Brian (London: Penguin, 1977); and her account of her mother's terminal illness, *A Very Easy Death*, trans. Patrick O'Brian (New York: Pantheon, 1985). For further biographical information, see Francis Jeanson, *Simone de Beauvoir ou l'enterprise de vivre* (Paris: Seuil, 1966); Deirdre Bair, *Simone de Beauvoir: A Biography* (New York: Summit, 1990); and Carol Ascher, *Simon de Beauvoir: A Life of Freedom* (Boston: Beacon, 1981).

embodiment to the ways it is molded through psychological development and historical, social, and economic conditions, she also explores
how somatic life is both represented and reshaped by myth and literature. Though sometimes outdated by scientific and social progress, her
views on analytic somaesthetics remain significant, especially in terms of
their bearing on the chapter's main focus: pragmatic somaesthetics and
its liberational potential.

Beauvoir shrinks from advocating somatic cultivation as a key means
for liberating the subjugated subjects of difference and domination.
Recognizing that bodily strength and health can be empowering, she
nonetheless downplays the value of heightened attention to the body,
while highlighting its dangers as a distracting hindrance to real emancipatory progress. Her problematic relationship to somatic cultivation will be
examined in terms of the different categories of pragmatic somaesthetics
delineated earlier: *representational* (primarily concerned with the body's
surface forms or representations), *experiential* (principally focused on the
quality and perceptive consciousness of one's somatic experience), and
performative (essentially devoted to building bodily power, performance,
and skill).

Beauvoir's studies of woman and old age reveal considerable homolo-
gies in the factors that subordinate these somatically marked, socially
dominated subjects. Perceived bodily differences (whether diminished
muscle strength or the disruptions of menstruation, pregnancy, and childbirth) are immediately seen as significant *weaknesses* by being grasped
through the discriminatory perspective of an entrenched sociocultural
matrix. This network of institutions, habits, beliefs, practices, and values reflects the socially subordinate status of women and the aged, while
reinforcing and justifying their domination in terms of their somatic difference of comparative weakness. One could imagine a radically alternative society, free from male dominance, that might conversely regard
the unruly power of high testosterone as a physiological weakness socially
marking the males as less qualified for positions of power that require
tranquil composure. *The Second Sex* and *The Coming of Age* are also similar
in expositional structure, the argument beginning with biology, history,
and myth before proceeding to the situation of contemporary subjects
and the way today's women and elderly inhabit and experience their subordinate situation. However, there are also clear differences in Beauvoir's
treatment of women and old age, so we will consider these subjects sep-
arately, beginning with *The Second Sex*, surely her most influential book
and a feminist classic.

II

Ambiguity, a key concept in Beauvoir's philosophy, is salient in her somatic theory. *The Second Sex* is pervaded by two different conceptions of the body, whose uneasy tension seems reflected in the conflictual discomforts that she argues are particularly acute in women's experience of embodiment. On the one hand, Beauvoir defines the body in the very positive terms of Merleau-Ponty's existential phenomenology – as not a merely material thing but the positive, enabling, instrumental situation of our grasping and having a world. "If the body is not a *thing*, it is a situation," "the instrument of our grasp upon the world" (SS, 34). Challenging the Freudian presumption that our bodies are most primally sexual, she asserts that "the body is first of all the radiation of a subjectivity, the instrument that makes possible the comprehension of the world" (SS, 267). On the other hand, alongside this active, intentional body subjectivity we find a more negative, Sartrian characterization of the body that is equally pervasive and perhaps ultimately triumphant in her book: the body as mere flesh, as an inactive material immanence, a passive contingent object that is defined and dominated by the actively subjective gaze of others.[5] Although women, because of their subjugated

[5] Though Sartre recognizes an active-acting body expressing the subjectivity of transcendence that could be distinguished from the body as mere passive flesh, he tends to devalorize the body in general as immanent facticity in contrast to transcendent consciousness, as infected by obscurity and weakness and as the material, visible dimension of a person that exposes that person to the gaze of the other and thus to the threat of being objectified as a thing and dominated by the other's subjectivity. As Moi and others note, the devalorizing rhetoric and problematic views that Beauvoir expresses with respect to the body (and especially the female body) bear the influence of Sartre. See Toril Moi, *Simone de Beauvoir: The Making of an Intellectual Woman* (Oxford: Blackwell, 1994), 152–153, 170. Moreover, in interviews about *The Second Sex*, where Beauvoir affirmed the dominant influence of Sartre's philosophy on her own, she also insisted that her view on the body was basically Sartrian. See the interviews in Simons, *Beauvoir and* The Second Sex, chs. 1, 4, 5. However, Simons and other feminist philosophers, such as Bergoffen and Karen Vintges, refuse to take Beauvoir at her word and rightly insist that Beauvoir's philosophy "redefined and transcended" Sartre's ideas (Simons, *Beauvoir and* The Second Sex, 2). Bergoffen and Vintges argue in particular that Beauvoir's somatic philosophy departs significantly from Sartre's, even though she deployed Sartrian concepts and rhetoric. Not only does Beauvoir go beyond Sartre's focus on the body's general ontology by providing a rich physiological, historical, social, and political analysis of women's bodies, but she also emphasizes far more than Sartre (and more like Merleau-Ponty) the body's ambiguity as intentionality and flesh and the positive aspects of this ambiguity. In other words, she was more accepting of the flesh, its vulnerability, and the emotional possibilities that such vulnerability could provide. See especially Bergoffen, *The Philosophy of Simone de Beauvoir*, 11–42, 141–181; and Karen Vintges, *Philosophy as Passion: The Thinking of Simone de Beauvoir* (Bloomington: Indiana University Press, 1996), 25, 39–45. Beauvoir

social situation, are especially inclined to feel their body as "a prey" of "passive" flesh (SS, 377), "a carnal object" (SS, 648) or "fleshly prey" (SS, 410), Beauvoir insists that "men and women all feel the shame of their flesh; in its pure, inactive presence, its unjustified immanence, the flesh exists, under the gaze of others, in its absurd contingence, and yet it is oneself: oh, to prevent it from existing for others, oh, to deny it!"(SS, 381).

Beauvoir thus ambiguously affirms that man is his body while rhetorically implying that human subjectivity is something other than body and even opposed to it, making the person seem deeply divided between carnality and consciousness, objecthood and subjecthood, inactive material immanence and the active transcendence of conscious will.[6] The case for woman's personhood is portrayed as even more problematically divided, because woman, under patriarchy, is not merely torn between body and consciousness but divided within her body itself. "Woman, like man, *is* her body; but her body is something other than herself" (SS, 29). From the onset of puberty and throughout the years of birth-giving, nursing, and motherhood, Beauvoir argues, the biological demand of the human species powerfully reasserts itself against the will of the individual female, and her body is the site of this inexorable takeover. The monthly "curse" of menstruation, whose hormonal reactions affect the "whole female organism," including her nervous system and consciousness, appears as an alien force that captures both body and mind, making the woman "more irritable" and more prone to "serious psychic disturbance" (SS, 27, 28, 29). At such times especially, "she feels her body most painfully as an obscure, alien thing; it is, indeed, the prey of a stubborn and foreign life that each month constructs and then tears down a cradle within it" (SS, 29).

herself acknowledges, on occasion, her divergence from Sartre's view of the body. "I criticized Sartre for regarding his body as a mere bundle of striated muscles, and for having cut it out of his emotional world. If you gave way to tears or nerves or seasickness, he said, you were simply being weak. I, on the other hand, claimed that stomach and tear ducts, indeed the head itself, were all subject to irresistible forces on occasion" (Beauvoir, *The Prime of Life*, 129).

[6] Debra Bergoffen describes this sort of tension in *The Second Sex* in terms of a tension between Beauvoir's "dominant voice" (that identifies subjectivity with transcendence) and her "muted voice" that "challenges the equation subjectivity equals transcendence" and instead sees subjectivity in terms of "the ambiguity of the body" that is both transcendence and immanence. This tension has further repercussions. "The dominant voice of *The Second Sex* urges women to pursue economic independence. The muted voice urges us all to retrieve the erotics of generosity." The dominant voice privileges violence and the transcendent "project ethic of liberation," the muted voice expresses "her erotic ethic of generosity" that highlights the concern for our bodily "bond" with others. See Bergoffen, *The Philosophy of Simone de Beauvoir*, 12, 36, 160, 173.

Conception is no escape, only a more extreme alienation in which the woman's body is no longer fully her own but instead inhabited by another living creature, a parasite who feeds on her bodily resources, and whose presence results in various bodily ailments, hardships, and risks of disease that range from the trivial to the very serious.[7] "Childbirth itself is painful and dangerous," and "nursing is also a tiring service" (the original French word is the far more negative "servitude," which connotes slavery) that further depletes the nutrients the mother needs to restore her own somatic health, while limiting the foods she can enjoy to rebuild her strength (SS, 30). Only at the late age of menopause, can woman finally escape her "bondage . . . to the species" (SS, 35).

Beauvoir, however, shrewdly resists the temptations of a crude biological determinism.[8] The biological facts are "insufficient for setting up a hierarchy of the sexes; they fail to explain why woman is the Other; they do not condemn her to remain in this subordinate role forever" (SS, 32–33). "It is not nature that defines woman; it is she who defines herself by dealing with nature on her own account in her emotional life" (SS, 38). "In human history grasp upon the world has never been defined by the naked body" (SS, 53); so "the facts of biology [must be seen] in the light of an ontological, economic, social, and psychological context" (SS, 36). The human body, she argues, is the malleable expression of a creature not entirely fixed or purely natural but significantly shaped by

---

[7] Describing pregnancy's ailments as expressing the "revolt of the organism against the invading species" (SS, 29–30), Beauvoir portrays the fetus as alien to the pregnant woman, "a growth arising from her flesh but foreign to it" (SS, 498) and notes how it can seem "rather horrible that a parasitic body should proliferate within her [own] body" (SS, 299).

[8] Whether she adequately resists the temptations of biological positivism is more debatable. In an instructive article that examines Beauvoir's treatment of biology in the light of recent feminist science and philosophy of science, Charlene Haddock Seigfried objects that "Beauvoir recognized only the distortive use of biological facts by various interpreters [to justify woman's subjugation] and did not consider whether the research programs from which the biological facts emerged were also distorted by these same cultural prejudices" of patriarchy. Beauvoir's account of the biological facts thus, for Seigfried, too uncritically absorbs their patriarchal bias and consequently "suffers from the same distortions," for example, in the so-called facts of maternity as an enslaving, alienating, cause of weakness. Considered from the perspective of evolutionary biology, where success is measured by the transmission of genes to a new generation through the production of viable offspring, women – by being "so much more responsible for reproductive success than men" – should be considered biologically "more favored." See Charlene Haddock Seigfried, "*Second Sex: Second Thoughts*," in *Hypatia Reborn: Essays in Feminist Philosophy*, ed. Azizah Al-Hibri and Margaret Simons (Bloomington: Indiana University Press, 1984), 305–322; citations 307–308, 312.

historical situations and societal conditions. If woman's bodily difference
and suffering were not reinforced by social and economic structures that
exploit that difference and suffering while marking them with meanings
of inferiority and exclusion from the dominant centers of action, then
these distinguishing biological features would not in themselves confine
woman to her oppression. Drawing on existentialist themes from Nietzsche and Merleau-Ponty, she claims that "man is defined as a being who
is not fixed, who makes himself what he is"; "man is not a natural species:
he is a historical idea"(SS, 34).[9] In the same way, "woman is not a completed reality, but rather a becoming" (ibid.). A creature whose life and
bodily experience are shaped not merely by biology but by the changing historical situations in which she exists, woman is also an "existent"
who can act to transcend and transform her initial situation. So the most
important question about woman and her body is not what she historically
or biologically is but what she can become; "that is to say, her *possibilities*
should be defined," and they should be defined in ways that expand those
possibilities and powers in the future (ibid.).

Beauvoir's future-looking, activist, meliorist approach to our open, malleable human nature (itself shaped by a malleable world that is partly the
product of human interventions) is an existentialist orientation conver-
gent with the pragmatist tradition that motivates somaesthetics.[10] Can
pragmatic somaesthetics, then, usefully treat the problematic limitations
that Beauvoir identifies as hampering women's self-realization while also
enhancing some of the distinctive capacities she attributes to women?
To make a case for such value, we need to examine Beauvoir's analysis
of women's distinctive problems of subjugational embodiment together
with the somaesthetic means to address them, some of which she notices
but firmly criticizes. Since *The Second Sex* persistently assimilates performative forms of somaesthetics into representational ones, my discussion

[9] Compare the remark from Maurice Merleau-Ponty's chapter on "The Body in its Sexual
Being," from his *Phenomenology of Perception*, trans. Colin Smith (London: Routledge, 1986,
170): "Man is a historical idea and not a natural species." Rejecting any sort of biological
determinism with respect to human existence, Beauvoir elsewhere remarks that "nothing
that happens to a man is ever natural, since his presence calls the world into question."
Beauvoir, *A Very Easy Death*, 106.

[10] Beauvoir's existentialism also converges with pragmatism on other points. Like pragmatist aesthetics, she criticizes "the aesthetic attitude" of "detached contemplation" as
"a position of withdrawal" from the world, noting how the artist creates "not in the
name of pure contemplation, but of a definite project," relating to his active situation
in the world; "man never contemplates; he does." See Beauvoir, *The Ethics of Ambiguity*,
74–77.

of her arguments will be divided into two sections, respectively relating to representational and experiential issues.

III

Representations, in their most basic philosophical sense, are objects of perception as grasped by subjects. To the extent that Beauvoir accepts a radical dualism between subject and object, the very idea of viewing a person in terms of representational properties would seem a way of negating that person's subjectivity by reducing that person to the status of a perceived or representational object. In other words, the active, perceiving, dominating subjectivity of the perceiving self would render the other, represented, human subject as a mere object, a product of subjectivity's representational objectifying gaze. For men, this problem is not without remedy, because they can strongly identify themselves as active, dominating subjects through their dynamic activity and power in the world. Although this remedy is clearly less available to men of dominated classes, races, and ethnicities, they still can assert their subjective dominance with respect to the women of their own (and other) dominated social groups.

But if men are traditionally seen as bearing the marks of subjecthood and transcendence (such as intellect, will, and action), woman, Beauvoir argues, is usually identified in contrast as *object*. She is essentially seen as her body and flesh – a material vehicle for man's desire and delight and for the procreation of the species. Woman, in short, is that subject whom patriarchy has made the quintessential object of the dominating subject's gaze and thus "the inessential" "Other" (SS, xxxv). Though men also have bodies that fall under the category of representational objects, the representational properties of their bodies, according to Beauvoir, imply transcendence and active, powerful subjectivity. Man's virile properties and bigger muscles suggest this dynamic power, as does "the identification of phallus and transcendence" (SS, 682) because of the active, dominant, directive, penetrating, willful role that the penis is seen as having – not only in sex but in urination (SS, 274, 385). These representational properties of male somatic strength help reinforce men's social power as dominating subjects. Perceived as strong, not only by others but also by themselves, their bodies give men the confidence to assert a strong subjectivity in the world and have it granted by others.

Woman's situation is unhappily quite different. Not only has patriarchal society taught "her to identify herself with her whole body," it has also taught her to view that body as mere "carnal passivity," "a carnal object" (SS, 648, 718). For Beauvoir, "to feel oneself a woman is to feel oneself a desirable object" but also a weak, passive one – the "fleshly prey" of a stronger desiring subject (SS, 410, 637). If "handsome appearance in the male suggests transcendence" through virile engagement with the world, it contrastingly suggests, "in the female, the passivity of immanence," an object of "the gaze" that "can hence be captured" (SS, 631). Traditional fashions of feminine beauty – that highlight delicacy, daintiness, softness, and frilly attire impractical for dynamic action – reinforce this image of woman as a fragile, weak, and fleshly passive prey. Such fashions encourage women to conform not only their visual appearance but also their bodily comportment to this image of weak feminine beauty – to take the passive role in sex, to sit or walk like a woman, to throw like a girl. In short, the established aesthetic ideology of the female body serves to reinforce female weakness, passivity, and meekness, while such submissiveness is reciprocally used to justify the permanent and natural rightness of the traditional feminine aesthetic and the "myth" of "the Eternal Feminine" (SS, 253).

Couldn't a somaesthetic critique of this ideology and the development of new somaesthetic ideals be helpful for breaking out of this vicious circle? Beauvoir initially seems to affirm this possibility. Writing in 1949, she celebrates fashion's "new" somaesthetic challenge to the traditional feminine ideal of pale, soft, and opulent flesh draped in impractical attire.

> A new aesthetics has already been born. If the fashion of flat chests and narrow hips – the boyish form – has had its brief season, at least the overopulent ideal of past centuries has not returned. The feminine body is asked to be flesh, but with discretion; it is to be slender and not loaded with fat; muscular, supple, strong, it is bound to suggest transcendence; it must not be pale like a too shaded hothouse plant, but preferably tanned like a workman's torso from being bared to the open sun. Woman's dress in becoming practical need not make her appear sexless: on the contrary, short skirts made the most of legs and thighs as never before. There is no reason why working should take away woman's sex appeal. (SS, 262)

Clearly, the message here is that a change of somaesthetic representations can help change not only the bodies of women but also improve their overall self-image and empower them toward greater transcendence.

Beauvoir suggests the same sort of argument with respect to sports and other performative forms of somatic discipline that have clear representational aspects and aims. The external representation of bodily power, "to climb higher than a playmate, to force an arm to yield and bend, is to assert one's sovereignty over the world in general. Such masterful behaviour is not for girls, especially when it involves violence" (SS, 330).[11] Moreover, for woman, "this lack of physical power leads to a more general timidity: she has no faith in a force she has not experienced in her body; she does not dare to be enterprising, to revolt, to invent" (SS, 331). If woman's "muscular weakness disposes her to passivity" (SS, 712), then male-dominated society is only too happy to confirm her disposition. Beauvoir cogently concludes: "Not to have confidence in one's body is to lose confidence in oneself. One needs only to see the importance young men place in their muscles to understand that every subject regards his body as his objective expression" (SS, 332).

The practical upshot of this argument should be a somaesthetic program aimed at developing women's general sense of strength by developing their somatic powers and endowing their bodies with the representational aesthetic qualities suggestive of such power. And Beauvoir seems initially to endorse this way for woman to "assert herself through her body and face the world" with transcendent power: "Let her swim, climb mountain peaks, pilot an airplane, battle against the elements . . . and she will not feel before the world that timidity" fostered by her bodily weakness (SS, 333). Beauvoir's claim that "technique may annul the muscular inequality of man and woman" (SS, 53) likewise suggests that women should cultivate somatic disciplines that specifically develop techniques to neutralize the advantage of brute strength, especially techniques like judo and other martial arts that can be deployed in what she sees as the crucial realm of violence.[12]

---

[11] Beauvoir is often strikingly outspoken about the value of violence. "Violence is the authentic proof of each one's loyalty to himself, to his passions, to his own will," she insists, while complaining that even "the sportswoman never knows the conquering pride of a boy who pins one's opponent's shoulders to the ground" (SS, 330, 331). In a passage that understandably shocks many feminists, she writes: "For it is not in giving life but in risking life that man is raised above the animal; that is why superiority has been accorded in humanity not to the sex that brings forth life but to that which kills" (SS, 64). In her interpretation of the Marquis de Sade as "a great moralist," Beauvoir affirms his view that violence, as an essential truth of nature, is a crucial means for the individual to experience the truth, to make it his own, and to communicate it to his victim, thereby establishing a bond between separate individuals. With such knowledge also comes greater delight: "One must do violence to the object of one's desire; when it surrenders, the pleasure is greater." Simone de Beauvoir, *Must We Burn de Sade*, trans. Annette Michelson (London: Peter Nevill, 1953), 47, 58; cf. 84–85.

[12] In an interview given to two biographers in May 1985, Beauvoir urges: "Young girls must learn karate at school, we must support a Tour de France for women." Quoted in Francis and Gontier, *Simone de Beauvoir: A Life, a Love Story*, 358.

Women can even overcome, to a large extent, their physical, muscular weakness by practicing somatic disciplines that develop strength as well as technique. In a passage that strikingly runs together performative and representational forms of somaesthetics (by blending ideas of active, powerful function and attractive, visible form), Beauvoir explains:

> Today, more than formerly, woman knows the joy of developing her body through sports, gymnastics, baths, massage, and health diets; she decides what her weight, her figure, and the color of her skin shall be. Modern aesthetic concepts permit her to combine beauty and activity: she has a right to trained muscles, she declines to get fat; in physical culture she finds self-affirmation as subject and in a measure frees herself from her contingent flesh. (SS 534–535)

If these words suggest that a blend of representational-performative somaesthetics provides a promising direction toward female liberation, Beauvoir is quick to counter (in the very same sentence) that this idea is a risky illusion. Any somatically oriented means of female "liberation easily falls back into dependence" (SS, 535), because it deploys the female body that is so deeply and stubbornly marked as mere object, flesh, and passive immanence in contrast to the true transcendence of consciousness and action in the world that real freedom requires. "The Hollywood star triumphs over nature, but she becomes a passive object again in the producer's hands," Beauvoir argues (SS, 535). "The subjection of Hollywood stars is well known. Their bodies are not their own; the producer decides on the color of their hair, their weight, their figure, their type; to change the curve of a cheek, their teeth may be pulled. Dieting, gymnastics, fittings, constitute a daily burden" (SS, 570). Although women can achieve a certain power by maximizing their beauty to wield the influence of being desired, Beauvoir insists that because such power depends on the woman's face and figure, it is built on a foundation of "flesh that time will disfigure" and relies on the admiring, desiring gaze of others; hence, it tends to reproduce woman's "dependence" (SS, 640). Not only is "her body . . . an object that deteriorates with time," but "routine makes drudgery of beauty care and the upkeep of the wardrobe" (SS, 535). "The American woman, who would be men's idol, makes herself the slave of her admirers; she dresses, lives, breathes, only through men and for them" (SS, 640). Thus despite occasional, provisional "victories" of self-affirmation through body care "in which woman may rightly rejoice" (SS, 535), representational and performative somaesthetics fail, in her view, to provide a real or reliable tool of woman's liberation.

Beauvoir's argument can be challenged. Her running together the performative and the representational projects of somaesthetics wrongly suggests that woman's work on strengthening the body is ultimately or essentially aimed at making it look good for others rather than making it feel stronger and perform better for herself. One can also counter that male actors face similar problems of having to objectify and submit themselves to the will of directors and producers while also worrying about keeping their figure and their hair to remain an attractive representational object for the female and male gaze. Moreover, it is wrong to think that only the body and flesh are subject to disfigurement by time. Our minds are also eventually diminished by time, indeed by the body's aging, even if the proud idealist tradition of philosophy has stubbornly sought to deny this. But these objections are marginal to what I think is the main point behind Beauvoir's argument.

Beauvoir resists a full endorsement of performative and representational somaesthetics because she rightly wants to insist that full female liberation cannot be achieved merely by the means of isolated individuals engaging in somatic cultivation. It can be won only through a "collective" political effort that "requires first of all...the economic evolution of woman's condition" and their active engagement in politics that projects their freedom "through positive action into human society" (627, 678). In short, woman's liberation cannot rely on changing the individual body but only on changing the larger situation that defines what women's bodies and selves can be. Beauvoir is right about the prime importance of the social, political, and economic conditions that constitute the situation through which the embodied self is shaped. But if the total concrete situation is what determines the meaning of the female self, it is also true that bodily practices form part of that wider situation (as "the body of woman is one of the essential elements in her situation in the world" [SS, 37]) and thus such practices can help transform that situation. This truth holds not merely for those unique individuals whose distinctive forms of bodily excellence (in beauty, sport, dance, and so forth) can be directly converted into economic and social capital. All women can become more empowered to face the world and its social and economic problems by learning to be, to feel, and to look stronger through somaesthetic disciplines.

It is a widely shared psychological insight (urged by thinkers as diverse as William James and Wilhelm Reich) that particular bodily postures both reflect and reciprocally induce certain related mental attitudes. By generating new habits of bodily comportment through disciplines of exercise that not only build strength and skill but also give feelings of power and efficacy, women can attain a better body image that gives them more confidence to act assertively and overcome the timidity that Beauvoir sees as enslaving them. Such represented body power and the confident attitude it inspires will also be perceived by men who may then be more disposed to respect these women as powerfully competent. Moreover, since increased bodily competence gives women greater efficacy in performing what they wish to perform, it will also boost their self-assurance for more ambitious projects of engagement with the world. In short, performative-representational somaesthetic activities oriented toward displaying power, skill, and an attractively dynamic self-presentation should promote Beauvoir's goal of promoting women's confidence for engaging in greater action in the world. By pragmatist logic, if we value the goal, we should also, *ceteris paribus*, respect the means necessary for achieving it. So, even if it is far from the highest end of female liberation, somaesthetics' cultivation of the body should at least be endorsed for its contribution as a useful (though certainly not the only useful) means.

Feminist theorists working in the tradition of Simone de Beauvoir and Merleau-Ponty seem to recognize this line of argument, and they develop it in different ways. In her brilliant essay, "Throwing Like a Girl," Iris Marion Young elaborates how "women often approach a physical engagement with things with timidity, uncertainty, and hesitancy" because they "lack an entire trust in [their] bodies." Feelings of weakness and "a fear of getting hurt" produce in many women a sense "of incapacity, frustration, and self-consciousness" that actually interferes in their somatic performance as a form of self-fulfilling belief in their impotence. This dimension of bodily weakness – which Young attributes largely to "lack of practice in using the body [for] performing tasks" involving "gross movement" – is also, she suggests, a source of "the general lack of confidence that we [women] frequently have about our cognitive or leadership abilities."[13] From a different but complementary direction, Judith Butler's arguments for the somatic performativity of gender parody (as in drag and cross-dressing)

---

[13] Iris Marion Young, "Throwing Like a Girl," in *The Thinking Muse: Feminism and Modern French Philosophy*, ed. Jeffner Allen and Iris Marion Young (Bloomington: Indiana University Press, 1989), 51–70, citations from 57, 58, 67. Though appreciative of Beauvoir's feminist recognition of the body's general situatedness, Young criticizes her for "largely ignoring the situatedness of the woman's actual bodily movement and orientation to its surroundings and its world" (53).

show how dramatically different aesthetic representations of female bodies can be used to transgress and subvert the conventional notions of gender identity, thus helping to emancipate women from the oppressive constraints that the ideology of a fixed and subordinate gender essence has imposed on them.[14]

To reassert the challenge of Beauvoir's arguments against all these promising uses of performative-representational somaesthetics, one might argue that any programmatic absorption in the body is dangerously problematic because it distracts women from the truest and most potent form of transcendence – namely, political action in the public world. But this kind of argument wrongly makes *the best* invalidate *the good*. Somatic development need not threaten robust political praxis; on the contrary, as Beauvoir recognizes, it can create the confidence and power that encourage such praxis. Moreover, her argument from distraction would also militate against the value of any other programmatic pursuit than political praxis, such as the reading and writing of philosophy.

It cannot therefore be mere distraction that renders somatic cultivation a danger. Besides temporarily distracting woman from "professional success" because "she must devote considerable time to her appearance," woman's cultivation of the body "means that her vital interests are divided" between transcendence in the world and care for her objectified, immanent flesh (SS, 369). The crucial problem, for Beauvoir, is that attention to the body means a *distraction toward immanence,* a regression toward objecthood that stands in opposition to the free subjectivity of transcendence. This is because, despite her initial endorsement of Merleau-Ponty's vision of the body as subjectivity, the dominant somatic rhetoric of *The Second Sex* (which sadly reflects the values of patriarchy and often seems largely ensnared by them) tends to construe the body as passive flesh, particularly where women's bodies are concerned. We can see this still more clearly in Beauvoir's views regarding experiential somaesthetics.

IV

Feminists have good reason to affirm experiential somaesthetics because it resists our culture's obsession with the representational domain of the

[14] Judith Butler, *Gender Trouble: Feminism and the Subversion of Identity* (New York: Routledge, 1990), 128–149.

objectifying gaze by offering an enriching alternative to specular body pleasures. Rather than focusing on how one's body looks to others and trying to make it conform to external stereotypes of beauty that seem designed to exercise power over us, experiential somaesthetics concentrates on examining and improving one's own inner somatic experience. Beauvoir's attitude, however, is again ambiguous and ambivalent. Arguing, on the one hand, that women are distinctively close to and interested in their somatic experience, she also claims they are particularly alienated from their bodies and woefully in the dark about their inner somatic feelings and processes. Similarly, while Beauvoir clearly suggests that ignorance of one's bodily experience is a major source of women's weakness, she does not recommend a program of greater somatic self-awareness to remedy this weakness. Quite the contrary, she even claims that women would do better by leaving their bodies outside the realm of their experiential scrutiny so as to concentrate their attention on projects of transcendence in the world.

Beauvoir astutely argues that woman's sense of bodily weakness is not simply a lack of physical strength exacerbated by social discrimination. It is also a problem of what could be called woman's "cognitive weakness" regarding her body, the sense that her body is something mysterious and not sufficiently known to her. Unlike the boy who can easily identify with his bodily self in terms of his penis as an "alter ego," the girl has no external point of identification with her body and is thus turned especially toward its hidden "insides" (SS, 48, 278). "She is extremely concerned about everything that happens inside of her, she is from the start much more opaque to her own eyes, more profoundly immersed in the obscure mystery of life, than is the male" (SS, 278). And since her body's inner mysteries harbor such painful and uncontrollable surprises as menstruation, conception, and childbirth, the woman's inner body of experience constitutes a great source of anxiety.

As she reaches adolescence, a woman perceives her mysterious insides as the source of "unclean alchemies" (SS, 307) that oppose her sense of self or autonomy. She "feels that her body is getting away from her, . . . it becomes foreign to her" (SS, 308). She feels not only mystery but disgust with her insides; every month "the same disgust at this flat and stagnant odor emanating from her – an odor of the swamp, of wilted violets – disgust at this blood, less red, more dubious, than that which flowed from her childish abrasions" (SS, 312). As the young girl becomes a woman, her body's sexual "mystery becomes agonizing," especially since her desire is forced to express itself in the role of passive flesh; "she suffers from the disturbance as from a shameful illness; it is not active" (SS, 321).[15] As in illness, so in female sexuality "the body is borne like a burden; a hostile stranger" (SS, 337), experienced as something strange, disgusting, inhumanly animal. Unlike the male sex organ "that is simple and neat as a finger" and "is readily visible and often exhibited to comrades with proud rivalry," "the feminine sex organ is mysterious even to the woman herself, concealed, mucous, and humid, as it is; it bleeds each month, it is often sullied with body fluids, it has a secret and perilous life of its own. Woman does not recognize herself in it, and this explains in large part why she does not recognize its desires as hers" (SS, 386). Rather than the expression of transcendent human subjectivity, "feminine sex desire is the soft throbbing of a mollusc," a humiliating passive "leak" or "viscous" "bog" (SS, 386). Moreover, because "the feminine body is peculiarly psychosomatic" (SS, 391), Beauvoir argues that women's deep cognitive weakness (with its consequent anxiety and disgust) about inner body experience actually tends to aggravate their physical weakness and generate real physical suffering beyond what would normally arise through purely organic causes.[16]

The practical upshot of this argument should be to urge women to know their own bodies better. They should not concede such knowledge entirely to the male-dominated medical institution, which typically treats

---

[15] Beauvoir insists that woman's sexual desire (at least under patriarchy) must remain passive, thus causing woman further inner conflict. "To *make* oneself an object, to *make* oneself passive is a very different thing from *being* a passive object." If the woman takes too active and dynamic a role in sexual intercourse, she will "break the spell" that gives her pleasure: "all voluntary effort prevents the feminine flesh from being 'taken'; this is why woman spontaneously declines the forms of coition which demand effort and tension on her part; too sudden or too many changes in position, any call for consciously directed activities – whether words or behavior – tend to break the spell" (SS, 379). But later, through the new female somaesthetics exemplified by Brigitte Bardot, Beauvoir seems to see the possibility of "a new type of eroticism" for woman, as assertively active as man's. "Her flesh does not have the abundance that, in others, symbolizes passivity . . . Her eroticism is not magical, but aggressive. In the game of love, she is as much a hunter as she is a prey. The male is an object to her, just as she is to him." Simone de Beauvoir, *Brigitte Bardot and the Lolita Syndrome*, trans. Bernard Frechtman (New York: Arno Press, 1972), 8, 20.

[16] Beauvoir here invokes the claim that "gynecologists agree that nine tenths of their patients are imaginary invalids; that is, either their illnesses have no physiological reality at all or the organic disorder is itself brought on by a psychic state: it is psychosomatic. It is in great part the anxiety of being a woman that devastates the feminine body" (SS, 332–333). Without contesting the importance of psychosomatic ailments, one wonders whether Beauvoir should uncritically accept the "facts" affirmed by the traditionally male-dominated, woman-dominating medical profession.

the body as an objectified machine of flesh rather than as lived subjectivity, and which traditionally has preferred to leave women in the dark about their bodies so as to exploit these mysteries to sustain women's sense of weakness and the doctor's sense of authoritative power. By paying more positive attention to one's bodily experience, one can render its mysterious processes more familiar and more understandable. As such, they can become less disgusting, threatening, and disempowering. Imagined fearful mysteries are usually much more frightening than familiar realities one has explored for oneself. Moreover, given the strong psychosomatic nexus that Beauvoir affirms, a woman's greater knowledge of her body can be translated into increased physical power and confidence because the debilitating clouds of mysterious anxieties are then dissipated.

Besides, as Beauvoir recognizes, there are strong elements of joy and delight in woman's bodily experience. Greater attention to these somatic pleasures, through the focusing awareness of experiential somaesthetics, could further boost women's confidence by raising their spirits. Woman, Beauvoir insists, is better than man in such inner somatic attention; "being occupied with herself" in that way is "that pleasure which [woman] prefers to all others . . . She listens to her heartbeats, she notes the thrills of her flesh, justified by the presence of God's grace within her as is the pregnant woman by that of her fruit" (SS, 623). If "the well-known 'feminine sensitivity' derives somewhat from myth, . . . it is also a fact that woman is more attentive than man to herself and to the world" (SS, 625); more able and more inclined to examine her feelings, "to study her sensations and unravel their meaning"(SS, 626). "The call of the flesh is no louder in her than in the male, but she catches its least murmurs and amplifies them" (SS, 603). This inclination toward greater somatic attentiveness explains why many women find "a marvelous peace" in the later stages of pregnancy: "they feel justified. Previously they had always felt a desire to observe themselves, to scrutinize their bodies; but they had not dared to indulge this interest too freely, from a sense of social propriety. Now it is their right; everything they do for their own benefit they are doing also for the child" (SS, 501).

Beauvoir's analysis of eroticism suggests further reasons why heightened attention to woman's bodily feelings could be an empowering experience. In contrast to male sexual pleasure, which she sees as localized in the genitals and terminated in orgasm, "feminine sex enjoyment," she writes, "radiates throughout the whole body . . . Because no definite term is set, woman's sex feeling extends toward infinity" (SS, 395–396). Moreover, because of her different sexuality and the objectified role she is trained to play in the sexual arena, woman is also more sensitive than man to the rich ambiguity of human subjectivity and objecthood that is displayed most strikingly in the domain of sex. "The erotic experience is one that most poignantly discloses to human beings the ambiguity of their condition; in it they are aware of themselves as flesh and as spirit, as the other and as subject" (SS, 402). Woman should be more aware of this than man because she is continuously reminded that she is not only desiring consciousness but desired, objectified flesh; and "she wants to remain subject while she is made an object" (SS, 397); to "regain her dignity as transcendent and free subject while assuming her carnal condition – an enterprise fraught with difficulty and danger, and one that often fails" (SS, 402).

Yet even in failure, attention to this ambiguous somatic experience can provide women a clearer insight into the fundamental ambiguity of the human condition. Beauvoir thus can claim: "Woman has a more authentic experience of herself," of her complex, painful, but enabling ambiguity, while man, "an easy dupe of the deceptive privileges accorded him by his aggressive role and by the lonely satisfaction of the orgasm[,] . . . hesitates to see himself fully as flesh" (SS, 402) and thus remains blind to an essential part of the human condition.[17] As authentic living is a prime goal of existentialist ethics, one might expect Beauvoir to urge heightened attention to somatic experience because it evokes a more authentic recognition of human ambiguity. Moreover, since blindness to our ontological condition is an obstacle to realizing true freedom, she has another reason for recognizing how better experiential somatic awareness could be useful in advancing woman's liberation.

Beauvoir, however, is very far from advocating such a program of somaesthetic cultivation. Instead, she ultimately deplores an intensified focus on body experience as both a contributing cause and a product of woman's oppression and confinement to immanence. She even suggests that women are better off by paying less attention to their bodily feelings, especially when it comes to the often unpleasant feelings associated with woman's special condition. "I am convinced," Beauvoir writes, "that the greater part of the discomforts and maladies that overburden women are due to psychic causes, as gynecologists, indeed, have told me" (SS, 697). Rather than self-examining self-care of one's somatic feelings

---

[17] See the original French, *Le deuxième sexe* (Paris: Gallimard, 1949), 2:191: "La femme a d'elle-même une expérience plus authentique," which Parshley mistranslates as "Woman lives her love in more genuine fashion" (SS, 402).

to manage them better or transform them through knowledge, it is best for woman to "take little notice of them." Hence, "work will improve her physical condition by preventing her from being ceaselessly preoccupied with it" (SS, 697).[18] More generally, Beauvoir argues that woman should avoid intense "subjective" analysis and instead cultivate a "forgetfulness of herself," since self-analysis diverts too much time and energy from accomplishing the sort of valued work in the world that will secure her independence. "Newly come into the world of men, poorly seconded by them, woman is still too busily occupied to search for herself" (SS, 702).

Respected work in the public world is, of course, crucially important for the full realization of woman's freedom, as it is for man's. But even the superior importance of respected work and economic independence does not gainsay the value of heightened somatic awareness, whose lessons can enable us to function much more successfully in the public and economic world by freeing the body from bad habits of use that hinder its efficiency and skill while burdening it with pain. Here again, the mere argument of temporary distraction from praxis cannot refute the value of disciplined somatic attention. It is clearly possible to absorb oneself in experiential somaesthetics for certain periods and then redirect oneself to renewed action in the world, better prepared for such action through what one has learned about oneself. What seems to make heightened somatic attention especially problematic, for Beauvoir, is the body's identification with immanence and passivity, so that scrutiny of one's bodily experience would tend to reinforce such immanence and passivity by identifying oneself with this inferiority of one's flesh. Examining one's mind in the quest for critical self-knowledge is not similarly condemned as passive immanence because Beauvoir regards it as belonging to the active transcendence of consciousness that is basic to her phenomenological existentialist perspective.

With Beauvoir, this asymmetry cannot merely be the product of traditional mind/body dualism, for she affirms the ambiguity of the body as both subjectivity and object. Her feminist worry about intensified attention to bodily feelings is better explained by the body's role in symbolizing and reinforcing woman's inferior status (under patriarchy) as passivity or

---

[18] In arguing that woman's psychosomatic ailments reflect her unhappy situation, Beauvoir claims that "the situation does not depend on the body; the reverse is true" (SS, 697). She is right that the total social situation wields a greater power, but the influence runs in both directions, partly because one's body is always part of one's situation. As Beauvoir herself claims: "the body of woman is one of the essential elements in her situation in the world" (SS, 37).

flesh, as a mere tool of natural reproduction and a mere object of man's desire. If woman is more skilled at attending to her bodily existence and at enjoying it, "it is because her situation leads her to attach extreme importance to her animal nature[,] . . . because immanence is her lot" (SS, 603). If "she experiences more passionately, more movingly, the reality in which she is submerged," this comes "from the fact that she is passive" (SS, 626).

Beauvoir seems to be arguing that by improving their awareness of bodily experience, women would be reinforcing their passivity and withdrawal from the world into immanence as well as underlining the very dimension of their being (namely, bodily experience) that most expresses their oppression. Being identified with the body and the passive interiority of its feelings, women find it more difficult to assert themselves in the public world of action and intellectual projects. Such critique of focused attention to inner somatic experience is endorsed even by feminists who advocate increased attention to performative disciplines of somaesthetics for women's empowerment.

Judith Butler's insistence on transgressive representational performances with the body is coupled with an argument against "the illusion of an interior" of somatic experience that could serve as a legitimate focus for critical study and transformation. Inner body experience is explained away as the effect of discursive regimes and performances that work with the body's external surfaces.[19] Being an effect, however, does not mean being an illusion. From a different angle, Iris Marion Young warns against reflective somatic "self-consciousness" as a hindrance to women's using their bodies more actively and freely. "We feel as though we must have our attention directed upon our body to make sure it is doing what we wish it to do, rather than paying attention to what we want to do *through* our bodies." Reflective attention to bodily experience thus contributes to women's somatic "timidity, uncertainty, and hesitancy," their "feeling of incapacity." Moreover, by objectifying the body as an object of consciousness, experiential self-scrutiny keeps woman on guard to "keep . . . her[self] in her place" and explains "why women frequently tend not to move openly, keeping their limbs enclosed around themselves."[20] In short, the argument seems to be that focused attention to one's bodily experience invariably turns oneself into a mere object of scrutiny, diverting the somatically self-examining woman

[19] Butler, *Gender Trouble*, 134–141, quotation on 136.
[20] Young, "Throwing Like a Girl," 57, 66–67.

from engagement in the world and thus relegating her to the immanence and passivity that Beauvoir condemned as undermining woman's freedom.

Why should scrutiny of one's somatic experience necessarily confine oneself to immanence and passivity? If it were some intrinsic logical relationship between objectifying somatic consciousness and the properties of immanence and passivity, then men should similarly be affected. But Beauvoir does not claim that they are, instead insisting that the self-knowledge and "mastery over his body acquired by an Indian fakir does not make him the slave of it" (SS, 673). In any case, the argument that scrutiny of one's somatic experience necessarily turns one into a mere immanent and passive object is grounded in false dichotomies of mind/body, subject/object, self/world, activity/passivity that Beauvoir's more subtle appreciation of the body's ambiguity puts in question. Experiential somaesthetics involves one's active body-mind in perception and active movement (even when this is merely the movement of one's breath in seated meditation or the contracting of facial muscles in concentrating one's attention). Somatic self-awareness activates the whole person, as subject and object.

Beauvoir's argument also fails because attention to one's somatic perceptions is always more than mere immanence of the self; such perceptions always go beyond the self by including the environmental context in which the soma is situated. Bodies, as Beauvoir realizes, are foci of larger situations that shape and condition those bodies. Just as our world cannot make sense without a body, our bodies make no sense without a world. Strictly speaking, we can never feel our body purely in itself; we always feel the world with it. As already noted, if I remain motionless and try to scan and sense my body in itself, I will still feel the chair or the floor on which my body's weight rests; I will feel the air that fills its lungs, the effects of gravity, and other external forces on my nervous system. For such reasons, we should acknowledge Merleau-Ponty's claim that consciousness (which includes body consciousness) always is "active transcendence. The consciousness I have of seeing or feeling is no passive noting of some psychic event hermetically sealed upon itself, an event leaving me in doubt about the reality of the thing seen or felt.... It is the deep-seated momentum of transcendence which is my very being, the simultaneous contact with my own being and with the world's being."[21] Beauvoir herself affirms this when she defines the body as "the radiation

[21] Merleau-Ponty, *Phenomenology of Perception*, 376–377.

of a subjectivity, the instrument that makes possible the comprehension of the world" (SS, 267).

Though Beauvoir's rejection of the empowering and emancipatory potential of somaesthetics is unconvincing, there is value in her pointing to the dangers and snares that women risk through heightened cultivation of the body and somatic self-consciousness. The idea of woman's somaesthetic care can be easily misconstrued and degraded as the mere provision of a pretty face and figure for a desiring man, and a fertile womb and nourishing breasts for the propagation of the species. Such ever-present risks were surely more threatening in 1949 when Beauvoir wrote the book, before the sexual revolution of the sixties and the women's movement of the following decades, and before today's proliferation of interest in many different forms of body disciplines and sexualities.[22] Beauvoir's cautionary arguments against somaesthetic cultivation, therefore, seem more pragmatically justified for the women of her time than for ours.[23] Even today, she is right that group-directed political action rather than isolated individual efforts of personal salvation will be more productive of lasting progress for women and other underprivileged groups.

Nonetheless, as personal feelings of strength and self-awareness feed into more collective feelings of power and solidarity, so individual efforts of consciousness-raising and empowerment through somaesthetics (especially when undertaken with an awareness of the wider social contexts that structure one's bodily life) can fruitfully contribute to the larger political struggles whose results will shape the somatic experience of women in the future. Indeed, improved somatic cultivation should be recognized as essential to those struggles, once we appreciate the body's irreplaceable instrumentality for all our action and the irreplaceable role of the

[22] In France, as late as 1943, a female abortionist was guillotined. "Married women had to wait until 1965 before gaining the right to open a personal bank account, or to exercise a profession without the permission of their husbands. Before 1965, moreover, the husband alone had the right to decide where the couple should live . . . : contraception was only legalized in France in 1967, and abortion remained outlawed until 1974." See Moi, *Simone de Beauvoir: The Making of an Intellectual Woman,* 187.

[23] Beauvoir also offers (albeit in what Bergoffen calls her muted rather than dominant voice) a very positive glimpse of how women (and men) might revel in their bodies once they are freed of the repressive ideology of patriarchy that infects our loving experience with conflicts of domination rather than erotics of generosity. "Eroticism and love would take on the nature of free transcendence," in which each of the lovers, man and woman, "in the midst of the carnal fever, is a consenting, a voluntary gift, an activity" living out "the strange ambiguity of existence made body"; "the humanity of tomorrow will be living in its flesh and in its conscious liberty" (SS, 727, 728, 730).

individual in the larger domains of social praxis.[24] Moreover, granting greater importance to broad political progress in the public sphere in no way negates the value of somaesthetic disciplines for achieving personal fulfillment and aesthetic richness as an embodied self, whether we pursue these goals through a male or female body.

V

What value has somaesthetics for empowering, enriching, and emancipating a subjugated somatic subjectivity shared by hundreds of millions of men and women – the embodied consciousness of old age? Once again, despite Beauvoir's skepticism toward pragmatic remedies of somatic cultivation, her detailed analyses of the problems besetting the elderly strongly suggest that such remedies should indeed be useful. Though not as influential or rigorously argued as *The Second Sex*, her 1970 book *La Vieillesse* (more mildly titled in English as *The Coming of Age*) is remarkably rich in information and insight, while passionately exposing a problem of subjugated otherness that philosophy had largely ignored and still neglects today. Parallel to her views on woman's domination, Beauvoir effectively argues that while bodily differences and weaknesses play an important role in the subordinate status and dominated consciousness of the aged, this is not simply a case of natural necessity where physiology is destiny. Though *our* society "looks upon old age as a kind of shameful secret that it is unseemly to mention" (CA, 1), Beauvoir shows that in certain other cultures and historical periods the elderly were held in high esteem. This elevated status, however, like that of admired women is "never *won* but always *granted*" by what she regards as the real powers of society – the adult males, who may have reasons to affirm the value of old age, for example, as a means to insure tradition and cultural conservatism and to preserve their own power as they age (CA, 85). But even such granted authority (which itself needs somehow to be earned or vindicated) clearly implies that the subjugation of old age is not a mere matter of natural necessity but the product of an entire social, institutional, and ideological framework.

[24] As one ancient Chinese classic puts it, "The ancients who wished to manifest their clear character to the world would first bring order to their states. Those who wished to bring order to their states would first regulate their families. Those who wished to regulate their families would first cultivate their personal lives." *The Great Learning (Ta-Hsueh)* in *A Sourcebook in Chinese Philosophy*, trans. Wing-tsit Chan (Princeton, NJ: Princeton University Press, 1963), 86.

When a culture evolves very slowly and gives great respect to the experience of tradition and the ancestral dead, then the elderly who embody that traditional experience and are closest to the dead are consequently invested with greater authority. But in societies that privilege transformation and this-worldly values, it is youth and the prime of life that are idolized (since they represent the promise and agency of change), while the elderly are dismissed as useless hangers-on, overrun by progress. Not surprisingly in our culture, "the standing of old age has been markedly lowered since the notion of experience has been discredited" (CA, 210). Modern technological society, with its ever-accelerated pace of invention, means that one's past experience and old skills cannot be usefully accumulated and applied but instead becomes an outdated burden that slows one's speed in keeping up with the new. Despite the growing old-age market, capitalism's hungry search for new generations of young consumers (eager to try new commodities and promising many more years of consumption) reinforces our culture's devaluation of the aged. As Beauvoir recognizes, it is the meaning that the people of a culture "attribute to their life, it is their entire system of values that define the meaning and the value of old age." Conversely, a society's "real principles and aims" are revealed in how they treat the old (CA, 87).

If the unhappily dominated condition of the aged is essentially the product of social power, not of bodily limitations (which are simply the occasions or tools for marking and naturalizing this power), then, Beauvoir argues, the only way to empower the elderly is through a global transformation of society and its values. Our "scandalous" treatment of old age she sees as emerging inevitably from the scandalous treatment that society inflicts on people already in their youth and maturity. "It prefabricates the maimed and wretched state that is theirs when they are old. It is the fault of society that the decline of old age begins too early, that it is rapid, physically painful and, because they enter in upon it with empty hands, morally atrocious." Exploited by a rapaciously profit-hungry society while they have strength to labor, the working classes "inevitably become 'throwouts,' 'rejects,' once their strength has failed them." The pervasiveness of this social oppression, contends Beauvoir, vitiates all piecemeal methods to improve old age; such "remedies" are a "mockery," since these people's lives and health "cannot be given back." "We cannot satisfy ourselves with calling for a more generous 'old-age policy', higher pensions, decent housing and organized leisure. It is the whole system that is at issue and our claim cannot be otherwise than radical – change life itself" (CA, 542–543).

Social factors are undeniably dominant in the subjugation of old age, and Beauvoir's call for a global remaking of society to ensure greater justice for young and old is undeniably inspirational. Less compelling is her scornful disregard of piecemeal remedies, particularly because such partial or limited solutions provide necessary building blocks and encouraging models for achieving more global social change. I confine myself here to Beauvoir's disregard for somaesthetic methods that could help delay, overcome, or even turn back the bodily incapacities that come with increasing age and that determine in large part the sense of negativity and decline that defines old age in our culture.[25] Her own analysis of the problems of old age, I shall argue, clearly implies the value of somatic cultivation.

First, what exactly is old age for Beauvoir? She never gives this concept a rigorous logical analysis. Claiming that old age "is not solely a biological, but also a cultural fact," she nevertheless, for purposes of clarity (and given the common retirement age of her time) defines the terms "old, elderly, and aged" in objective chronological terms as "people of sixty-five and over" (CA, 13). On the one hand, Beauvoir seems sensitive to the ambiguity of the concept of age, recognizing that "chronological and biological ages do not always coincide" so that a person of sixty-five may be more physically fit and in this sense physiologically younger than a fifty-five year old. On the other hand, she insists "the words 'a sixty-year old' interpret the same fact for everybody. They correspond to biological phenomena that may be detected by examination" (CA, 30, 284). There is also the age one looks, which can be distinguished from one's biological age; and Beauvoir seems to give this sense of representational or manifest age considerable significance: "physical appearance tells more about the number of years we have lived than physiological examination" (CA, 30).

Besides these chronological, physiological, and representational senses of age, a proper analysis of this concept should further include an experiential sense of age (the feelings of being old or middle-aged or in one's prime) and also a performative sense relating to one's abilities to function in ways that distinguish a person in the prime of life from one with the functional limits associated with old age. Beauvoir's discussion of old age

---

[25] In contrast, Beauvoir claims that *intellectual* powers can be maintained by systematic exercise so as to delay or defy their decline in old age: "the higher the subject's intellectual level, the slower and less marked is the decline of his powers"; "there is a great deal of intellectual work performed without any relation to age" and "some very old people ... prove more effectual than the young" in such work. Generally, for example, "the philosopher's thought grows richer with age" (CA, 34–35, 396).

ranges over these different senses without distinguishing them clearly and consistently. Though chronological age is an objective baseline that cannot be affected (apart from the still barely imaginable exceptions of time travel and cryonics), other dimensions of aging are far more amenable to somatic cultivation than Beauvoir recognizes.

VI

One of her more striking claims about old age is its being only knowable and defined from the outside. It cannot be directly experienced in the "for-itself" mode of pure subjectivity but can only be grasped indirectly as an objectified condition of the self from the perspective of the defining gaze of other subjects outside oneself who regard that self as old. For Beauvoir, old age "is a dialectic relationship between my being as [the outside other] defines it objectively and the awareness of myself that I acquire by means of him. Within me it is the Other – that is to say the person I am for the outsider – who is old: and that Other is myself" (CA, 284). Old age is thus always experienced as something alien that is imposed on oneself by the gaze of others, similar to the way women have their identity as inessential Other imposed on them by the socially privileged and defining male gaze. "The aged person comes to feel that he is old by means of others, and without having experienced important changes." Lacking a proper "inward experience" of aging, "his inner being" has trouble accepting and inhabiting the outer-generated label, so "he no longer knows who he is"; hence, the discomforting confusion and embarrassed alienation of old age (CA, 291–292). This troubling disharmony and alienating disconnect between outer and inner, this inability to experience from the inside the somatic feelings of aging, clearly demands the meliorative methods of *experiential* somaesthetics that enhance our abilities to know, inhabit, and even to some extent modify the qualitative experience and proprioceptive signals of advanced age.

Before pursuing this point, note how the value of *representational* somaesthetics is likewise implied in Beauvoir's claim that old age is essentially defined by the gaze of the external observer. Since such observers do not determine our age by reading our birth certificates but by judging our appearance, if we do not look like old men and women in decline, then we will not be treated as such. Hence, by working to keep our bodily appearance different from that of aged decrepitude, we can better and longer avoid that discriminatory label and the social subjugation it tends to bring.

Millions of men and women (from diverse ethnicities, cultures, and classes) clearly appreciate this logic, devoting enormous time and expense to cosmetic treatments and other methods designed to make them look younger than their chronological age (if not also their physiological and performative age). Should we simply condemn them for selling out to society's concern for surface appearances? This facile response unfairly ignores the fact that some surface appearances (including those of old age) are richly freighted with deep meanings that significantly shape social reality; they cannot properly be ignored but need to be negotiated or deployed to sustain an individual's social power. A business executive whose success requires projecting strength, dynamism, energy, and future promise cannot maintain that image (and consequently his position) if he looks too old and weak. So he preserves his social authority by working on a more youthful, dynamic appearance, which, without lying about his age, refutes the presumption that advanced age entails physical feebleness. Such personal efforts can have more than personal effects. If more elderly people successfully projected an image of prime-of-life vigor and fitness, then the automatic association of old age with unattractive decrepitude would be undermined, and with it much of old age's social stigma that contributes to its disempowerment.

This does not mean that seventy-year-olds should try to look seventeen or even thirty-seven. The ridiculous futility of such attempts in no way negates the value of representational somaesthetics for empowering the aged. On the contrary, it shows that somaesthetic attention is needed to develop new images of vigorous and able-bodied good looks that are appropriate for seniors, while also exploring the best methods to realize them in practice. With stereotypes of beauty confined to the forms it takes in one's teens through forties, there is no apparent option for an attractive elderly appearance whose power and dignity can serve the social authority of seniors. As millions of baby boomers approach old age, reluctant to relinquish their self-image of energetic dynamism spawned by the dominant youth culture that formed their psyches, there is increasingly urgent interest in finding such models of attractively healthful aging. While Beauvoir recognizes that women's sense of power has been boosted by "a new aesthetics" of somatic appearance that transformed the established stereotype of soft, passive, female flesh into a new bodily image that is "muscular, supple, strong [and] ... bound to suggest transcendence" and activity (SS, 262), she fails to make a parallel argument for the transformative value of a new empowering somaesthetics of aging.

Methods for improving bodily appearance often overlap with disciplines aimed at enhancing strength, health, and performance. Although bodybuilding, for example, may focus primarily on external looks, its techniques and benefits extend into the strength training of performative somaesthetics, whose goal is not the mere image of functional potency and healthy vigor but their lived reality and utilization in actual practice. Most dieters are primarily concerned with a more attractively slender appearance, but their weight loss, exercise, and more wholesome eating habits typically result in better health, greater energy, and consequently improved performance. Because our culture prizes functionality, performative power is essential to sustaining the personal effectiveness needed for full social recognition, which the aged, in their ineffectual feebleness, are so often denied.

Alert to this fundamental insight, Beauvoir astutely identifies and refutes a pervasively influential philosophical argument for shrugging off the problem of old-age weakness by construing its somatic enfeeblement as instead a blessing in disguise. Ever since Plato affirmed that old age relieves us from unruly passions fueled by youthful bodily vigor, philosophers have often argued that bodily weakness or affliction promotes the strength of the soul, by encouraging us to focus on this higher part of us. Beauvoir vehemently contests this claim as wishful "nonsense" that is "indecent" in its refusal to confront the genuine experience and conditions of old age (CA, 316).

Though age brings decline in the sexual glands and consequent reduction of genital function, Beauvoir offers ample evidence that the elderly are not released from sexual desire and other passions (CA, 317–352). Because sexual desire and activity are not confined to genital behavior, they can continue well into old age. The libido, moreover, is not a merely physical drive but "psychosomatic" and shaped by one's sociocultural context (CA, 317, 323). Nonetheless, it thrives on physical health (as also mental energy ultimately does). Since sexuality forms an important part of our sense of self, the loss of libido through aging's somatic weakness "is a mutilation that brings other mutilations with it: sexuality, vitality, and activity are indissolubly linked" (CA, 350). Yet, Beauvoir does not draw the conclusion that the elderly should systematically work on their fitness in order to heighten the energy resources needed to nurture a stronger libido and the performative power to exercise it rewardingly in erotic contact, whose active pleasures, in turn, reinforce a person's sense of dynamic, energetic well-being.[26]

---

[26] Beauvoir fails to recognize the role of somatic vigor and energy when she argues that manual workers remain sexually active far longer than "brain workers." This claim (which seems contestable and which she does not support with empirical data) she explains as

Beyond the realm of sexual experience, it is equally clear that bodily infirmity does not liberate the mind but instead burdens consciousness with incessant worries relating to ailments and pain, while depleting the energy needed for sustained or effortful thinking. As Rousseau once put it, "the weaker the body, the more it commands" the soul.[27] "The old man's tragedy," writes Beauvoir, "is that often he is no longer capable of what he desires. He forms a project, and then just when it is to be carried out his body fails him" (CA, 315). While emphasizing how the somatic weaknesses of old age incapacitate performance and thus diminish self-confidence and social standing, Beauvoir notes that aging *athletes* can often nonetheless succeed in "compensating for [their] lost powers to a very considerable age," because of their previously acquired "technical experience" and "precise knowledge of their own bodies." They thus can "keep their form" and the social respect such ability commands (CA, 31). But she never seems to realize that systematic training (in both performative and experiential techniques) could improve the somatic functioning of the general elderly population, even though this remedy clearly follows from the causes she gives for decline in old age.

If loss of social status and self-worth results from diminished functionality through deficient strength, health, and energy, then these losses can be deferred and mitigated through methods that develop somatic skill and vigor. Pain and suffering from age-related illnesses, many of which can be prevented through improved somatic fitness, should likewise inspire the study of health-promoting disciplines of somatic self-care. In the same way, skills of experiential somaesthetics can address the self-alienation generated from the inability to accurately feel and effectively inhabit one's aging body. If the aged have lost their zest for activity because of insufficient strength and energy for successfully performing their projects, then their plight can be countered by somatic methods to sustain and even build strength and energy. The stale sadness of old age, Beauvoir asserts, is not because of the weight of our memories, but "because our vision is no longer given life by fresh projects" that stimulate activity and interest but reciprocally require it. "The old man's want of curiosity and his lack of interest are aggravated by his biological condition," she admits. "Paying

resulting from manual workers being simpler in their desires and "less dominated by erotic myths" that demand a beautiful sexual object (CA, 323). A more convincing and direct explanation would be that manual workers, by leading a more physically active life, have more capacity and inclination for physical expression and performance, including that of sex.

[27] Jean-Jacques Rousseau, *Emile*, trans. A. Bloom (New York: Basic Books, 1979), 54.

attention to the world tires him. Often he no longer has the strength to assert even those values which gave his life a meaning" (CA, 451, 453).

Yet, Beauvoir fails to advocate a systematic training of the body to maintain the biological vigor and strength needed for pursuing projects that invest one's life with interest, meaning, and value. Though conceding that "Psychologically, old athletes' perseverance [in sport] has a tonic effect" and may also help their somatic functioning, she emphasizes sport's physiological dangers and ineffectiveness for preserving the health of the elderly. "For two-thirds of them sport is dangerous after sixty . . . [and] does not delay the ageing of the organs" (CA, 314–315).

Today's science of aging provides a welcome revision of Beauvoir's views on these matters, and increasingly more seniors thus recognize that vigorous exercise is not just reserved for an elite group of former athletes but constitutes a crucial means for all sorts of older people to improve their functioning and health. Exercise not only delays age-related weakening of the body but can sometimes even reverse such weakening. Aging of the skeletal system, expressed in the frequently hunched and crooked figures of the elderly, is primarily the result of "the loss of calcium from bone" and is "more severe in older women than in men." Though the actual cause of this loss "is not known, and there are no certain methods of preventing it . . . , numerous studies have shown that exercising regularly can significantly reduce the rate of calcium loss."[28] Studies clearly show that a systematic program of exercise is "the best defense against muscle atrophy" and can "actually increase the strength of the muscles – even in persons in their 70s," while also apparently improving "the general metabolic activity of exercised muscle cells" and "the ability of nerves to stimulate muscle fibers."[29] The major cardiovascular problems of old age include a decrease of heart rate, stroke volume, and maximal oxygen consumption (all associated with weakened left-ventricular functioning), together with high blood pressure (due to decreased elasticity and internal diameter of the arteries). Numerous studies demonstrate that these declines can be mitigated through programmatic regimes of vigorous exercise and (for blood pressure) also of diet. Some findings indicate that "individuals as old as 70 years can increase their maximum oxygen consumption by following an endurance exercise training program, and

[28] Alexander Spence, *Biology of Human Aging*, 2nd ed. (New York: Prentice Hall, 1994), 57. "One study showed that 45 minutes of moderate weight-bearing exercise three times a week greatly slows the loss of calcium in older women and, if continued for a year, can reverse the demineralization that has occurred." (ibid., 63)

[29] Ibid., 71–72.

the intensity of training necessary to achieve this improvement is lower than is necessary in younger persons."[30]

Performative somaesthetics is not limited to vigorous exercise and strength training. Subtle somaesthetic methods requiring no sweat-producing effort can often remedy age-related functional disabilities that burden the elderly with pain, incapacity, and a sense of powerlessness, thus hampering their pursuit of projects to enrich their lives with greater meaning, action, and value. Let me provide an example from my work as a Feldenkrais practitioner. An elderly man over eighty years old came to me for help because of soreness in the knees that made it painful and difficult for him to stand up from sitting. He was particularly frustrated and depressed by the way this problem inhibited his normally dynamic and energetic behavior, such that every frequent impulse to get up to do something – even simply to get a drink of water or a book to read – had to be reconsidered for its cost of pain. The pills and injections that doctors prescribed for him were of no help, and he was advised that he would just have to bear the pain as the price of his longevity. When I examined the way he stood up from his chair, I noticed he used the same basic mechanics that most of us use when we are young and strong: raising ourselves straight up vertically by pressing our feet hard into the ground and pushing through our knees. This involves considerable effort and pressure on the knee joints, which can easily cause pain when the joints are injured or simply weak and old.

However, one can also learn to rise from a sitting position by bringing one's head, shoulders, arms, and torso to the fore and letting these upper body parts sink, provisionally, forward and toward the ground. This shifting of upper-body weight (since the body is anatomically top heavy) will pull the lower body and legs easily up to standing without requiring us to push through the knees. After a couple of lessons my octogenarian was able to master this new way of standing up so that he could habituate it into daily life. The knee problem disappeared. His greater power of standing was not due to increased muscular strength or effort. It came from the force of gravity, working through the now less skeletally supported upper body. Enhanced performative agency is here achieved not

---

[30] Ibid., 122. See also A. A. Ehsani et al., "Exercise Training Improves Left Ventricular Systolic Function in Older Men," *Circulation*, 83, no. 1 (1991): 96–103; and P. A. Beere et al, "Aerobic Exercise Training Can Reverse Age-Related Peripheral Circulatory Changes in Healthy Older Men," *Circulation*, 100, no. 10 (1999), 1085–1094.

by building the body's autonomous power but by learning a more intelligent method of utilizing the larger powers of nature that intersect and
inhabit the individual whose body and self are always more than one's
own.

To master this method of standing up, the octogenarian had to learn
greater proprioceptive awareness of the positions of his head, limbs, and
torso and acquire a more conscious sense of balance with his upper-body
weight unsupported and his head much closer to the floor, a position that
initially can feel frighteningly like falling. This need of heightened experiential awareness for improving motor skills exemplifies the interactive
overlap of performative and experiential somaesthetics. As the weight
lifter needs to discern experientially the pain that builds muscle from
the pain that signals damage, so the elderly exerciser needs to develop a
better experiential sense of her bodily self to avoid injury caused by over-
straining or misusing herself in exercise. Improving one's inner somatic
self-awareness through somaesthetic training thus crucially combines the
famous philosophical demand to "know yourself" with a second Delphic
maxim "nothing too much" that insists on discerning due measure.

One of the root problems of old age, claims Beauvoir, is our fundamental experiential inability to feel it properly in our own terms *from
the inside*, so that it "takes us by surprise" as a condition imposed on us
"from the outside" through the objectifying judgment of others: "our private, inward experience does not tell us [we are aging or] ... show us the
decline of age" (CA, 284). Hence, the awkward confusion and discouraging alienation of old age, in which one feels it must be some "Other
within us who is old," not one's own inner being or true self (CA, 288).
But if we skillfully apply certain techniques of experiential somaesthetics
that heighten somatic awareness (such as body-scanning meditation or
the Feldenkrais Method), we can become more proficient in identifying and diagnosing our bodily feelings and thus better able to perceive
and monitor the somatic transformations of aging from the inside. We
could then more comfortably inhabit our age without feeling it an unwel-
come, undecipherable foreign identity imposed on us from others; even
unwanted limitations are easier to handle if they are they are perceived
as part of us rather than inflicted from without.

Sharper somaesthetic awareness also improves our powers to distinguish between the changes of mere decline induced by advancing age
and those caused by actual disease or dysfunction that may (or may
not) be age related. We can therefore better diagnose and remedy those

disease-induced ailments rather than assuming they are simply part of the inevitable process of aging. Recognizing that the health of the elderly is seriously threatened by their own neglect because of their tendency "to confuse some curable disease with irreversible old age" (CA, 284), Beauvoir however fails to recommend any effort of somaesthetic attention to distinguish feelings of illness and injury from those of mere weakening old age.

Why does she refuse this option of heightened knowledge and power for the aged? Here again, just as for women, Beauvoir fears that somatic self-consciousness encourages immanence while discouraging what she regards as the key to life's meaning and value – transcendence through projects. If focused attention to bodily feelings implies remaining within the passive immanence of the flesh in contrast to the dynamically transcendent "ego," then meaningful projects in old age cannot include increasing our somatic self-knowledge of aging in order to live our age more effectively. "Projects," she insists, "have to do only with our activities. Undergoing age is not an activity. Growing, ripening, ageing, dying – the passing of time is predestined, inevitable" (CA, 540).

But cultivating somaesthetic acuity to know and monitor one's aging is no passive inevitability, but rather an active project of cognitive searching and probing, as is the disciplined pursuit of aging wisely, skillfully, and healthfully, even if, like other projects, it is vulnerable to failure. To "give our existence a meaning" in old age, Beauvoir however insists, "There is only one solution . . . – devotion to individuals, to groups or to causes, social, political, intellectual or creative work." So we need "passions strong enough [to pursue such projects and] to prevent us turning in upon ourselves," such inward turning being a sin of immanence, of stifling, isolated, withdrawal from the world (ibid). But again, since somatic self-consciousness always involves an environmental field significantly larger than the self, the problem of autistic isolation lies not with somaesthetic self-cultivation per se, but with failing to recognize how much the self depends on and incorporates the environments that shape it. Besides, as the very capacity to have "passions strong enough" for significant projects requires an adequate "biological condition" of energy or strength (CA, 453), so old age becomes increasingly reliant on somatic self-cultivation and self-care for sustaining such potency. Even if securing personal somatic health is merely a means to far nobler ends beyond the individual, it still remains, through its crucial instrumentality, a worthwhile project.

Taking instrumentalities seriously because one values the ends they serve is a key pragmatist principle. But before turning to the embodied pragmatism of William James and John Dewey, we devote the next chapter to the somatic theory of Ludwig Wittgenstein, whose enormously influential work in analytic philosophy of mind includes a fascinating inquiry on the role of bodily feelings.

4

Wittgenstein's Somaesthetics

Explanation and Melioration in Philosophy of Mind,
Art, and Politics

I

In his *Vermischte Bemerkungen*, in the course of a political discussion concerning nationalism, antisemitism, power, and property, Ludwig Wittgenstein speaks of one's having an "aesthetic feeling for one's body [*aesthetische Gefühl für seinen Körper*]."[1] This phrase naturally attracted my attention because of my interest in somaesthetics as a discipline concerned with the aesthetics of bodily feelings. But Wittgenstein's phrase particularly intrigued me because his philosophy is famous for refuting the centrality of bodily feelings in explaining the key concepts of philosophy for which those feelings are often invoked: concepts of action, emotion, will, and aesthetic judgment. He thinks that philosophers invent them as primitive explanations for the complexities of mental life. "When we do philosophy, we should like to hypostatize feelings where there are none. They serve to explain our thoughts to us. '*Here* explanation of our

---

[1] See the bilingual edition of this work, translated by Peter Winch and entitled *Culture and Value* (Oxford: Blackwell, 1980), 21, hereafter CV. I will occasionally provide my own translation from the German when it seems clearer or more accurate. Some of the book's problematic translations have been corrected in a later revised edition published by Blackwell in 1998, but I prefer to cite from the earlier, more familiar edition that is less encumbered with scholarly notations. The second edition, when referred to, will be designated as RCV. Other Wittgenstein texts frequently cited in this chapter refer to the following works and editions: *Philosophical Investigations*, trans. G. E. M. Anscombe (Oxford: Blackwell, 1968), hereafter PI (this famous work is divided into two parts; references to the first part are to numbered sections, while the second part is referred to by page number, preceded by "p."); *Zettel*, trans. G. E. M. Anscombe (Oxford: Blackwell, 1967), references are to fragment number; *Lectures and Conversations on Aesthetics, Psychology, and Religious Belief* (Oxford: Blackwell, 1970), hereafter LA; *Denkebewegung: Tagebücher, 1930–1932, 1936–1937* (Innsbruck: Haymon, 1997), hereafter TB.

thinking demands a feeling!' It is as if our conviction were simply consequent upon this requirement" (PI, 598).

In contrast to traditional theories that have used feelings or sensations (whether corporeal or allegedly more purely mental) to explain
the causes and meanings of our psychological and aesthetic concepts,
Wittgenstein argues that such complex concepts are better understood
in terms of their use. They are grounded and expressed in the sedimented
social practices or consensual forms of life of a community of language-
users. "*Practice* gives the words their sense," (CV, 85) and such practice
involves "agreement... in form of life" (PI, 241).

Because Wittgenstein provides powerful arguments for rejecting theories of sensationalism and psychologism with respect to mental concepts and aesthetic judgment, there is a tendency or a temptation to
conclude that he thought bodily sensations were cognitively insignificant
and unworthy of philosophical attention. This chapter makes a case for
resisting this temptation. Despite his devastating critiques of sensationalism, Wittgenstein recognizes the role of somaesthetic feelings in fields as
varied as philosophy of mind, aesthetics, ethics, and politics. That such
feelings cannot provide an adequate conceptual analysis of our concepts
does not entail that they lack other cognitive value and are therefore
irrelevant for philosophy. We may be tempted to make this inference if
we equate philosophy narrowly with conceptual analysis. However, like
Wittgenstein, I think otherwise. Philosophy has a much wider meaning;
it concerns what Wittgenstein called "the problem of life" and the self-
critical task of improving the self: "Working in philosophy – like work
in architecture in many respects – is really more a working on oneself"
(CV, 4, 16).[2]

If philosophy involves the tasks of self-improvement and of self-
knowledge (which seems necessary for self-improvement), then we
should find an important role for somaesthetic perceptions, explicitly
conscious bodily feelings. While examining the various ways Wittgenstein
recognizes the positive role of such feelings, this chapter goes beyond
Wittgenstein to advocate how these feelings should be more widely and
powerfully employed. To understand these positive uses properly, we
need to distinguish them from Wittgenstein's sharp critique of the use

[2] For my account of philosophy as a way of life and of how Wittgenstein so conceived
and practiced it, see *Practicing Philosophy: Pragmatism and the Philosophical Life* (New York:
Routledge, 1997), ch. 1.

of somatic feelings for explaining central concepts of aesthetics, politics, and philosophy of mind. First, however, it may be necessary to explain how key concepts and issues in these different philosophical disciplines are in fact closely related. Modernity's logic of professionalization and specialization tends to compartmentalize aesthetics, politics, and philosophy of mind and thus obscure their fundamental connection in philosophy's pursuit of better thinking and living, a connection that was powerfully affirmed and cultivated in ancient times.

To appreciate how strongly philosophy once tied aesthetics and philosophy of mind to political theory, we need only recall the paradigm text that largely established political philosophy and still helps define it today – Plato's dialogue, the *Republic* or *Politeia*, one of the most widely read of philosophical texts and one which in late antiquity bore the subtitle "On Justice." In this seminal work, Socrates argues that justice is essentially a virtue, that is, a special psychological achievement and disposition rather than a mere external social contract (as his interlocutors argue against him in the dialogue). A good part of the *Republic* is therefore devoted to philosophy of mind, analyzing the soul's basic faculties, needs, and desires in order to see whether the psychological underpinnings of Socrates' political theory or those of his rivals are more correct. Arguing that justice as a mental virtue is essentially the ruling of the proper order in the human soul, Socrates projects that view of the right ruling order onto the public order of the state. A state is just when it is ruled by the proper order of its different kinds of citizens, each group doing what it can do best for the better benefit of the whole community, the philosophers being charged with the highest role of governing guidance, teaching the ruling group of guardians.

But to secure the proper education of the guardians and ensure more generally the proper order of mind that constitutes the virtue of justice in the individual, Socrates insists that we must address aesthetic issues. Not only our intellects but our feelings and desires must be educated to recognize and appreciate the right order, so that we will desire and love it. The harmonies of beauty are therefore advocated as crucially instrumental in such education. Conversely, Plato's notorious condemnation of art is similarly motivated by his moral psychology and political theory. Art is dangerous politically, he argues, not only because it purveys imitative falsehoods, but because it appeals to the baser parts of the soul and overstimulates those unruly emotions that disturb right order in the mind of the individual and the polis in general.

This integral connection of aesthetics, politics, and philosophy of mind is reaffirmed by Friedrich Schiller, who argues that art is the necessary key to improving both mental and political order. In his *On the Aesthetic Education of Man*, written after the French revolution had turned into the Reign of Terror, Schiller posed the dilemma that a just society requires "the ennobling of character" to create more virtuous people, yet how can we ennoble character without already relying on a just political society to educate people toward virtue? Schiller's famous answer is "aesthetic education"; the "instrument is Fine Art," whose exemplars of beauty and perfection inspire and elevate our characters. Art's educational value for virtue and justice is again explained in terms of human psychology. If man's mind is torn between an earthy, sensual, material drive (*Stofftrieb*) and an intellectual, transcendental formal drive (*Formtrieb*), then art's expression of a mediating play drive (*Spieltrieb*) provides a crucial reconciling force, since in this drive "both the others work in concert." "Taste alone brings harmony into society, because it fosters harmony in the individual... only the aesthetic mode of communication unites society, because it relates to that which is common to all."[3]

The same nexus of moral psychology, aesthetics, and politics could also be shown in later thinkers like Dewey and Adorno. It, moreover, forms the core of the Chinese philosophical tradition.[4] But I trust that the linkage between these disciplines is now sufficiently clear to warrant examining how bodily feelings play a significant role in Wittgenstein's thought, extending from philosophy of mind and aesthetics to his ethical and political theory. Since Wittgenstein repudiates the view that bodily feelings can explain the meaning of our central mental and aesthetic concepts, let us begin with his critique of this view before considering the positive roles he allows for bodily feelings.

---

[3] Friedrich Schiller, *On the Aesthetic Education of Man*, trans. E. M. Wilkinson and L. A. Willoughby (Oxford: Clarendon, 1982), 55–57, 79–81, 97, 215.

[4] This is especially evident, for example, in the ideas of attractive, harmonizing order in Confucius and Xunzi. See *The Analects of Confucius: A Philosophical Translation*, trans. R. T. Ames and Henry Rosemont Jr. (New York: Ballantine, 1998); and Xunzi's "Discourse on Ritual Principles" and "Discourse on Music" in *Xunzi: A Translation and Study of the Complete Works*, trans. John Knoblock, Stanford: Stanford University Press, 1994), vol. 3, where we read that "music is the most perfect method of bringing order to men" (84). I explore how somaesthetics relates to the East-Asian nexus of aesthetics, moral psychology, and politics in "Pragmatism and East-Asian Thought," in *The Range of Pragmatism and the Limits of Philosophy* (Oxford: Blackwell, 2004), 13–42.

II

In critiquing the use of somatic feelings for explaining crucial mental concepts like emotion and will, Wittgenstein takes the pragmatist philosopher William James as his prime target. James influenced Wittgenstein more than any of the other classical pragmatists did, and we know that Wittgenstein greatly appreciated James's thought on religious issues.[5] But here Wittgenstein uses the somatic sensationalism of James's psychology as a critical foil to develop his own theories. James is famous for his corporeal explanation of emotion: Not only are "the general causes of the emotions . . . indubitably physiological," but the emotions themselves are identified with the feelings we have of these physiological excitations. When we perceive something exciting, "*bodily changes follow directly the perception of the exciting fact, and . . . our feeling of the same changes as they occur IS the emotion;* . . . we feel sorry because we cry, angry because we strike, afraid because we tremble, and not that we cry, strike, or tremble, because we are sorry, angry, or fearful, as the case may be. Without the bodily states following on the perception, the latter would be purely cognitive in form, pale, colorless, destitute of emotional warmth."[6]

If James one-sidedly equates emotions with bodily sensations,[7] then Wittgenstein's response is emphatically to reject this identification by insisting that emotions "are not sensations" of the body, since they are neither localized nor diffuse, and always have an object (which is different than a bodily cause). Emotions are "in the mind," "expressed in thoughts," and experienced and aroused by thought, "not body pain." In contrast to James, Wittgenstein "should almost like to say: One no more feels sorrow in one's body than one feels seeing in one's eyes" (*Zettel,* 495). My fear of the dark may sometimes manifest itself in my consciousness of shallowness in my breathing and of a clenching of the jaw and face muscles, but sometimes it may not be so manifested. Even if such bodily feeling is always present, this does not mean that it is the cause of my fear, nor its object. I am not afraid of shallow breathing or of these muscle contractions, but instead of the dark. "If fear is frightful and if while it

---

[5] See *Ludwig Wittgenstein: Cambridge Letters,* ed. B. McGuinness and G. H. von Wright (Blackwell: Oxford, 1996), 14, 140.

[6] William James, *Principles of Psychology* (Cambridge, MA: Harvard University Press, 1983), 1065–1066, hereafter PP.

[7] A full and sympathetic reading of James's different formulations of his theory would deny that he simply identifies emotions entirely with bodily feelings or sensations. See the more detailed account of his theory in Chapter 5.

goes on I am conscious of my breathing and of a tension in my facial muscles – is that to say that I find *these feelings* frightful? Might they not even be a mitigation?" (*Zettel*, 499). Wittgenstein is surely right that our emotions are not reducible to bodily feelings nor to any mere sensation; emotions instead involve a whole context of behavior and a background of language games, a whole form of life in which the emotion plays a part.

Bodily feelings, Wittgenstein claims, are also incapable of explaining will. Here again James is the target of critique. In the chapter on will in *Principles of Psychology*, James argues that our voluntary movements rely on more primary bodily functions and are guided by "*kinaesthetic impressions*" of our proprioceptive system that have sedimented into a "*kinaesthetic idea*" or "memory-image": "*whether or no there be anything else in the mind at the moment when we consciously will a certain act, a mental conception made up of the memory-images of these sensations, defining which special act it is, must be there.*" James goes on to insist that "*there need be nothing else*, and that *in perfectly simple voluntary acts there is nothing else, in the mind, but the kinaesthetic idea, thus defined, of what the act is to be*" (PP, 1100–1104).

Though James's kinaesthetic theory might be criticized as "inflationary" in positing the need for a special conscious feeling to explain and accompany every act of will, he actually intended his theory to be a deflationary challenge to the still more bloated account of will proposed by philosopher-scientists like Wundt, Helmholtz, and Mach. In addition to the kinaesthetic feelings, they posited a special active "*feeling of innervation,*" that accompanies the "special current of energy going out from the brain into the appropriate muscles during the act" of will, while James maintained that the more passive "*kinaesthetic images*" he described were enough to induce the action (PP, 1104, 1107).

Though appreciative of James's efforts of theoretical economy, I prefer to economize further by endorsing Wittgenstein's claim that specific kinaesthetic ideas or other conscious visceral feelings constitute neither the sufficient nor necessary cause of voluntary action and cannot adequately explain the will. Recall Wittgenstein's famous posing of the problem in *Philosophical Investigations* (which clearly evokes James): "what is left over if I subtract the fact that my arm goes up from the fact that I raise my arm? ((Are the kinaesthetic sensations my willing?)) . . . When I raise my arm I do not usually *try* to raise it" (PI, 621–622).

Voluntary action does not typically involve any conscious effort of "trying" nor any related conscious kinaesthetic impressions of "willing," whether actual or remembered. Most voluntary action is produced spontaneously or automatically from our intentions without any attention at all to any visceral feelings or bodily processes that could occur when initiating the action. "Writing is certainly a voluntary movement and yet an automatic one. And of course there is no question of a feeling of each movement in writing. One feels something, but could not possibly analyse the feeling. One's hand writes; it does not write because one wills, but one wills what it writes. One does not watch it in astonishment or with interest while writing; does not think 'What will it write now?'" (*Zettel*, 586). In fact, Wittgenstein adds, such attention to one's movements and feelings can hinder the smooth execution of willed action: "self-observation makes my action, my movements, uncertain" (*Zettel*, 592)

Like our emotions, then, acts of the will cannot be explained by or identified with the particular kinaesthetic feelings that may sometimes accompany them. Voluntary action (just like emotion) can only be explained in terms of a whole surrounding context of life, aims, and practices, "the whole hurly-burly of human actions, the background against which we see any action." "What is voluntary is certain movements with their normal *surrounding* of intention, learning, trying, acting" (*Zettel*, 567, 577).

There is also a third important area where Wittgenstein challenges the use of visceral feelings as essential to understanding key concepts of our mental life. This area concerns the concept of self and self-knowledge of one's bodily state or position. Once again, James is the explicit target. He is attacked for identifying the self with basic somatic sensations that can be discerned by introspection, for "the idea that the 'self' consisted mainly of 'peculiar motions in the head and between the head and throat'" (PI, 413).[8] This, unfortunately, is an ungenerous distortion of James's concept of self, which indeed includes a vast variety of dimensions – from the body parts, clothes, property, and diverse social relations that form our material and social selves to the various mental faculties of what he calls our "spiritual self."[9]

What James described in terms of bodily feelings in the head (ascertained through his own personal introspection) is only *one*, though allegedly the most basic, part of the self, which he called "the central active self," "the nuclear self," or "the Self of selves." The full concept of

---

[8] Wittgenstein adds that "James' introspection shewed, not the meaning of the word 'self' (so far as it means something like 'person,' 'human being,' 'he himself,' 'I myself'), nor any analysis of such a thing, but the state of a philosopher's attention when he says the word 'self' to himself and tries to analyse its meaning. (And a good deal could be learned from this.)" (PI, 413).

[9] For more details on James's account of the self, see Chapter 5 of this book.

self, as both James and Wittgenstein realize, is not reducible to any kind of basic sensations in the head or anywhere else. A whole background of social life and practices is needed to define it. Most of the time, as James himself asserts, we are entirely unaware of these "head feelings" – which typically "are swallowed up in [the] larger mass" of other things that claim more conscious attention than these primitive background motions of the self (PP, 288–289) – yet, we are not therefore most of the time unaware of ourselves and unconscious of where we are and what we do. Wittgenstein, however, is far clearer than James about this, and he wisely avoids the positing of a nuclear self that would be identified with or identifiable by particular head sensations, for such homuncular theories can encourage many essentialist confusions. One is much more than one's head, and even one's mental life extends far beyond one's head sensations.[10]

Wittgenstein, moreover, emphatically insists (much like Merleau-Ponty) that knowing one's bodily position does not require paying special attention to somaesthetic feelings of one's body parts and then inferring from them the particular location and orientation of the body and its limbs. Instead, we have an immediate sense of our somatic position. "One *knows* the position of one's limbs and their movements... [with] no local sign about the sensation" (*Zettel*, 483). In performing ordinary tasks like washing or feeding ourselves, climbing stairs, riding a bicycle, or driving a car, we do not usually need to consult the separate feelings of our body parts in order to calculate the necessary movements to achieve the action we will (e.g., what parts need to be moved, in which direction, distance, speed, articulation, and degree of muscle contraction).[11]

---

[10] In his early masterpiece, *Tractatus Logico-Philosophicus*, Wittgenstein deploys the body to argue against the very idea of "the philosophical self" or "subject" as something in the world that can be investigated by psychology. "If I wrote a book called *The World as I found it*, I should have to report therein about my body and say which members are subordinate to my will and which are not, etc., this being a method of isolating the subject, or rather of showing that in an important sense there is no subject; for it alone could *not* be mentioned in that book." "The philosophical self is not the human being, not the human body, or the human soul, with which psychology deals, but rather the metaphysical subject, the limit of the world – not part of it." Ludwig Wittgenstein, *Tractatus Logico-Philosophicus*, bilingual edition, trans. D. F. Pears and B. F. McGuinness (London: Routledge, 1969), sections 5.631, 5.641 (translation of the first citation slightly revised).

[11] In fairness to James, we should recall that he, too, insisted that we typically do (and should) perform our ordinary bodily actions through unreflective habit without any explicit attention to our body feelings or any thematized awareness of the location of our body parts. See, for example, PP, 109–131, and my more general discussion of his views on habit and somatic reflection in Chapter 5.

Wittgenstein's refutes the thesis that "My kinaesthetic sensations advise me of the movement and position of my limbs" (PI, p. 185) by engaging in some somaesthetic introspection of his own:

> I let my index finger make an easy pendulum movement of small amplitude. I either hardly feel it, or don't feel it at all. Perhaps a little in the tip of the finger, as a slight tension. (Not at all in the joint.) And this sensation advises me of the movement? – for I can describe the movement exactly.
>
> "But after all, you must feel it, otherwise you wouldn't know (without looking) how your finger was moving." But "knowing" it only means: being able to describe it. – I may be able to tell the direction from which a sound comes only because it affects one ear more strongly than the other, but I don't feel this in my ears; yet it has its effect: I *know* the direction from which the sound comes; for instance, I look in that direction.
>
> It is the same with the idea that it must be some feature of our pain that advises us of the whereabouts of the pain in the body, and some feature of our memory image that tells us the time to which it belongs. (PI, p. 185)

In short, our knowledge of bodily location and movement is typically immediate and nonreflective. It is not always accompanied by conscious kinaesthetic feelings that we attend to; nor is it usually derived from such feelings when they are in fact present. Nor does successful voluntary action require the mediation of attention to somaesthetic feelings. Such feelings may also be absent from much of our experience of will, emotion, and self. It is tempting, therefore, to conclude that they are unimportant for these topics of philosophy of mind and that a behaviorist skepticism about their role in mental life might be appropriate.

But that would be a mistake, even from Wittgenstein's perspective. Such feelings, despite their inadequacy for explaining mental concepts, remain a real part of the phenomenology of mental life that philosophy should describe. Kinaesthetic sensations are not theoretical nothings like phlogiston, but elements of experience that can be properly or improperly described. "We feel our movements. Yes, we really *feel* them; the sensation is similar, not to a sensation of taste or heat, but to one of touch: to the sensation when skin and muscles are squeezed, pulled, displaced." And we can also, though we don't always have to, feel the position of our limbs through a distinct "body-feeling" ("*Körpergefühl*"), for example, "'the body-feeling' of the arm . . . [in] such-and-such a *position*" (*Zettel*, 479–481). Indeed, in certain circumstances we can even learn of our movements and position through the mediation of feelings, as when a perceived tension in the neck informs us that our shoulders are hunched up near our ears. Though Wittgenstein rightly insists that we typically neither require nor use such somaesthetic clues to know about our bodily position, he recognizes that they can, on occasion, provide such knowledge and he provides his own characteristically "painful" example: "A sensation *can* advise us of the movement or position of a limb. (For example, if . . . your arm is stretched out, you might find out by a piercing pain in the elbow.) – In the same way the character of a pain can tell us where the injury is" (PI, p. 185).

I want to go further by insisting that, in the same way, attention to somaesthetic feelings can sometimes usefully inform us about our emotions and our will. It is a commonplace that a person may be angry, upset, anxious, or fearful before he is consciously aware of it. He often, however, becomes aware of his emotional state when someone else, noticing his movements, gestures, breathing, tone of voice, inquires whether there is something bothering him. Behaviorism finds support in this phenomenon for claiming that emotions are not defined by what we are aware of feeling and that introspection is not the true arbiter of our emotional state. Observers from "the outside" can inform us of an emotional state of which we are not yet consciously aware. But we should realize that introspective attention to our somaesthetic feelings (shortness of breath, clenching in the chest or jaws) can also provide us with such observation.

In certain situations, where I am not initially aware of my anxiety or fear and when I am still unconscious of their having a specific object, I can learn that I am anxious or fearful by noticing my shallow, rapid breathing and the heightened muscle contraction in my neck, shoulders, and pelvis. Of course, different people have somewhat different patterns of muscle contraction and of breathing-change when undergoing emotional stress. But this does not negate the fact that an individual can know her own pattern and infer from it that she is in a heightened emotional state (and often which emotional state it is), even before she is conscious of that state having a specific object – the particular thing about which she is angry or anxious or fearful. Wittgenstein admits: "My own behaviour is sometimes – but *rarely* – the object of my own observation" (*Zettel*, 591). Somaesthetic feelings provide us with helpful tools for such self-observation through which we can better attain philosophy's classic goal of self-knowledge. Of course, one often needs a sustained effort of training to learn how properly to read one's own somaesthetics signs, but disciplines of somatic education such as the Feldenkrais Method or yoga can provide such training.

The role of somaesthetic feelings and discipline goes still further, once we realize that attention to these feelings can give us not only knowledge of our emotional states, but, through that knowledge, the possible means to cope with them better. Once emotions are thematized in consciousness, we can take a critical distance and thus both understand and manage them with greater mastery (which does not mean with greater repression). Moreover, because emotions are (at least empirically) closely linked with certain somatic states and feelings, we can influence our emotions indirectly by changing our somatic sensations by consciously exercising somaesthetic control. We can regulate our breathing to make it deeper and slower, just as we can learn to relax certain muscle tensions that reinforce a feeling of nervousness by their long-conditioned association with states of nervousness. These strategies are familiar from ancient practices of meditation but are also employed in more modern strategies of stress management.

The effective understanding of the will and voluntary action can also be enhanced through disciplined attention to somaesthetic feelings. Successful willed action depends on somatic efficacy, which in turn, as we have seen, depends on accurate somatic perception. Recall the struggling golfer example from Chapter 1. She ardently wants to perform the voluntary action of keeping her head down and her eyes on the ball while swinging the club so as to hit the ball properly, yet she nonetheless always lifts her head and fails in her swing. She even fails to notice that she is lifting her head and therefore cannot correct the problem, because she is insufficiently attentive to her head positions and eye movements, which she could indeed sense if she were more somaesthetically disciplined and skilled. This golfer's head goes up against her will, though no external force or internal instinct is forcing her to lift it, just the force of unconscious bad habits that are reinforced in their blindness through insufficient somatic self-consciousness and what F. M. Alexander described as "debauched *kinaesthetic* systems" with faulty "sense-appreciation."[12] This failure to do what she consciously wills and is physically capable of doing could be overcome if she had a better grasp of her body position and movement through more attention to somaesthetic feelings of proprioception and kinaesthesis. The same kind of impotence of will is evident in

---

[12] F. M. Alexander, *Man's Supreme Inheritance*, 2nd edition, (New York: Dutton, 1918), 22, 89. He elaborates the case of the head-lifting golfer in *The Use of the Self*, (New York: Dutton, 1932)

the insomniac who wants to relax but whose blindly effortful striving to do so serves only to aggravate his state of tension and insomnia, because he does not know how to relax his muscles and breathing just as he cannot feel how they are tense.

But doesn't such attention to bodily feelings and movements distract the golfer from hitting the ball or the insomniac from fully relaxing? Experience (with proper training) shows the contrary.[13] In any case, somaesthetic attention does not need (nor is meant) to be a permanent focus that distracts from other goals. Because once the feelings of faulty movements are attended to, the movements can be analyzed, corrected, and replaced by proper ones accompanied by other somaesthetic feelings that can be habituated and then allowed to slip into unreflective but intelligent habit.[14] If philosophy involves not merely knowledge of one's mind, but ameliorative self-mastery (as Wittgenstein fervently believed), then attention to somaesthetic feelings should be crucial to philosophy's task of "working on oneself." This project of self-mastery is central to the field of ethics, but let us first turn to aesthetics, since Wittgenstein closely identifies these two domains of value, even to the point of regarding the quest of the good life in largely aesthetic terms.[15]

III

Like his philosophy of mind, Wittgenstein's aesthetics presents a critique of sensation-based psychologism. Aesthetic explanations are not

---

[13] The clinical work of Alexander and Feldenkrais provides ample evidence that trained somaesthetic awareness need not interfere with motor performance. Insomnia therapists explicitly deploy attention to breathing and subtle body movements not only to relax the body but also to distract one's troubled mind from the relentless thoughts that keep one frustratingly awake.

[14] In arguing that focused somaesthetic attention is most needed for remedying faulty habits and may be subsequently diminished once the new habit is successfully adopted, I do not wish to deny the further claim that it can sometimes also be helpful when deploying a well-functioning intelligent habit in actual performance; for example, an expert dancer's focused proprioceptive attention in performing a dance she knows well. With respect to this issue of interference versus value in performance, so much depends on the skill, quality, and focus of the somaesthetic attention. I suspect that many errors allegedly caused by explicit attention to one's bodily movements and feelings are in fact due to poor somaesthetic skills of focused attention and to the unnoticed distraction of attention (with consequent anxiety) toward the successful results of one's action.

[15] I provide a detailed argument for this claim in *Practicing Philosophy*, ch. 1. Recall Wittgenstein's famous dictum: "Ethics and aesthetics are one," from his *Tractatus Logico-Philosophicus*, 6.421.

causal ones and, like the aesthetic judgments they explain, "have nothing to do with psychological experiments" (LA, 17). As with emotions
and other mental states, aesthetic judgments and experiences cannot be
explained in terms of the artist's or audience's somatic sensations, "their
organic feelings – tension of the muscles in their chest" (LA, 33). We can
explain aesthetic experiences and judgments much better by describing the particular artworks that are being judged and experienced, as
well as describing the behavior of the artists and audience, including ourselves. Gestures are also very effective in conveying how the artwork makes
us feel.

In any case, our appreciation of art is not an appreciation of any separable somatic sensations that art can give us (just as it is not an appreciation of associations that are independent of the artwork). Otherwise,
we could imagine foregoing any interest in the artwork simply to get the
sensations (or associations) more directly through some other means
(say, some drug). But we cannot separate our aesthetic experience of art
from the object of that experience; and that object is art, not our somatic
sensations. Finally, the appeal to "kinaesthetic feelings" to explain our aesthetic judgments is logically unsatisfactory because these feelings themselves are not adequately describable or individuated without appealing
either to the artwork itself or to some set of gestures that we feel expresses
them. For Wittgenstein, there seems to be no "technique of describing
kinaesthetic sensations" of aesthetic experience more accurately than by
our gestures. Moreover, he argues, even if we did devise a new system of
describing "kinaesthetic sensations" in order to determine what would
count as "the same kinaesthetic impressions," it is not clear that its results
would correspond with our current aesthetic judgments and their gestural expression (LA, 37–40).

If somatic feelings are neither the object nor the explanation of our
judgments and experience of art, this does not entail, however, that such
feelings are not aesthetically important. Wittgenstein, as we have seen, is
clearly attentive to somatic feelings, and he acknowledges their aesthetic
value in a number of ways. First, they form the mediating focus (if not also
the precise object) of aesthetic satisfactions derived from experiencing
our bodies. Wittgenstein highlights "the delightful way the various parts
of a human body differ in temperature" (CV, 11). Second, kinaesthetic
feelings may help us derive a greater fullness, intensity, or precision in our
experience of art because (at least for some of us) aesthetic imagination
or attention is facilitated or heightened by certain bodily movements that

somehow feel as if they correspond to the artwork. Wittgenstein provides his own example:

> When I imagine a piece of music, as I often do every day, I always, so I believe, grind my upper and lower teeth together rhythmically. I have noticed this before though I usually do it quite unconsciously. What's more, it's as though the notes I am imagining are produced by this movement. I believe this may be a very common way of imagining music internally. Of course I can imagine without moving my teeth too, but in that case the notes are much ghostlier, more blurred and less pronounced.[16] (CV, 28)

"If art serves 'to arouse feelings,'" Wittgenstein later asks, "is, in the end, perceiving it sensually [*ihre sinnliche Wahrnehmung*] to be included amongst these feelings?" (CV, 36) This cryptic, apparently rhetorical, question reminds us that aesthetic perceptions must always be achieved through the bodily senses, and it could be recommending a more embodied and sensually attentive use of art. In other words, we might sharpen our appreciation of art through more attention to our somaesthetic feelings involved in perceiving art instead of narrowly identifying artistic feelings with the familiar kind of emotions (such as sadness, joy, melancholy, regret, etc.) that often make art appreciation degenerate into a gushy, vague romanticism. Wittgenstein's remark is not at all clear, and my interpretation may be more or other than what he intended. But independent of Wittgenstein, the point can be validly made. If better somaesthetic awareness and discipline can improve our perception in general by giving us better control of the sense organs through which we perceive, then it can also, *ceteris paribus*, give us better perception in aesthetic contexts.

For Wittgenstein, the body may have a crucial aesthetic role that goes deeper than any conscious somaesthetic feeling or expression. As with Merleau-Ponty, the body serves Wittgenstein as a central instance and symbol of what forms the crucial, silent, mysterious background for all that can be expressed in language or in art, the unreflective source for all that can be consciously grasped in reflective thought or representation. "The purely corporeal can be uncanny." "Perhaps what is inexpressible (what I find mysterious and am not able to express) is the background against which whatever I could express has its meaning" (CV, 16, 50). Music's inexpressible depth of meaning and its grand,

---

[16] It may be that Wittgenstein's habits as a clarinet player had something to do with these somaesthetic feelings because playing this instrument involves holding the teeth together.

mysterious power derive from the body's silent role as creative ground and intensifying background. That is how a surface of ephemeral sounds can touch the very depths of human experience. "Music, with its few notes & rhythms, seems to some people a primitive art. But only its surface [its foreground] is simple, while the body which makes possible the interpretation of this manifest content has all the infinite complexity that is suggested in the external forms of other arts & which music conceals. In a certain sense it is the most sophisticated art of all" (CV, 8–9).[17]

Here again, I think Wittgenstein's recognition of the body's crucial role needs to be taken a step further in a pragmatic direction. More than guitars or violins or pianos or even drums, our bodies are the primary instrument for the making of music. And more than records, radios, tapes, or CD's, bodies are the basic, irreplaceable medium for its appreciation. If our bodies are the ultimate and necessary instrument for music, if one's body – in its senses, feelings, and movements – is capable of being more finely tuned to perceive, respond, and perform aesthetically, then is it not a reasonable idea to learn and train this "instrument of instruments" by more careful attention to somaesthetic feelings?

The value of such somaesthetic training (as I have already argued in *Practicing Philosophy* and *Performing Live*) extends far beyond the realm of fine art, enriching our cognition and our global art of living. Improved perception of our somatic feelings not only gives us greater knowledge of ourselves but also enables greater somatic skill, facility, and range of movement that can afford our sensory organs greater scope in giving us knowledge of the world. Besides augmenting our own possibilities of pleasure, such improved somatic functioning and awareness can give us greater power in performing virtuous acts for the benefit of others, since all action somehow depends on the efficacy of our bodily instrument. Earlier in this chapter I noted how the ideas of proper mental order and the proper aesthetic education of taste to appreciate right order have traditionally been very important for ethics and political philosophy. If bodily feelings have a significant place in Wittgenstein's philosophy of mind and aesthetics, do they play an equally meaningful role in his ethical and political thought?

[17] The parenthetical term "foreground" refers to the German "*Vordergrund*," which was a textual variant to "surface" [*Oberfläche*] in the manuscripts. See the revised second edition of *Culture and Value* (RCV, 11).

IV

Wittgenstein's discussion of somatic feelings with respect to ethics and politics is rather limited but nonetheless noteworthy. First, our sense of the body, he argues, provides the ground and often the symbol for our concept of what it means to be human. "The human body is the best picture of the human soul" (PI, p. 178).[18] Our basic existential situation as embodied beings, moreover, implies how we are limited by the constraints and weakness of our mortal flesh: "We are prisoners of our skin" (TB, 63). But our appreciative feeling for the body (as the Greeks and even idealists like Hegel recognized) is also crucial to our sense of human dignity and integrity and value. Our bodies give us substance and form without which our mental life could not enjoy such a varied, robust, nuanced, and noble expression. "It is humiliating to have to appear like an empty tube which is simply inflated by a mind" (CV, 11). Our ethical concepts of human rights, the sanctity of life, our high ideals of moral worth and of philosophical, and aesthetic achievement all depend, Wittgenstein argues, on a form of life that takes as a premise the ways we experience our bodies and the ways that others treat them. Consider this strikingly brutal passage from his Cambridge Notebooks, whose evocation of violence reminds one of Foucault (though without Foucault's apparent relish and utopian hope for positive change through radical body transformation):

> Mutilate a man completely, cut off his arms & legs, nose & ears, & then see what remains of his self-respect and his dignity, and to what point his concepts of these things are still the same. We don't suspect at all, how these concepts depend on the habitual, normal state of our bodies. What would happen to them if we were led by leash attached to a ring through our tongues? How much then still remains in him of being human? Into what state does such a person sink? We don't know that we are standing on a high narrow rock, & surrounded by precipices, in which everything looks different. (TB, 139–140, my translation)

If the familiar forms and normal feelings of our body ground our form of life, which in turn grounds our ethical concepts and attitudes toward others, then we can perhaps better understand some of our irrational political enmities. The fanatical kind of hatred or fear that some people have for certain foreign races, cultures, classes, and nations does display

---

[18] Moreover, embodied passions form part of the soul whose care and salvation are so important to Wittgenstein: "it is my soul with its passions, as it were with its flesh and blood, that needs to be saved, not my abstract mind" (CV, 33).

a deep visceral quality, which suggests that such enmity may reflect profound concerns about the integrity and purity of the familiar body in a given culture. Such anxieties can be unconsciously translated into hostility toward foreigners who challenge that familiar body and threaten its corruption through ethnic and cultural mixing that can alter the body in both external appearance and behavior.

Wittgenstein may be suggesting something like this as an explanation for the stubborn persistence of rabid antisemitism in the apparently most rational countries of Europe. This seemingly irrational hatred of the Jews may in fact have a deep compelling logic of its own that seems to operate on a visceral model or analogy. The Jews, in this unhappily familiar analogy, are a diseased tumor (*Beule*) in Europe, though Wittgenstein is prudent enough not to call this tumor a fatal cancer.

> "Look on this tumor as a perfectly normal part of your body!" Can one do that, to order? Do I have the power to decide at will to have, or not to have, an ideal conception of my body?
>
> Within the history of the peoples of Europe the history of the Jews is not treated as circumstantially as their intervention in European affairs would actually merit, because within this history they are experienced as a sort of disease, and anomaly, and no one wants to put a disease on the same level as normal life [and no one wants to speak of a disease as if it had the same rights as healthy bodily processes (even painful ones)]. We may say: people can only regard this tumor as a natural part of the body if their whole feeling for the body changes (if the whole national feeling for the body changes). Otherwise the best they can do is *put up with* it.
>
> You can expect an individual man to display this sort of tolerance, or else to disregard such things; but you cannot expect this of a nation, because it is precisely not disregarding such things that make it a nation. I.e. there is a contradiction in expecting someone *both* to retain his former aesthetic feeling for his body [*aesthetische Gefühl für seinen Körper*] and *also* to make the tumor welcome. (CV, 20–21)

After a half-century of efforts to overcome the horrors of the Holocaust with arguments for multicultural tolerance, should we simply endorse the apparent political implications of this alleged contradiction and argue that it is unreasonable for European nations to tolerate the Jews or other alien minorities that are experienced as tumors? If we respect Wittgenstein's intelligence and ethical integrity (and how could we not!), should we read this private notebook entry from 1931 as Wittgenstein's final view on the Jewish question, asserting that a nation's essential function or duty is to preserve the ethnic purity of its body politic? We can reject this purist conclusion without denying the explanatory links between political enmity against the Other and the concern for our familiar body feelings and practices. Instead, Wittgenstein's remarks on the politics of somaesthetic feelings can be given a much richer and more politically progressive interpretation.

It is a commonplace of anthropology that maintaining the intact boundaries and purity of the body can play an important symbolic and pragmatic role in preserving the unity, strength, and survival of a social group. Thus, for example, in trying to ensure the social identity of the young Hebrew nation, the early books of the Old Testament are full of meticulous injunctions for the Hebrews about body purity with respect to diet, sexual behavior, and the cleanliness of intact body boundaries. Bodily "issues" like bleeding, pus, spit, semen, vomit, and menstrual discharge defile all those who come in contact with them, and the unclean need to be separated and cleansed. "Thus shall ye separate the children of Israel from their uncleanness" (Leviticus 15). Incest, bestiality, homosexuality, adultery, and the eating of foods declared unclean are similar defilements. "Defile not ye yourselves in any of these things for in all these the nations are defiled which I cast out before you" (Leviticus 18). Foreign nations are portrayed as unclean dangers of contamination that threaten the purity and health of the Hebrew people. As Wittgenstein's tumor analogy suggests, the same metaphorical logic of unclean disease has been turned *against* the Jews in the symbolic unconsciousness of Europe. Jews are stereotyped as dark, hairy, malodorous, unclean, and unhealthy; yet, nonetheless mysteriously thriving in their filthy darkness like a tumor, while the true nation or folk is idealized as essentially pure or unmixed. And the ugly tumor of antisemitism similarly thrives through the dark power of such symbolism rather than through the critical light of rational analysis.

It is precisely because antisemitism (like other forms of ethnic hatred) has this compellingly sinister symbolism – a picture that holds whole nations captive – that rational arguments for multicultural tolerance always seem to fail, since the hatred is acquired not by rational means but by the captivating aesthetic power of images. Yet, as Schiller long ago claimed, aesthetic education may be able to achieve ethical-political transformation where rational arguments still find no purchase. So if Wittgenstein is right that it is contradictory to expect a person to welcome a tumor while retaining his former aesthetic feeling for the body, this does not mean that the tumor must be exterminated. An alternative would be to modify that person's aesthetic feeling for the body and the body politic.

In such ethical and political matters, the discipline of somaesthetics can offer once again a productive pragmatic step. If racial and ethnic enmity resists resolution through logical means of verbal persuasion because it has a visceral basis of discomforting unfamiliarity, then as long as we do not consciously attend to these deep visceral feelings we can neither overcome them nor the enmity they generate and foster. Disciplines of somaesthetic awareness, involving a focused, systematic scanning of our bodily feelings, is first helpful in identifying these disturbing somatic sensations so that we can better control, neutralize, or overcome them. If we can do no more than merely "put up with" them, in Wittgenstein's words, we have at least the ability to identify and isolate them in our consciousness, which better enables us to take a critical distance from them and avert their infecting our political judgments.

But somaesthetic efforts could go further than the remedy of diagnosis and isolation by actually transforming the undesirable, "intolerant" bodily feelings. Somatic feelings can be transformed through training because they are already the product of training. One's normal feelings and tastes are largely the result of learning rather than innate instinct; as habits derived from our experience and sociocultural formation, they are malleable to efforts of reformation.[19] Disciplines of somaesthetic training can therefore reconstruct our attitudes or habits of feeling and also give us greater flexibility and tolerance to different kinds of somatic feeling and behavior. This is a commonplace of gastronomy, athletics, and somatic therapies; but modern philosophical ethics and political theory have not given it enough attention.

Part of the problem may be that philosophers who do suggest that greater tolerance can be achieved through disciplines of somatic transformation – figures like Wilhelm Reich or Michel Foucault (and many of Foucault's followers in queer theory) – focus their sociopolitical advocacy of somatic discipline on the radical transformation of sexual practice. However useful and needed their reformatory proposals may be, their concentration on the sensitive issue of sex and transgression creates a cloud of controversy and polemics that distracts most mainstream philosophers (and the general public) from the general notion and value

[19] It is a common experience of negotiations between extremely hostile groups that mutual understanding is greatly improved once the negotiators actually spend enough agreeable time together to get somaesthetically comfortable with each other, which is why the sharing of meals and entertainment can be a fruitful part of the negotiating process. This was quite evident, for example, in the more successful negotiations between Israel and its Arab enemies.

of transformative somaesthetic discipline. The whole promise of improving social tolerance and political understanding through somaesthetic means should not be so narrowly tied to the sensationally charged but still rather limited issue of sexual behavior. For all the joys of sex (and despite the brilliant insights of Freud), there is a great deal more of interest and of value in our bodily life than our experience of sexual activity and desire. This is something that Wittgenstein must have known, since sexuality hardly seems to constitute the dominating center of his work and life, even though his rather hidden, largely repressed, and guiltily troubled homosexuality must have been an enduring concern.[20]

In this context, we should note that the hostility, fear, torment, and social stigmatization associated with homophobia can also be addressed by somaesthetic mindfulness, since homophobic prejudice shares the same visceral logic of racial and ethnic enmity. Here too, antagonism and intolerance are fueled by uncomfortable but often unacknowledged visceral reactions, feelings that homosexual acts and appetites are alien and threatening to the familiar, established forms of bodily desire and behavior. Many people who in principle might recognize that consenting adults should be free to discreetly pursue their alternative sexual preferences, nevertheless are actually unable to tolerate homosexuality because of the somatic reactions of discomfort and disgust (including the revulsion of repressed guilty desires) that even imagined homosexuality generates. Here again, somaesthetic mindfulness can offer the means to recognize and control these visceral reactions and thus can also provide a bridge toward transforming them into less negative feelings about homosexuality. Somaesthetic reflection can likewise empower those homosexuals who are confused or troubled about having erotic desires and encounters that deviate from the heterosexual norm. By giving individuals greater clarity about their feelings, such mindful body consciousness can enable anyone with deviant desires to acknowledge, inhabit, and manage these feelings better (which need not mean to stifle them).

If the seductive image of body purity and uniformity fuels the deep prejudice that incites fear and hatred toward alien groups (whether of racial, ethnic, or sexual difference), then one strategy for overcoming the problem would be to make vividly clear and visible the impure and mixed nature of all human bodies, including our own. Somaesthetic disciplines can give us such a heightened experiential awareness of the

---

[20] On Wittgenstein's troubled sexuality, see, for example, the biography by Ray Monk, *Ludwig Wittgenstein: The Duty of Genius* (London: Penguin, 1991).

What a whopper of a quote from Buddhism!

impure mixture of our bodily constitution and remind us that our body boundaries are never absolute but rather porous. The body is a messy container of all sorts of solids, liquids, and gases; it is always being penetrated by things coming from the outside in the air we breathe and the food we eat, just as we continuously expel materials from within our bodies. The somaesthetic strategy of focusing on our impure bodily mixture can already be found in the Buddha's sermon advocating heightened mindfulness of the body: "a bhikkhu reflects on this very body enveloped by the skin and full of manifold impurity, from the sole up, and from the top of the hair down, thinking thus: 'There are in this body hair of the head, hair of the body, nails, teeth, skin, flesh, sinews, bones, marrow, kidneys, heart, liver, midriff, spleen, lungs, intestines, mesentery, stomach, faeces, bile, phlegm, pus, blood, sweat, fat, tears, grease, saliva, nasal mucus, synovial fluid, urine.' ... Thus, he lives observing the body."[21]

Having indicated my general arguments for the ethical and political potential of somaesthetic mindfulness, I shall not here pursue a more detailed account of its diverse disciplines or methods[22]; for Wittgenstein provides no analysis of mindfulness practices, ancient or modern. We can, however, conclude this chapter by considering a Wittgensteinian theme that helps underline the pertinence of somaesthetics not just for the integrated branches of philosophy we have so far examined, but for philosophy as a whole.

V

Wittgenstein frequently insists on the crucial importance of slowness for properly doing philosophy. Philosophers often err by jumping to wrong conclusions by misinterpreting the gross surface structure of language in terms of some primitive scheme and then inferring something that seems at once necessary and impossible. Instead of rushing "like savages, primitive people" to "put a false interpretation" on language "and then draw the queerest conclusions from it," the key to good philosophical work is taking the time to carefully untangle the knots of conceptual confusion caused by such hasty conclusions from language. We do

[21] See the Buddha's "The Foundations of Mindfulness," in Walpola Rahula, trans. *What the Buddha Taught* (New York: Grove Press, 1974), reprinted in *A Sourcebook of Asian Philosophy*, ed. John Koller and Patricia Koller (Upper Saddle River, NJ: Prentice Hall, 1991), 206.

[22] I treat some of these methods in *Performing Live* (Ithaca, NY: Cornell University Press, 2000), ch. 8.

this by patiently "clearing up" the complexities of our language, "by arranging what we have always known," by "assembling reminders," "to bring words back from their metaphysical to their everyday use," and thus "uncovering ... one or another piece of plain nonsense and ... bumps that the understanding has got by running its head up against the limits of language" (PI, 109, 116, 119, 127, 194). This work of painstaking linguistic analysis requires slow, patient labor and thus demands a sort of practiced, disciplined slowness. Wittgenstein therefore cautions that "someone unpracticed in philosophy passes by all the spots where difficulties are hidden in the grass, whereas the practiced [philosopher] will pause and sense that there is a difficulty close by even though he cannot see it yet" (CV, 29).

Hence, Wittgenstein's appreciation of slowness: "The salutation of philosophers to each other should be: 'Take your time!'" Wittgenstein's manner of reading and writing aims at attaining this slowness. "I really want my copious punctuation marks to slow down the speed of reading. Because I should like to be read slowly. (As I myself read.)" "My sentences are all supposed to be read slowly" (CV, 57, 68, 80). We know, however, that Wittgenstein's temperament was the opposite of patient. Exceedingly quick of mind and movement, he had great difficulty in either sitting or standing still.[23] Fiery and quick-tempered, he contrastingly insisted "My ideal is a certain coolness" a state of tranquillity where "conflict is dissipated" and one achieves "peace in one's thoughts" (CV, 2, 9, 43).

But how can we achieve a better mastery of slowness and tranquility without drugging ourselves with mind-deadening tranquillizers? Self-isolation in a quiet, foreign place that is far from familiar and unwanted distractions is one traditional method, and Wittgenstein indeed applied it in his periods of hermit life far up on the Sogna Fjord in Norway. But another ancient answer has been a focused attention to and consequent regulation of our breathing. Since breathing has a profound effect on our entire nervous system, by slowing or calming our breathing, we can bring greater slowness and tranquillity to our minds. In the same way, by noticing and then relaxing certain muscle contractions that are not only unnecessary but also distractive to thinking because of the pain or fatigue they create, we can strengthen the focus of our mental concentration, and

---

[23] Memoirs of Wittgenstein often attest to this. See, for example, Fania Pascal, "Wittgenstein: A Personal Memoir," in *Recollections of Wittgenstein*, ed. Rush Rhees (Oxford: Oxford University Press, 1984), 18; and Norman Malcolm, *Wittgenstein: A Memoir* (Oxford: Oxford University Press, 1958, 2nd ed., 1985), 29.

build its patient endurance for sustained philosophical meditations. We can then afford to take our time.

Attention to bodily feelings cannot explain our thinking, our emotions, or our will. But it can improve them. Somaesthetic sensations neither explain nor justify our aesthetic judgments, but they can help us enhance our aesthetic capacities and even our ethical powers. Sensation is not the mysterious explanatory "*something*" that defines the fundamental mechanism of all mental life, but, as Wittgenstein recognizes, it "is not a *nothing* either!" (PI, 304). However much somaesthetic feeling and somatic self-consciousness count for Wittgenstein, I hope to have shown that they should count for something more, at least for a pragmatism that seeks to improve the quality of our thought and life, including the thoughtful lives we lead as active ethical and political beings.

5

Deeper into the Storm Center

The Somatic Philosophy of William James

I

"The body," writes William James, "is the storm centre, the origin of co-ordinates, the constant place of stress in [our] experience-train. Every-thing circles round it, and is felt from its point of view." "The world experienced," he elaborates, "comes at all times with our body as its cen-tre, centre of vision, centre of action, centre of interest."[1] For purposes of survival, if not also for other reasons, "all minds must . . . take an intense interest in the bodies to which they are yoked . . . My own body and what ministers to its needs are thus the primitive object, instinctively deter-mined, of my egoistic interests. Other objects may become interesting derivatively through association" with it.[2]

Despite such powerful pronouncements and his many arguments to back them up, William James is rarely celebrated as a body philoso-pher, though he surely gives more careful attention to body conscious-ness than do more famously somatic philosophers such as Nietzsche, Merleau-Ponty, or Foucault. Perhaps his stature as a body philosopher has been eclipsed because the bulk of his somatic research is concen-trated in his early book on psychology (of 1890) and because he devoted much of his later energy to topics of metaphysics, religious belief, and spiritualism. However, James's affirmation of the body's central impor-tance extends throughout his entire career. The quote that opens this chapter comes from an essay of 1905 that James later appended to

---

[1] See William James, "The Experience of Activity," in *Essays in Radical Empiricism* (Cambridge, MA: Harvard University Press, 1976), 86. Reference to this book of essays, first published in 1912, will be to this edition, hereafter RE.

[2] William James, *The Principles of Psychology* (1890; Cambridge, MA: Harvard University Press, 1983), 308, hereafter PP.

A Pluralistic Universe, which was published in 1909, the year before he died. In "The Moral Equivalent of War," written in 1910, James can still be found touting the body by lauding the "ideals of hardihood," the "virtues" of "physical health and vigor" and "the tradition . . . of physical fitness" that make the martial life irresistibly attractive and that must be incorporated into a more moral substitute for war.[3]

Three reasons can explain James's intense interest in the body and his keen sensitivity to its expressive role in mental and moral life. One was his early pursuit of a career in painting, which he formally studied between 1858 and 1861. "'Art' is my vocation," he declared to a friend in 1860 at the age of eighteen.[4] Though this vocation was soon to be replaced by science and later by philosophy, James's acutely discriminating attention to bodily form and subtleties of expression, together with his skill in visualizing and depicting states of mind and feelings, were no doubt developed by his youthful passion for drawing and the study of art, which his long and frequent stays in the cultural centers of Europe helped inspire.

James's special sensitivity to the body's pervasive influence on our mental and moral states was surely also a product of his own enormous burden of nagging, recurrent bodily ailments, which for many years threatened to rob him of any career at all. In what should have been the healthy years of early manhood, he very often suffered from chronic gastritis, headaches, constipation, insomnia, listless fatigue, nervous depression, and severe back pains. He also was plagued by debilitating eye problems that sometimes limited his reading to only forty-five minutes in a row and no more than two hours a day.[5] Forced to give up his career plans for laboratory science, since he physically could not endure the strain of laboratory work, James chose to become a doctor despite his lower regard of this profession as full of "humbug" and "tenth-rate" minds.[6] Of the five years he took to complete the degree at Harvard Medical School, only two were spent in school. The rest were devoted to seeking – primarily through rest and water cures in various spas of Europe – the bodily and mental health

[3] William James, "The Moral Equivalent of War," in *The Writings of William James*, ed. John McDermott (Chicago: University of Chicago Press, 1977), 664, 665, 670.

[4] *The Correspondence of William James*, ed. I. Skrupskelis and E. Berkeley (Charlottesville: University Press of Virginia, 1992–2004), 4:33. Hereafter C followed by volume and page numbers will designate page references to this twelve-volume work.

[5] These health problems are expressed in voluminous detail in James's letters, but see also Howard Feinstein, *Becoming William James* (Ithaca, NY: Cornell University Press, 1984).

[6] See his letters to friends, as presented in Ralph Barton Perry, *The Thought and Character of William James*, 2 vols. (Boston: Little, Brown, 1935), 1:216; and also in *The Letters of William James*, ed. Henry James III, 2 vols. (Boston: Atlantic Monthly Press, 1926), 1:79.

that could allow him to achieve a successful professional life. Four years after the degree, James was still, at thirty-one, a jobless dependent "nursing ill health in his father's house," until his friend Henry Bowditch, a Harvard physiologist, offered James a job as his temporary replacement. Harvard's new president, Charles Eliot, who had been James's chemistry teacher (and was a neighbor and friend of the family) approved the idea and eventually arranged for James a regular post in physiology.[7]

An avowed victim of "neurasthenia" (now regarded as a mythical disease), James realized that many of his ailments were psychosomatic, the result of what he repeatedly described as his "miserable nervous system" (C2:108). His problematic nerves generated bodily disorders that in turn increased his nervous stress, which then stimulated further somatic complaints and mental anxiety in a vicious spiral of incapacity. How could James not be deeply impressed by the powerfully reciprocal influences of mind and body when they were played out so often and so dramatically in his own painful experience of infirmity and when they were so carefully monitored by him as a medical school student and young doctor whose primary occupation was to heal himself so that he could eventually begin a career beyond that of a studious invalid? Biographers have sometimes attributed the onset of these psychosomatic ailments to James's problem of choosing a profession and particularly his reluctance to give up a career in art for one in science and medicine.[8] But whatever their cause, the fact that many of these ailments continued long after James was well launched into his hugely happy career as a professional philosopher must have kept the body's mental and moral importance pervasively present in his philosophical thinking.

The matter of professional career also suggests a third reason that could have been crucial in prompting James to emphasize the body's central philosophical role. His university training and first professional work were in anatomy and physiology; and this somatic knowledge was precisely what enabled him to enter the academic profession of philosophy, despite his having had no formal training in it. Though Nietzsche criticized philosophers for "lack ... [of] knowledge of physiology,"[9] James began his illustrious career as a Harvard philosopher by teaching physiology in the Medical School in 1873. He then used this expertise in physiology as the key wedge to maneuver himself slowly but surely into

---

[7] Feinstein, *Becoming William James*, 318, 321.
[8] This is a central thesis in Feinstein's instructive biography.
[9] Friedrich Nietzsche, *The Will to Power* (New York: Vintage, 1967), para. 408.

a professorship in the Harvard philosophy department, overcoming his lack of official philosophical credentials and the stubborn opposition of some important department members.[10]

Physiology was increasingly recognized to be central to new research in psychology (which was still considered a subbranch of philosophy), but the Harvard philosophy department had no faculty who was qualified to teach this new scientific approach to the mind; so James was able to convince Harvard's president and Board of Overseers that his teaching of psychology was essential to keep the philosophy department competitively up to date. In 1874, James was able to offer a course on "The Relations between Physiology and Psychology," in the physiology department; by 1877, he was permitted to teach a course on Herbert Spencer's psychology in the philosophy department; and by 1879, James was able to give his first purely philosophical course (on Charles Renouvier) and leave all teaching of physiology. Finally, in 1880, his (assistant) professorship was officially transferred to the philosophy department. Since James's professional aspirations as a philosopher so heavily relied on the view that physiology was crucial to the philosophical study of mind, it is only natural that his philosophy would give the body a very prominent role.

That personal factors helped fuel James's somatic emphasis should not discredit his theories. If the quest for knowledge is always guided by interest, then heightened personal interest can generate better theory by promoting more penetratingly vigilant attention, more subtle awareness, and keener sensitivity. Worries about his own body-mind attunement prompted James to seek more than a purely theoretical and speculative understanding of how physical life and mental life are related. His somatic philosophy was thus deepened by extensive explorations into a wide variety of pragmatic methodologies aimed at improving the harmonious functioning of the self's body-mind nexus.

James not only read and wrote about these pragmatic therapies, exhorting the philosophical community to explore them more seriously.[11] He also boldly tested many of them on his own flesh. James's letters reveal his experiments with an impressively broad range of often contradictory

---

[10] James's maneuvers are described in Feinstein, *Becoming William James*, 332–340.

[11] In his presidential lecture to the American Philosophical Association in 1906 ("The Energies of Men"), James urged philosophers to undertake a sustained program of research that would systematically explore the wide-ranging means (such as yoga), by which we human beings are able to tap into our normally dormant "deeper levels of energy" so as to improve our physical and mental capacities of performance. See "The Energies of Men," in *William James: Writings 1902–1910*, ed. Bruce Kuklick (New York: Viking, 1987), 1230.

methods: ice and blistering (for counter-irritation), corsets, varieties of weight lifting, electric shock, absolute bed-rest, diverse water cures, vigorous walking, rapid mountain climbing, systematic chewing, magnetic healing, hypnosis and "mind-cure" therapy, relaxation, spinal vibrations, vapor inhalations, homeopathic remedies, lessons in mental focusing to minimize muscular contractions, diverse programs of medically prescribed gymnastics, cannabis, nitrous oxide, mescaline, strychnine, and varieties of hormonal injections. James's palette of somatic experiments was surely as varied and daring for his time as Michel Foucault's was for ours, and often just as defiant of mainstream opinion. However, true to his Puritan-Victorian context, James's experimentalism avoided the explosive area of sexuality, where his views were as conservative and sexist as Foucault's were radically transgressive.[12] Still, no less than the French poststructuralist, the New England pragmatist was an admirably adventurous explorer in all three branches of somaesthetics: the *analytic* study of the body's role in perception, experience, and action and thus in our mental, moral, and social life; the *pragmatic* study of methodologies to improve our body-mind functioning and thus expand our capacities of self-fashioning; and the *practical* branch that investigates such pragmatic methods by testing them on our own flesh in concrete experience and practice.

This chapter first examines the contributions James made to analytic somaesthetics through his theories on the body's central role in mental and moral life. Next his pragmatic views on somatic methodologies of meliorism must be considered, especially because he construed philosophy as an instrument and art of living aimed at improving our experience. Finally, we shall see how the problematic limitations of James's somatic methods are sometimes reflected in his own practical efforts to heal himself through body-mind attunement.

II

The best entry into James's somatic philosophy is through his first book and mammoth masterpiece, *The Principles of Psychology* (1890). Its opening chapter introduces what will be the guiding hypothesis of James's philosophy of embodied mind: "the general law that *no mental modification ever*

---

[12] James strikingly argues for the existence of what he calls "the *anti-sexual instinct*" – "the actual repulsiveness to us of the idea of intimate contact with most of the persons we meet, especially those of our own sex" (PP, 1053–1054).

occurs which is not accompanied or followed by a bodily change" (PP, 18). Since the brain is the most crucial body part for mental life, the book's next two chapters explain brain functioning and the general physiological conditions of brain activity. James then devotes the subsequent chapter to the topic of habit. Beginning with habit, we shall analyze the major topics through which James develops his arguments for the centrality of bodily experience in our mental and social life, deploying also his texts beyond the *Principles*.

Habit

Habits are an apt topic for exploring the body-mind connection, since we speak of both bodily and mental habits. Moreover, habits can be understood as the expression of mental attitudes incorporated in bodily dispositions or conversely as bodily tendencies reflecting mental life and purpose. James's famous theory of habit evinces the striking way that his insight into the basic bodily dimension of life is elaborated into ever widening circles of human significance, like the ever-expanding ripples of a single well-cast stone, which soon encompass an entire pond. From the simple but crucial physiological fact that our malleable bodily constitution permits habit formation, the body of habit grows into a key factor not only shaping the individual's mental and moral life but also more broadly structuring human society as a whole.

At the most fundamental physical level, "*the phenomena of habit in living beings are due to the plasticity of the organic materials of which their bodies are composed,*" which includes, for James, the inner nervous system as well as "outer form" (PP, 110). "*Our nervous system grows to the modes in which it has been exercised*" (PP, 117), so our embodied selves are shaped into habits of mind and action that perform for us automatically what once required considerable thought, time, and effort. Because habits thus provide the principal direction of thought and behavior, we can be described as "mere walking bundles of habits" (PP, 130). By allowing us to diminish "conscious attention" to what they themselves can successfully perform through "the effortless custody of automatism," habits also enable us to concentrate "our higher powers of mind" on more problematic aspects of our experience that need more focused attention (PP, 119–126).

From these premises, James draws a strong moral: We should make every effort to develop the best possible habits while our body or nervous system is still flexible enough to be most easily shaped. The key "*is to make our nervous system our ally instead of our enemy . . . For this we must make automatic and habitual, as early as possible, as many useful actions as we can,* and guard against the growing into ways that are likely to be disadvantageous to us, as we should guard against the plague" (PP, 126). Such training of embodied action, James argues, requires a good measure of "asceticism" to push our nervous system further into the right directions it may not yet be prone to take (PP, 130).

But the role of the disciplined habit-body extends far beyond the personal ethical efforts of self-improvement; it sustains the entire social structure through which habit is itself shaped and in which individual efforts find their place and limit. Prefiguring Foucault's theory of disciplined, docile bodies and Pierre Bourdieu's theory of *habitus*, James asserts: "Habit is thus the enormous fly-wheel of society, its most precious conservative agent. It alone is what keeps us all within the bounds of ordinance, and saves the children of fortune from the envious uprisings of the poor." Habit, James continues, "keeps the fisherman and the deckhand at sea through the winter; it holds the miner in his darkness...It dooms us all to fight out the battle of life upon the lines of our nurture or our early choice, and to make the best of a pursuit that disagrees, because there is no other for which we are fitted, and it is too late to begin again. It keeps different social strata from mixing." Even if a man acquires the wealth to dress his body "like a gentleman-born," "he simply *cannot* buy the right things. An invisible law, as strong as gravitation, keeps him within his orbit, arrayed this year as he was the last" (PP, 125, 126). Likewise, a body habituated to timid, subservient, inhibited expression will find it almost impossible to express itself suddenly in the kind of bold and defiantly assertive action needed to challenge social structures that pervasively inculcate inferiority through somatic habit formation that shapes mental attitudes and not merely body postures.

Change and Unity in the Stream of Thought
From this broad social panorama, let us turn to the more private theatre of personal thought in which philosophers rarely grant the body a central role. James proves a remarkable exception. Asserting that each individual's consciousness exists in "absolute insulation" from others (PP, 221), James argues that personal consciousness is not merely pervaded by somatic feelings but ultimately depends on them for its distinctive sense of continuous flux and unity. His celebrated notion of the stream of consciousness affirms "thought is in constant change" (PP, 224). Our sensations are always slightly changing, even if we think that we are having exactly the same sensation as we continue to regard the same blue sky. We have this impression because we confuse having "*the same bodily sensation*," with having a sensation of "*the same* OBJECT" (PP, 225), here the blue sky; and because our minds are far more interested in (and

habituated to focus on) noticing objects rather than sensations. But since one's physiological "sensibility is altering all the time," the same object cannot continuously give exactly the same sensation. "The eye's sensibility to light . . . blunts itself with surprising rapidity," and the state of one's brain, which surely affects our experienced sensation, is also continuously modified to some extent, since even the mere flux of experience and brain activity will leave new neural traces. "For an identical sensation to recur it would have to occur the second time *in an unmodified brain.*" But this, notes James, "is a physiological impossibility." "Experience is remoulding us every moment"; and as our nervous system is continuously modified, so is the flow of our sensations, feelings, and thoughts (PP, 226, 227, 228).

James's view of the pervasively somatic dimension in the ever-changing stream of consciousness finds support from contemporary neuroscience. The neurologist Antonio Damasio explains "the ever-changing modulation of affect" that characterizes normal human consciousness as ultimately a function of "the ever-changing landscape of your body." Feelings result from the brain's "ongoing, uninterruptible representation of the body," its "continuous monitoring" through images "of what your body is doing *while* thoughts about specific contents roll by," and this "body landscape is always new," yet relatively stable. For alongside the ever changing "current," "dynamic body maps," there are also "more stable maps of general body structure" or tendency that help form our more abiding "notion of body image."[13]

Besides explaining the ever-changing stream of thought, the body conversely provides the ground of thought's unity. Our thoughts are united as being ours because "as we think we feel our bodily selves as the seat of the thinking. If the thinking be *our* thinking, it must be suffused through all its parts with that peculiar warmth and intimacy" that James regards as primarily constituted by "the feeling of the same old body always there," even though the body is never, strictly speaking, there in exactly the same unmodified state. Some sense of embodiment thus pervades all our knowledge, even if we are not attentive to it. "Our own bodily position, attitude, condition, is one of the things of which *some* awareness, however inattentive, invariably accompanies the knowledge of whatever else we know"; and our continuous somatic sensitivity is essential to the unity of our thinking even in nonsomatic matters, since it helps "form

[13] Antonio Damasio, *Descartes' Error: Emotion, Reason, and the Human Brain* (New York: Avon, 1994), 144–145, 151–152, 158, hereafter DE.

a *liaison* between all the things of which we become successively aware" (PP, 234–235). Although one's world of experiences and thoughts may be "a quasi-chaos" with "vastly more discontinuity... than we commonly suppose," this baffling complexity can be held together by "the objective nucleus of every man's experience, his own body, [which], is, it is true, a continuous percept" (RE, 33).

Damasio's neuroscientific research supports such claims. Though we are not often explicitly aware of "the ongoing, uninterruptible representation of the body," this is because "our focus of attention is usually elsewhere, where it is most needed for adaptive behavior." It "does not mean the body representation is absent, as you can easily confirm when the sudden onset of pain or minor discomfort shifts the focus back to it. The background body sense is continuous, although one may hardly notice it, since it represents not a specific part of anything in the body but rather an overall state of most everything in it." Yet Damasio concludes, "such an ongoing, unstoppable representation of the body state is what allows you to reply promptly to the specific question 'How do you *feel?*' with an answer that does relate to whether you feel fine or do not feel that well" (DE, 152). One of Damasio's key theories is that our continuous sense of bodily feelings is necessary for the successful performance of sustained reasoning, especially with respect to social and practical matters. Here again, his arguments are deeply inspired by James, who notoriously championed the somatic character of emotion while celebrating the importance of affect in the life of thought.

Sensation, Attention, and Sense of Time and Place
Before critically considering these controversial views in their Jamesian formulation, we should note some other ways James underlines the body's cognitive importance. Knowledge involves the selection and organization of content. The body's sense organs contribute to this process first by shaping our abilities and scope of perception. Serving as filters that are receptive to only some aspects of the physical world and only within a certain range of "velocity," our bodily sense organs select the sensations that can come into our thinking (PP, 273–274).[14] Real thought, of course, requires the further selection of conscious attention to some of

---

[14] Moreover, the body is not a mere passive register but an active integrator of such sense perceptions, so that the perception of a ball in one's hand involves an integration "of optical impressions of touch, of muscular adjustments of the eye, of the movements of our fingers, and of the muscular sensations which these yield" (PP, 708).

the manifold of sensations that are given in immediate experience. But attention is itself partly "a bodily disposition" (PP, 413). "When we look or listen we accommodate our eyes and ears involuntarily, and we turn our head and body as well" (PP, 411). Even what seems to be purely intellectual attention (such as trying to recall and focus on a memory or an idea or a line of reasoning) involves, James argues, distinctive muscular contractions in the head, eyeballs, eyelids, brow, and glottis. In addition, if the attention is in any way effortful, it will also involve "contractions of the jaw-muscles and of those of respiration," which then often radiate down from the throat and chest and into our lower back (PP, 287–288).

There is a practical consequence to this muscularity of thought that James fails to note here but that we have already suggested in previous chapters. The often painful strain of attention in what we presume to be purely mental work comes from the muscular tension involved in such allegedly "pure" thinking. We tend to feel such tension only when it reaches a certain threshold of pain or discomfort, feeling it in the strain of our eyes, our backs, and, if we are sufficiently sensitive, in the fatigue of our facial muscles. But greater somatic self-consciousness could provide us with a better monitoring of these muscular contractions so that we can learn to avoid or at least diminish those that are unnecessary or unnecessarily severe. By arresting or minimizing such pain-producing contractions before they are sustained long enough to generate the pain, we can enable ourselves to think longer and harder with greater ease and less distraction from discomfort and fatigue.

James further argues that bodily feelings are cognitively crucial in providing our sense of time, especially when it concerns the passage of so-called empty time. The phenomenological feeling of time passing can never be the sensation of pure duration without any content, since such a pure emptiness could not be perceived as moving or changing. Hence, some passing content must be being attended to in the passage of "empty time," and James (relying on both introspection and experimental findings) claims that the body – through its rhythms of "heart-beats," "breathing," and "feelings of muscular tension and relaxation" – provides this changing content that expresses time's passage (PP, 584).[15]

---

[15] James affirms Hugo Münsterberg's more specific view that up to a duration of one third of a second we can feel the sense of time in the fading memory image of an impression, but that beyond that threshold our sense of time's passage is a function of changes of muscular feelings (PP, 584).

As "the objective nucleus of every man's experience," the soma also establishes one's sense of place and positionality by organizing the experienced world around its center as "the origin of co-ordinates." James explains, "Where the body is is 'here'; when the body acts is 'now'; what the body touches is 'this'; all other things are 'there' and 'then' and 'that.' These words of emphasized position imply a systematization of things with reference to a focus of action and interest which lies in the body; and the systematization is now so instinctive (was it ever not so?) that no developed or active experience exists for us at all except in that ordered form" (RE, 33, 86). Our bodies, moreover, help create a sense of common space. When I see your body, I focus on a place and object that is also the focus of your experience, even though *your* experience of your body is from a different perspective. In the same way, bodies provide a common place for the meeting of minds, whose intentions, beliefs, desires, and feelings are expressed in bodily demeanor and behavior (RE, 38, 41).

The body also works to unify space by serving as a bridge between the spaces of inner self and outer nature, and between physical and mental events. It does so by ambiguously straddling these domains in our experience. I can regard my bleeding finger as an external object to be wrapped with a bandage, but I can also experience it as a throbbing painful part of me. And this throbbing I feel as the blood pulses and gushes forth, is it a physical feeling or a mental experience of pain? It seems to span both spaces, as does the surge of conjugal love I feel that makes my chest swell and my face beam with bright eyes and a broad smile. Such feelings (which James called "affectional facts") are "affections...of the mind" but also "simultaneously affections of the body" (RE, 69, 71), an ambiguity reflecting the exemplary ambiguity of the body itself, which is both what I am and what I have as something distinct from the "I" that regards it. As James explains, "Sometimes I treat my body purely as part of outer nature. Sometimes, again, I think of it as 'mine,' I sort it with the 'me,' and then certain local changes and determinations in it pass for spiritual happenings. Its breathing is my 'thinking,' its sensorial adjustments are my 'attention,' its kinaesthetic alterations are my 'efforts,' its visceral perturbations are my 'emotions'" (RE, 76). Such strong identification of spiritual and bodily processes is the most radical and controversial aspect of James's somatic philosophy, and we need to separate the truly valid points from the confusing rhetoric of exaggeration he sometimes used, pragmatically, to make them.

Emotion

James held that bodily feelings are not merely cognitively useful in organizing our experience but that they also constitute our most basic sense
of self. His account of the self is complex, ranging from the "phenomenal
self" or "Empirical Me" (which includes the material Self, the social
Self, and the spiritual Self) to the more ethereal "pure principle of
personal identity" that he identifies with the "*I* which knows" that Me
and that has been traditionally identified with the noumenal "soul" or
"pure ego" (PP, 280, 283, 314, 379). "The body," writes James, "is the
innermost part of *the material self* in each of us," followed by our clothes
and our immediate family, which we also tend to regard and care for
as "part of our very selves" (PP, 280). The body is also important for
one's social self, since that self involves one's "image" in the "eyes" or
"mind" of others, and one's body typically figures centrally in that image
(PP, 281–282).[16] Beyond these commonplace claims for the body, James
controversially contends that bodily feelings constitute an important
aspect of our spiritual self, of which emotions form a significant part.

The established psychological view of his time regarded emotions as
purely mental events, which are first experienced directly through perception and independently of bodily reactions, such reactions being construed as the mere subsequent effects or expression of the emotion. James
(and C. G. Lange, a Danish thinker who independently developed a very
similar theory in the same year of 1884), argued that bodily sensations
play a more essential role in generating and even constituting emotion,
at least with respect to the stronger emotions (such as grief, anger, fear,
joy, etc.).[17] When we notice something that makes us angry or fearful or

---

[16] James ranks our devotion to clothes so high as to suggest that their beauty may be more
important to us than that of our own body. "We so appropriate our clothes and identify
ourselves with them that there are few of us who, if asked to choose between having a
beautiful body clad in raiment perpetually shabby and unclean, and having an ugly and
blemished form always spotlessly attired, would not hesitate a moment before making
a decisive reply" (PP, 280). James notes that "*a man has as many social selves as there are
individuals who recognize him* and carry an image of him in their mind" (PP, 281–282), so
an individual's ability to display different body images – say as a nursing mother and a
demanding judo instructor – can contribute to her ability in developing a more varied
social self.

[17] Describing such emotions as "the *coarser* emotions," James allows there are also "*subtler*
emotions" (exemplified by certain "moral, intellectual, and aesthetic feelings") in which
"pleasure and displeasure" or even "rapture" result simply from the perception of certain sensory qualities without the intervening influence of felt bodily sensations. The
"aesthetic emotion" of "primary and immediate pleasure in certain pure sensations and
harmonious combinations of them" is thus purely "*cerebral.*" James notes, however, that

elated, James claimed, we do not first derive a purely mental emotion from that perception, which in turn issues in bodily reactions. Instead, *"bodily changes follow directly the perception of the exciting fact, and . . . our feeling of the same changes as they occur* IS *the emotion"* (PP, 1065). The constitutive intervening role of bodily reactions (such as quickened heartbeat, goose flesh, shallow breathing, flushing, trembling, or flight) are what distinguishes a real emotion of fear from a mere intellectual recognition that what we perceive is dangerous or frightening. "Without the bodily states following on the perception, the latter would be purely cognitive in form, pale, colourless, destitute of emotional warmth" (PP, 1066). Emotions "are in very truth constituted by, and made up of, those bodily changes which we ordinarily call their expression or consequence" (PP, 1068). "A purely disembodied human emotion," James concludes, "is a nonentity," even if it is not a logical impossibility and even if such emotion might be metaphysically realized by "pure spirits" beyond the human realm (PP, 1068).

Much of the notorious controversy concerning the so-called James-Lange theory stems from the conceptual sloppiness and stylistic exaggeration in James's earlier formulations. He later acknowledged "the slap-dash brevity of the language [he] used," whose rhetorical pith and flourish greatly sacrificed precision.[18] To make his point that bodily changes are formative and not merely gratuitous subsequent effects, James argued that when we perceive a sorrowful event or a frightening object we do not first experience a disembodied sorrow or fear and then only subsequently have the sorrow- or fear-related bodily reactions such as crying, trembling, or running; instead, we only experience real sorrow or fear when our bodily reactions to that object or event are felt to "kick in." Unfortunately, James first expressed this by saying "that we feel sorry

---

such emotion is so subtle that it "can hardly be called emotional at all." Moreover, on top of this primary pleasure of pure intellectually appreciated beauty is typically added "secondary pleasures" in which the "bodily sounding-board is at work," and only when they are added do we get a robustly emotional experience of art (PP, 1065, 1082–1085). Perhaps the assertion of a disembodied aesthetic emotion was a strategic concession to the conventions of refined aesthetic taste (exhibited so masterfully in his brother Henry's fiction), but it is hard to see, given James's views on the somatic dimension of perception and thought, how bodily feeling is not integrally involved in even the purest of our aesthetic pleasures.

[18] See William James, "The Physical Basis of Emotion" (1894), repr. in William James, *Collected Essays and Reviews* (New York: Longmans, 1920), 351. His earlier treatments include, "What Is an Emotion?" *Mind*, 9 (1884): 188–205, and the long chapter on emotions in *Principles of Psychology*.

because we cry, angry because we strike, afraid because we tremble, and not that we cry, strike, or tremble, because we are sorry, angry, or fearful, as the case may be" (PP, 1066). This catchy, oft-cited formula confusingly reduces the wealth of bodily reactions involved in emotion (many of which James realized were "invisible visceral ones"[19]) down to certain explicit, well-defined, large-scale body movements like crying, striking, running, trembling.

James's famous slogan also falsely suggests that each general emotion (such as fear, anger, sorrow, joy, etc.) has one fixed and easily observed bodily behavior that defines it and that emotions should thus be understood in essentially behavioristic terms. James in fact held neither of these views. Affirming that the bodily changes involved in a given emotion could vary significantly in different people and in different situations and that emotions themselves admit of unlimited variety despite our tendency to group them under a limited set of general names, James insisted that emotions are inward experiences that are not reducible to their "physiological ground" and therefore need to be studied also inwardly through more acute efforts of introspection. Indeed, he argued that critics rejected his theory largely because they were introspectively unable to discern the feelings of bodily changes he identified with emotion.[20]

James's theory suffers from further problems. He was not always adequately clear in distinguishing between mere bodily changes and the *feeling* of those changes as what causes or constitutes the emotion (note his remarks cited three paragraphs above). More seriously, in trying to define what emotion is, James did not sufficiently distinguish the organic constitution of emotion from the emotion's intentional content or object,

---

[19] James, "The Physical Basis of Emotion," 351, hereafter PE.

[20] James claims *"there is no limit to the number of possible different emotions which may exist"* and that *"the emotions of different individuals may vary indefinitely,* both as to their constitution and as to objects which call them forth" (PP, 1069). He thus urges us to "discriminate also between the various grades of emotion which we designate by one name," though recognizing that these grades should share "enough *functional* resemblance" to warrant their common name, which should not be understood as designating a fixed essence in an ontological or "entitative" sense (PE, 351, 354). Resisting the claim that his theory is materialistic, James stresses that "our emotions must always be *inwardly* what they are, whatever be the physiological ground of their apparition" (PP, 1068), and he defends his theory by claiming that its critics are insufficiently skilled at "introspection" to detect or "localize" the bodily feelings involved in emotional excitement, hence they conclude that this excitement must have a nonorganic source (PE, 360–362). James therefore insists that we should "sharpen our introspection" to improve our ability of localizing feelings (PP, 1070) and that many more people should provide careful reports of such introspective "observations" (PE, 357).

which can also be thought to define an emotion because it is what the emotion is about. This failure, we recall, forms the crux of Wittgenstein's attack on James's theory. My bodily sensations of trembling, loss of breath, muscle contraction may essentially contribute to my emotion of fearing an approaching lion (rather than my mere judging the lion to be dangerous), but the *object* of my fear is really the lion, not these bodily changes or my feelings of these changes.

Though his more sober reformulation gives such objects a vital role "as elements... in [the] total 'situations'" that generate or constitute emotion,[21] James's dominant tendency is to identify emotion with the single dimension he considered most distinctive – "the organic feeling which gives the rank character of commotion to the excitement" we feel in the "*seizure*" of strong emotion and which distinguishes the emotional commotion of real fear from the mere cognitive recognition of danger (PE, 361). This organic feeling of excited commotion, James rightly argues, depends on the bodily changes we feel in reaction to the object (or total situation) that frightens us. However, the fact that this bodily feeling is distinctive of the emotion does not justify inferring, as James does, that it simply "IS *the emotion*," as if to imply that the cognitive element is inessential. Such an inference commits what Dewey called "the fallacy of selective emphasis," taking one element that can be rightly emphasized as distinctively important in a given phenomenon but then wrongly concluding that it is *all* that is essential or definitive of that phenomenon.[22]

Despite his problematic overstatements, James is clearly correct in affirming an important bodily dimension to our emotions. Damasio's recent neurophysiological research confirms this, though Damasio is even less careful than James in suggesting a simple bodily essentialism about emotion. Damasio defines "the *essence* of emotion as the collection

---

[21] PE, 350. The core of James's theory of emotion, in terms of the context of psychological theory of his day, was that the emotions were the product of afferent nerve currents based on sensorial input from the outside world and from our bodies rather than being the pure product of efferent nerve currents going out toward the body and based on a purely cognitive judgment of the mind. So James also defined "the length and breadth" of his theory in a most modest "unpretending" way by the proposition that our emotional consciousness is always mediated by these incoming currents, some of which are "*organic sensations*" (PE, 359–360).

[22] John Dewey, *Experience and Nature* (Carbondale: Southern Illinois University Press, 1981), 31–32. Dewey did not, however, invoke this fallacy in his very appreciative critical analysis of James's theory of emotion. For a brief discussion of Dewey's critique, see Gerald Myers, *William James: His Life and Thought* (New Haven, CT: Yale University Press, 1986), 535–536.

of changes in body state that are induced in myriad organs by nerve cell terminals, under the control of a dedicated brain system, which is responding to the content of thoughts relative to a particular entity or event." Many of such changes are perceptible to an external observer, but some can only be perceived internally by the subject, who may also not perceive them. Damasio reserves "the term *feeling*" for "the perception" or "the experience of those changes" (DE, 139). This formulation problematically implies that we can be in an emotional state and not even feel it, which would not be the case in the more precise version of James's theory, where to have the emotion is to feel the bodily changes, though we could feel them and still not identify ourselves as having the emotion. For instance, we could feel angry (by feeling the appropriate bodily changes), yet not realize that we are angry or what we are angry about. The key insight to retain from James and Damasio is that the bodily changes resulting from the perception or thought of what provokes us emotionally are not mere gratuitous or subsequent expressions of that emotion but, rather, are part of its formative core as a mental state.

There are important pragmatic consequences to be drawn from James's theory. If there is an essential connection between our emotions and bodily changes, then improved awareness of the feelings of these changes can provide a tool for better recognizing our emotions. We can be anxious or distressed without really knowing it; of course, we feel something, but we do not explicitly recognize the feeling and thus do not identify it as anxiety or distress. But if we are sensitive to our body signs, we can recognize our emotional disturbance and deal with it, even before we know the precise thing or situation outside our bodies about which we are anxious or upset. James does not elaborate this pragmatic application of somaesthetic awareness, though he should have. Instead, he recommends managing the emotions, by other means, by actions aimed at transforming the bodily feelings involved in emotion.

Realizing that strong feelings can often be dangerously destructive (and undoubtedly aware of the ravages of his own bouts of depression), James is not an indiscriminate advocate of emotion.[23] But he does affirm passion's productive dimension far more than do most philosophers.

---

[23] Gerald Myers (*William James*, 227–230) describes James attitude toward emotion as "ambivalent," because James recognized emotions could sometimes be detrimental and because he did not explicitly regard them as part of the most spiritual core of the self. But that hardly amounts to serious ambivalence. In holding emotion to be essential to his ideal of a full human life of rich experience and thought, James must have regarded emotion as essentially a positive feature, even if some emotions could be negative in their consequences.

Rather than a sign of error and irrationality, strong feeling provides prima facie experiential evidence of reality and truth. In this basic experiential sense, "*reality means simply relation to our emotional and active life*" (PP, 924); what is most real for us is what we care most passionately and actively about,[24] even if such judgments of the real can be overruled by subsequent experience. Moreover, James argues, passion is not the enemy of reason but rather its potent aid in pursuing a line of thought. "If *focalization* of brain activity be the fundamental fact of reasonable thought, we see why intense interest or concentrated passion makes us think so much more truly and profoundly. The persistent *focalization* of motion in certain tracts is the cerebral fact corresponding to the persistent domination in consciousness of the important feature of the subject. When not 'focalized,' we are scatter-brained; but when thoroughly impassioned, we never wander from the point. None but congruous and relevant images arise" (PP, 989–990).

Once again, Damasio offers a scientifically updated version of James's argument. Since there is no single "Cartesian theater" where all brain input meets together for simultaneous processing, human thinking works "by synchronizing sets of neural activity in separate brain regions, in effect a trick of timing," involving "time binding" of images occurring in different places but "within approximately the same window of time." But this requires "maintaining focused activity at different sites for as long as necessary for meaningful combinations to be made and for reasoning and decision making to take place. In other words, time binding requires powerful and effective mechanisms of attention and working memory" (DE, 94–96). Damasio argues that emotions (through their somatic dimension) not only work "*as a booster for continued working memory and attention*" but also facilitate "deliberation by highlighting some options" and eliminating other possibilities (DE, 174, 198). Without emotion's "somatic markers" to give an energizing boost and helpfully selective bias to our thinking, we could not reason as quickly, effectively, and decisively as we do. We would get lost in all the logical possibilities of action and their possible consequences and thus would "lose track" or direction (DE, 172–173). Pure rationalist cold-bloodedness, like the cold-bloodedness of the brain-damaged patients Damasio treats, would make the "mental landscape" of working memory not only "hopelessly flat" but also "too shifty and unsustained for the time required... of the reasoning process" in any complex matter of thinking or decision making (DE, 51).

---

[24] "Coerciveness over attention" (a common experiential way of defining reality) is also explained by James as "the result of liveliness or emotional interest" (PP, 928, 929).

James's physiological-psychological argument for the productive role of passion in our reasoning seems to issue (nine years after its formulation in *Principles of Psychology*) in a far more striking and questionable epistemological claim: "wherever there is conflict of opinion and difference of vision, we are bound to believe that the truer side is the side that feels the more, and not the side that feels the less."[25] This view, which may be more deeply rooted in James's ethics of respect for individuals than in his psychological arguments about the focusing power of feelings, is clearly contestable, since we know how strong feelings often distort our judgments. Passion may indeed hold us steadily on track, but it may be a track that takes us further from the most rational direction or balanced perspective for treating a problem. James's assertion is best construed as a pragmatic overstatement of the more convincing claim that we should be more prone to pay attention to opinions that people feel strongly about and to give them, at least prima facie, the benefit of the doubt.

Personal Identity and the Spiritual Self
Even when considered as essentially mental events, emotions have always been associated with bodily passions and thus have never been regarded (not even by James) as the most spiritual expression of mind. The spiritual core was instead identified with one's will and the active consciousness directing one's attention or stream of thought. James's somatic philosophy thus reaches its radical peak by asserting that bodily feeling rather than "*any purely spiritual element*" provides our sense of "the *active* element in all consciousness" that manifests our subjectivity and "spontaneity," and "that is the source of effort and attention ... and ... the fiats of the will" (PP 284–287). Arguing from his own efforts of introspection, James asserts that when observing the activity of this core "Self of selves," in its key mental acts of "attending, assenting, negating, making an effort," and so on, "*all [he] can ever feel distinctly is some bodily process, for the most part taking place within the head,*" or "*between the head and throat*" (PP, 287, 288). These feelings, James explains, include the adjustments of the cephalic sense organs associated with the thought (such as pressure and orientation of the eyeballs) as well as muscular contractions of the brow, jaw, and glottis. James next maintains, that, if his experience is typical of human thought in general (and he presumes he is not psychologically aberrant), then "*our entire feeling of spiritual activity, or what commonly passes by that name, is*

[25] William James, "On a Certain Blindness," in *Talks To Teachers on Psychology and To Students on Some of Life's Ideals* (New York: Dover, 1962), 114.

really a feeling of bodily activities whose exact nature is by most men overlooked" (PP, 288).

This argument does not prove that the core spiritual self of active will and consciousness is itself bodily; nor did James intend it to. Given the psychological focus of his *Principles,* James did not presume to pronounce on the *metaphysical reality* of this spiritual self but only on how this innermost "nuclear self" (PP, 289) is actually *felt* in experience, for he held that we do indeed feel its activity, and feel it somatically. Though James admits the commonsense experience of "most men" would not identify the feeling of mental activity in terms of localizable bodily feelings, he claims the reason is simply our inadequate attentiveness and acuity in somatic introspection. It is "for want of attention and reflection" that these "cephalic motions" or "bodily activities" of thought "usually fail to be perceived and classed as what they are" (i.e., bodily feelings), so we assume they are felt in a purely spiritual way (PP, 288, 291–292).

Besides the feeling of one's core spiritual self, the body provides the initial core of self-interest; and the eventual range of such interest effectively determines the ethical scope of the self. For evolutionary reasons of "survival," James argues, a person's *"own body . . . first of all, its friends next, and finally its spiritual dispositions,* MUST *be the supremely interesting* OBJECTS *for each human mind"* from which *"other objects may become interesting derivatively* through association" (PP, 307–308). Our interest in friends and mental powers ultimately derives from their relation to caring for the body's needs as necessary for basic self-survival. *"My own body and what ministers to its needs are thus the primitive object, instinctively determined, of my egoistic interests"* from which other interests (including altruistic ones) evolve to greatly enlarge the self (PP, 308).

Bodily feelings are also claimed to be the nucleus of our sense of continuous self-identity and of the very unity of consciousness with which the thinking "I" is identified. What gives us, asks James, the sense that I am the same self that I was yesterday and that my present thought belongs to the same stream of consciousness as my earlier thoughts? He answers this psychological question (distinct from the epistemological question of what guarantees the truth of this sensed unity) in terms of feelings of "warmth and intimacy" that the present self (or current thought) feels toward its past counterparts; and these feelings James identifies as bodily: "we feel the whole cubic mass of our body all the while, it gives us an unceasing sense of personal existence" (PP, 316). "The past and present selves" are unified by "a uniform feeling of 'warmth,' of bodily existence (or an equally uniform feeling of pure psychic energy?) [that]

pervades them all . . . and gives them a *generic* unity," though "this generic
unity coexists with generic differences just as real as the unity" (PP, 318).[26]
Even the unity of consciousness of my present thought (which can then
appropriate past thoughts and selves as being mine) must, James argues,
be grounded in the body. Because my present thought's unity cannot be
explained as pure awareness of itself (since the pure thinking "I" cannot
be conscious of itself as an object), this unity must instead derive from
"the most intimately felt *part of its present Object, the body, and the central
adjustments*, which accompany the act of thinking, in the head. *These are
the real nucleus of our personal identity*" (PP, 323).

This somewhat tortured account of how the unity of consciousness
rests on embodied feeling is greatly simplified when James gives up the
more traditional dualistic language of his *Principles of Psychology* for the
experiential monism of his radical empiricism, which simply denies that
consciousness exists as a special spiritual entity, though it still exists as a
function of thinking or knowing. In other words, consciousness exists in
the sense that we surely have thoughts, but not in the sense that thoughts
are tied together by a continuous substance called consciousness that
is independent of its content or objects. My consciousness or "stream
of thinking," James asserts, relying once again on his introspection, "is
only a careless name for what, when scrutinized, reveals itself to consist
chiefly of the stream of my breathing. The 'I think' which Kant said must
be able to accompany all my objects, is the 'I breathe' which actually
does accompany them." Though noting the presence of other "muscular
adjustments," James concludes that "breath, which was ever the original
of 'spirit,' breath moving outwards, between the glottis and the nostrils, is,
I am persuaded, the essence out of which philosophers have constructed
the entity known to them as consciousness" (RE, 19).

This argument is not convincing. Relying merely on James's introspection, it also seems to confuse the question of how consciousness is felt
with the questions of how and whether consciousness exists. That we feel
something through our breathing movements does not mean that this
something is essentially no more than such movements. Of course, this
distinction is undermined if we are metaphysically committed to the view
that things can be nothing more than the way they are currently felt in
one's experience. But why should one accept this view, especially given
James's critique of our poor ability to recognize what we actually feel? Why,

[26] James's skepticism about such a feeling of pure psychic energy is indicated by his placing
it both in parenthesis and under the shadow of a question mark.

moreover, does James decide to limit the breath of thought to exhalation; for surely we can also feel our inhalations when we think. Though James surely exaggerates in defining breath as the essence of consciousness (for we clearly continue to breathe when we are unconscious), his overstatement does have pragmatic shock value in underlining an important truth: the powerful influence of breathing in the activity and effort of thinking. Mind-body disciplines, from ancient yoga and Zen to modern Feldenkrais Method, have effectively demonstrated this truth in practice by deploying focused breathing to insure a steady calmness that is crucial to sharpening consciousness so that one can perceive and think more clearly and deeply, yet with greater ease, even in situations of urgency and pressure.[27]

The Will

Philosophy often celebrates the will as the purest and strongest expression of human spirituality. Descartes, for example, defined it as the soul's "principal activity" and our "only . . . good reason for esteeming ourselves," since the will's freedom "can never be constrained."[28] Having identified thinking with the processes of breathing and subtle bodily movements in the head and throat, James might be expected to propose a bodily account of the will. But here James's somaticism of mental life comes to a sharp halt. Will, he insists, is a purely mental phenomenon that does not in any way involve the body's activity in executing what is willed. "In a word, volition is a psychic or moral fact pure and simple" (PP, 1165).

Why this exception for volition? Perhaps because free will loomed much larger than an abstract philosophical issue for James; it formed the essential cornerstone of his entire life of perfectionist striving. His early ambitions had long been defeated by deep bouts of depression that were generated not simply by "bad nerves" and multiple physical ailments, but by the philosophical specter of materialist determinism that threatened to condemn his whole future to a life sentence of despondency. If there was no free will for James to enlist to fight against his physical and mental miseries, then their hold on him would be inescapably paralyzing. The

---

[27] See, for example, Moshe Feldenkrais, "Thinking and Breathing," ch. 12 of *Awareness Through Movement* (New York: Harper and Row, 1972). Advocating the importance of proper breathing for the better overall functioning of the individual, Alexander Technique also urges a reeducation of our typically faulty breathing habits through "conscious control" of our breathing mechanisms until we establish better breathing habits. See F. M. Alexander, *Man's Supreme Inheritance* (New York: Dutton, 1918), 315–339.

[28] *The Philosophical Writings of Descartes*, 2 vols. trans. J. Cottingham, R. Stoothoff, and D. Murdoch (Cambridge: Cambridge University Press, 1985), 1:333,343,384.

way out of this "crisis in [his] life," James records in a diary entry of April 1870, was through the appeal of Charles Renouvier's "definition of free will – 'the sustaining of a thought *because I choose to* when I might have other thoughts.'" "My first act of free will," James momentously decides, "shall be to believe in free will," and this faith then inspired his life.[29] His monumental *Principles of Psychology*, a product of that faith, continues to affirm its power to make us "the lords of life," though James concedes that his belief in free will rests ultimately on ethical grounds, not psychological proof (PP, 1177, 1181).

If the will is purely mental, in what does it consist? James claims "attention with effort is all that any case of volition implies" (PP, 1166). It is entirely a matter of focusing the mind's attention on one idea rather than another; and this chosen attention alone, barring physical constraints, should be enough to initiate the voluntary action, because "consciousness is *in its very nature impulsive*" or prone to act on its ideas (PP, 1134). The act of willing "is absolutely completed when the stable state of the idea is there"[30]; so the consequent "supervention of motion [in the body] is a supernumerary phenomenon" that is not part of the willing proper (PP, 1165). The effort felt in difficult cases of exercising one's will is simply that of forcing oneself "*to* ATTEND *to a difficult object and hold it fast before the mind*" when strongly inclined to think of other things (PP, 1166). "*Effort of attention is thus the essential phenomenon of will,*" and "the volitional effort lies exclusively within the mental world. The whole drama is a mental drama. The whole difficulty is a mental difficulty, a difficulty with an object of our thought" (PP, 1167, 1168).

This psychic purism of the will is especially unconvincing because undermined by James's own previous arguments that clearly implicate the body in volition. If effort of attention is the essential phenomenon of will, then James should remember his arguments that such effort essentially involves bodily means. Not just attention to sensory input but even attention to purely intellectual ideas is constituted through bodily activities of

---

[29] Cited in Ralph Barton Perry, *The Thought and Character of William James*, abridged edition (Nashville, TN: Vanderbilt University Press, 1996), 121, hereafter TCWJ.

[30] James elsewhere notes that a further mental act of "*express consent*" to the idea attended to is sometimes needed (PP, 1172), for example, in cases when the "act of mental consent" is needed to overcome or displace antagonistic ideas in the mind (PP, 1134). Though James first claims that the mere "filling of the mind by an idea . . . *is* consent to the idea" (PP, 1169), he later identifies "*express consent*" and "the effort to *consent*" as being something more than mere attention to the idea (PP, 1172). In any case, this further act of consent is likewise construed as entirely mental.

concentration (such as those "adjustments" felt in the head and throat) that James describes and defends through introspection and other evidence. So if "strain of the attention is the fundamental act of will" (PP, 1168), it must have a clear bodily component or expression.[31]

The body is also implicated in James's account of voluntary action, which forms part of his analysis of will. In such action, James insists, there must be a *"kinaesthetic idea . . . of what the act is to be,"* an idea *"made up of memory-images of these sensations"* of movement with which the willed act is associated (PP, 1104). But we cannot make sense of these kinaesthetic images without invoking the bodily movements and feelings essential for experiencing such images and thus "equally essential" for recalling them. Thus, our mental imagining or remembering of the act of picking up a ball would include motor images of the relevant muscular contractions needed for the movement (PP, 708).

Similar considerations challenge the Jamesian claim that all bodily matters relating to execution are irrelevant to successful cases of willing, that "the *willing* terminates with the prevalence of the idea; and whether the act then follows or not is a matter quite immaterial, so far as the willing itself goes." James argues for this by asking us to consider three cases. "I will to write, and the act follows. I will to sneeze, and it does not. I will that the distant table slide over the floor towards me; it also does not. My willing representation can no more instigate my sneezing-centre than it can instigate the table to activity. But in both cases it is as true and good willing as it was when I willed to write" (PP, 1165).

This argument is highly questionable, since most people cannot even make sense of willing the table to move, as James, in a note, is forced to concede (PP, 1165). He thinks the reason is that their belief in the impossibility of successfully achieving the desired result renders them psychologically unable to will. But this cannot be the right explanation, because I also know I cannot make myself sneeze or fly; yet, I can make real sense of willing those things. What is the difference? I can will to sneeze

[31] James insists, in a note, that the will's *"effort of attention"* or *"volitional* effort pure and simple must be carefully distinguished from the *muscular* effort with which it is usually confounded" (PP, 1167). But these muscular efforts are described as "peripheral feelings" of "exertion," which suggests that they are different from the central cephalic movements of adjustments in attention, which involve such little muscular contraction that they are barely detected by most people and hardly could count as exertion, even if they bespeak effort. James, moreover, provides no way (not even in terms of his own introspection) of distinguishing the purely mental volitional effort from the muscular effort of which he speaks. He also admits the body's necessary role in *expressing* volition, since "the only *direct* outward effects of our will are bodily movements" (PP, 1098).

or to fly because I have some bodily sense (however vague or misguided) of how I might do this. I have a kinaesthetic idea of what it is like to sneeze and I can visualize or call up that idea in willing myself to sneeze. I also have a vague (even if confused and largely empathetic) kinaesthetic sense of what flying is like (perhaps from experiences of jumping, diving, flying in planes, watching birds or fictional flying superheroes that give me bodily ideas of lift-off), so that I can somehow make sense of willing myself to launch into flight. With making a distant table levitate or slide toward me, I draw a kinaesthetic blank as do most people (though James perhaps knew psychics who could provide an array of motor images to draw on).

The repressed idea of the will's bodily effort revealingly breaks through in his discussion of this problematic case. "Only by abstracting from the thought of the impossibility am I able to imagine strongly the table sliding over the floor, to make the bodily 'effort' which I do, and to will it to come towards me" (PP, 1165). If difficult acts of willing involve strong efforts of imagination, then they involve some sense of bodily activity and means. Modern somaesthetic disciplines, such as the Alexander Technique and the Feldenkrais Method, draw the pragmatic conclusion that our powers of volition can be rendered more effective by paying better attention to our bodily feelings of willed action and to the precise bodily means demanded of the action we wish to perform.

III

James studied, practiced, and discussed many different methods of improving somatic experience, but perhaps his greatest contribution to pragmatic somaesthetics can be found in his scattered but insightful remarks on what we could call somaesthetic introspection, the examination of one's own bodily feelings. A grand master at observing and vividly describing such feelings, James may have first acquired this skill through his sadly recurrent experience of diverse (and often subtle) psychosomatic ailments. But his powers of somaesthetic perception were further honed by his tireless experiments of introspection conducted within the framework of his scientific research in psychology. As Gerald Myers notes, introspection along with physiology were the two pillars of James scientific method in psychology.[32] In the early years of this modern science that James helped create, researchers were frequently obliged to perform

---

[32] See Myers, *William James*, 54, 224.

their observations and experiments on themselves by having themselves undergo an experience and then examining, often through introspection, its mental effects.[33]

"*Introspective Observation,*" James affirms with unfortunate overstatement, "*is what we have to rely on first and foremost and always*" in the study of mind (PP, 185), though admitting it is neither infallible nor all seeing. It is just as "*difficult and fallible*" as "*all observation of whatever kind*" is (PP, 191).[34] Like John Stuart Mill, James argues that introspection essentially means retrospection, since, in our ever-moving stream of thought, we can objectify and report on a specific mental event only by the time it has just passed (into the present act of introspection) but is still fresh in our memory. Moreover, because such reflective reporting requires descriptive or classificatory language, introspective observation can err not only in misremembering but also in misdescribing what it perceives. Knowing we are sometimes motivated by mental states we are not clearly conscious of, James repeatedly maintains that introspection is typically too superficial to detect all that the mind is actually feeling or doing. Recall how he defends the role of somatic feelings in emotion and thought by arguing that these feelings are simply overlooked because our introspection is insufficiently careful or acute. Moreover, any introspective focus will necessarily relegate some mental states to an unobserved background.

Though aware of its limitations, James regards introspection as too precious a tool to reject, at least for the fledgling science of psychology that possessed too few other resources. Urging that the introspective accounts of diverse individuals should be multiplied, pooled, tested, and compared to distinguish a common core of general truth from the scattered chaff of idiosyncratic experiences, James further claims that an individual's own

---

33 Lotze, Wundt, Münsterberg, Mach, and other psychologists James cites in his *Principles of Psychology* did the same, and James employs their introspective findings, noting where his own experience converges and differs.

34 The article on "Introspection, psychology of" in *The Routledge Encyclopedia of Philosophy* (London: Routledge, 1998), 4:843 wrongly claims that for James there are no "aspects of mind that are hidden from introspective awareness." What James asserted was that there could be no mental state without some consciousness that experienced it, but not that those states were always introspectively observable. For he realized that they may be too faint to be noticed or they may be blocked or repressed from an individual's introspective consciousness, as in hypnosis, multiple personality, and other such cases. James, however, did not share the Freudian notion of a general unconscious and rejected the idea of mental states that do not occur in any consciousness whatever. For more on these points, see Myers, *William James*, 59–60, 210–211. There is a continuing debate about whether introspection can be viewed as observation, since it is obviously different in significant ways from the visual observation of external objects.

personal efforts of introspection could be improved through more attentive, disciplined, and precise exercise of awareness. Most importantly, his
psychological analyses of attention, sensation, discrimination, and comparison provide key clues for concrete pragmatic strategies to improve
such awareness.

  1. The first way James guides us toward better introspection is by pointing out the "baleful" (PP, 237) difficulties we actually have with it; for
unless we realize how and why our introspection is problematic or inadequate, we will have no clear direction for improving it. James notes how
the vague, nameless "feelings of tendency" and "psychic transitions" that
exist in our stream of consciousness are "very difficult, introspectively, to
see" (PP, 236), because our attention always tends to focus on the "substantive" "resting-places" in that stream, which are fixed by words or by
clear, enduring "sensorial images" (PP, 236, 240, 244). Such nameless
feelings include bodily ones that are vaguely felt but not usually (or easily)
noticed by introspection. In contrast to the sharp throb of a toothache or
the prick of a pin (substantive, named feelings), there are subtle fleetingly
felt tendencies that escape our naming and explicit attention: a slight tilt
of our head, a faint expectation, a vague loosening of our pelvis, a gentle
easing of facial muscle tone as we open ourselves to some inviting person
or situation.

  James also indicates more specific problems of somaesthetic introspection. Feelings of "the beating of our hearts and arteries, our breathing,
[and even] certain steadfast bodily pains" are hard to focus on since they
tend to fade into the stable felt background that frames our conscious
focus, and that focus tends anyway to concentrate not on the discrimination of bodily feelings but on the discrimination of external things
(PP, 430). Particularly hard to examine are habitually concomitant sensations of bodily activities, whose different feelings – since they almost
always come together – are extremely difficult to introspectively single
out from the total combination of feelings to which they belong: "The
contraction of the diaphragm and the expansion of the lungs, the shortening of certain muscles and the rotation of certain joints, are examples"
(PP, 475). In the latter example, James further notes, we generally over-
look the feelings of both muscle contraction and joint rotation, because
our interest is instead absorbed with the movement of the limb, which is
felt concomitant with these other feelings. The practical nature of consciousness is what explains our strong tendency to focus on the limb's
movement rather than on the internal feelings of movement in the muscles and joints which actually initiate the limb's movement; our interest

naturally goes toward the limbs because they are more directly in contact with our goals of movement, such as reaching for an apple, kicking a ball, leaping over an obstacle (PP, 687, 829–830).[35]

2. Beyond targeting problems of somatic introspection, James suggests some practical ideas for making it more effective, strategies that are essentially derived from his study of two key principles of attention: change and interest. As human consciousness evolved to help us survive in an ever changing world, so its attention is accustomed to, and requires, change. *"No one can possibly attend continuously to an object that does not change"* (PP, 398), James explains, in pressing the paradoxical argument that in order to keep attention unchangingly fixed on the very same object of thought, one must somehow insure that some kind of change is introduced in the object, even if this is only a difference of the perspective from which it is examined as an object of thought. Similarly, as consciousness evolved to serve our interests, so continued interest is required to sustain attention. We cannot focus for long on things that do not interest us, and even one's interest in the thought of something one cares about (say, one's right hand) can soon be exhausted unless one finds some way of reviving that interest and introducing some change of consciousness. Though James does not formulate them clearly, seven distinct strategies of somaesthetic introspection can be derived from his discussions of attention, discrimination, and perception.

a. "The *conditio sine quâ non* of sustained attention to a given topic of thought is that we should roll it over and over incessantly and consider different aspects and relations of it in turn," James asserts; and one very useful means to do this is by asking a variety of *"new questions about the object"* on which we want to fix continued attention (PP, 400). Such questions provoke renewed interest in the object by prompting us to reconsider it in order to answer the questions. Moreover, the very effort of considering the questions effectively changes the way or aspect in which the object is perceived. It is hard, for example, to keep our attention focused on the feeling of our breathing. But if we ask ourselves a series of questions about it – is our breath deep or shallow, rapid or slow? is it felt more in the chest or in the diaphragm? what does it feel like in the mouth or in the nose? does the inhalation or exhalation feel longer? – then we will be

---

[35] These feelings of joint and muscles are felt but simply absorbed as signs of the limb's movement and thus they are typically ignored, since consciousness tends to leap immediately from the sign to the interesting thing signified. Indeed, even our awareness of the limb's movement tends to get occluded by our interest in the external object to which that movement is directed, the ball to be kicked, the apple to be picked, and so on.

able so sustain attention much longer and introspect our feelings more carefully.

b. The principles of change and interest are likewise basic to the intro-spective *body scan*. This important tool of somaesthetic reflection, which is deployed by numerous body-mind disciplines (from Asian-inspired varieties of meditation to Western techniques like Feldenkrais Method), involves systematically scanning or surveying one's own body, not by look-ing or touching from the outside but instead by introspectively, propri-oceptively feeling ourselves as we rest essentially motionless (apart from breathing), typically with our eyes at least partially closed. Though James does not use the term "body scan," he clearly grasps its core importance, basic logic, and its challenging difficulty. If we try to examine our "cor-poreal sensations... as we lie or sit motionless, we find it difficult to feel distinctly the length of our back or the direction of our feet from our shoulders." Even if we succeed "by a strong effort" to feel our whole self at once, such perception is remarkably "vague and ambiguous," and only "a few parts are strongly emphasized to consciousness" (PP, 788). The key to a more precise bodily introspection is therefore to systematically scan the body by subdividing it in our awareness – directing our focused attention first to one part then to another, so that each part can be given proper attention, and a clearer sense of the relations of parts to whole can be obtained.[36] The *transition of focus* not only provides the sense of change that continued attention requires, it also provides renewed interest with each newly examined part presenting a new challenge. Moreover, this transition of introspective probing from one body part to another helps in providing successive *contrasts of feeling*, and such contrasts help sharpen the discrimination of what we feel.

c. If asked to assess the felt heaviness of one of our shoulders as we lie on the floor, we are not likely to get a clear impression of this feeling. But if we first focus on one shoulder and then on the other, we can get a clearer impression of each by noticing which feels heavier and rests more firmly on the floor. Contrast makes feelings easier to discriminate,[37]

---

[36] James treats this as a principle for attention to any large whole. "*The bringing of subdivisions to consciousness constitutes, then, the entire process by which we pass from our first vague feeling of a total vastness to a cognition of the vastness in detail*" (PP, 793).

[37] James (PP, 463–464) notes two sorts of contrast: "*existential*" and "*differential*." The first is the simple contrast between whether the feeling (or, more generally, element) in question is actually there or is absent, without considering the specific nature of that element. Differential contrast is a matter of contrasting the nature of the existing feelings (or elements). Both kinds of contrast can be helpful in somaesthetic introspection. We can,

and contrasts of succession are more discriminating than simultaneous contrasts.[38] So focusing first on one shoulder and then the other is far more effective for noticing how our shoulders feel than the method of trying to combine our attention on the feeling of both shoulders in one simultaneous perception. When it comes to more global discriminations of body experience, as when trying to feel which parts of the body feel the heaviest or densest or tensest, it is even clearer that we cannot rely on a simultaneous comparative grasp of the feelings of all our body parts, but must instead proceed by successive examination and comparison of parts. That is what a body scan is all about.

d. Besides the use of focusing questions and the transitions, subdivisions, and contrasts of the body scan, James's discussion of attention suggests further strategies for maintaining the interest necessary for effective somaesthetic introspection. One is *associative interest.* Just as the faint knock of an expected lover will be heard over louder sounds because the listener is interested in hearing it (PP, 395), so we can stimulate attention to a bodily feeling by making its recognition a key to something we care about: for example, the recognition of a certain feeling of muscle relaxation or rhythm of breathing whose presence and perception can sustain a feeling of repose that leads into desired sleep.

e. Attention to bodily feelings can also be enhanced by the strategy of warding off competing interests, since any form of attention constitutes a focalization of consciousness that implies ignoring other things in order to concentrate on the object attended (PP, 381–382). That is why introspective body scans and other forms of meditation are performed with the eyes closed (or half-closed) so that our minds will not be stimulated by perceptions from the external world of sight that would distract our interest. Internal perception is thus indirectly improved by blunting external

---

for example, learn to discriminate a previously unnoticed feeling of chronic muscular contraction in our antigravity extensors by suddenly feeling what it is like to have those muscles relaxed (say, through the work of a somatic therapist who supports our weight) and thus to have a momentary absence of the contraction. But we can also learn to discriminate the degree of felt tension in, say, a clenched fist by the contrast of intensifying the fist's muscular contraction through one's own greater effort of flexion or through the therapist's squeezing of that fist (or even the other fist).

[38] James cites experimental evidence to show that among differential contrasts, those of succession are more discriminating than those of simultaneous perceptions. "In testing the local discrimination of the skin, by applying compass-points, it is found that they are felt to touch different spots much more readily when set down one after the other than when both are applied at once. In the latter case, they may be two or three inches apart on the back, thighs, etc., and still feel as if they were set down in one spot" (PP, 468).

perception. Somaesthetic introspection can also be sharpened by other methods of indirection. For example, when we are lying on the floor, we may be unable to feel which parts of our body are not making contact with the floor, but we can come to notice them by first attending to which parts of our body *are* felt to make such contact. Though James does not mention this indirect tactic of introspection, it could be accommodated by his strategy of contrast.

f. Still another technique for sharpening our attention to a feeling we are trying to discriminate is by preparing for or anticipating its perception, since "*preperception*... is half of the perception of the looked-for thing" (PP, 419). With respect to somatic introspection, such preparation (which in itself heightens interest) can take different forms. One can prepare oneself to discriminate a feeling by conceptualizing where in one's body to look for it or by imagining how it will be induced and felt there. Such conceptualization and imagining clearly involves linguistic thought, which means that language can be an aid to somaesthetic insight, though it can also be a distracting obstacle when the range of language is assumed to exhaust the entire range of experience. While emphasizing the limits of language and the importance of nameless feelings, James realizes that language can improve our perception of what we feel.

g. Linguistic tags or descriptions, for example, can make a very vague feeling less difficult to discriminate by tying that feeling to words, which are much more easily differentiated. James argues, for instance, that the different names of wines help us discriminate their subtly different flavors far more clearly and precisely than we could without the use of different names.[39] The rich and value-laden associations of words can, moreover, transform our feelings, even our bodily ones. For such reasons, the use of language to guide and sharpen somaesthetic introspection – through preparatory instructions, focusing questions, and imaginative descriptions of what will be (or was) experienced and how it will (or did) feel – is crucial even to those disciplines of somatic awareness that regard the

[39] James notes how the use of verbal description for a previously nameless quality can make the feeling of that quality more distinct: "the snow just fallen had a very odd look, different from the common appearance of snow. I presently called it a 'micaceous' look, and it seemed to me as if, the moment I did so, the difference grew more distinct and fixed than it was before" (PP, 484). In a very different context, T. S. Eliot argued that the poet's role, by forging new language, is to help us feel things that could not otherwise be felt, thus "making possible a much greater range of emotion and perception for other men, because he gives them the speech in which more can be expressed." See *T. S. Eliot, To Criticize the Critic* (London: Faber, 1978), 134.

range and meaning of our feelings as going well beyond the limits of language.

IV

A prominent feature of James's philosophy of mind is his tendency to translate the findings of his psychological research into moral maxims and practical methods for the improved conduct of life. His theories of habit, will, emotion, and self provide striking examples of this.[40] But for all his study, practice, and advocatory discussion of somaesthetic introspection, James does not develop his insights into practical ways of deploying its heightened awareness for enhancing our performance in the wider world of action. While James affirms other bodily-related methods of self-improvement, somaesthetic introspection remains confined to an observational role in psychological theory. Considering the robustly pragmatic tendency of his thought, this failure to transform theory into practice seems surprising and regrettable.

James, however, had reasons to doubt the value of such introspection for the practical business of life. First, it seems to conflict with his advocacy of leaving as much as possible of our practical daily life "to the effortless custody of automatism" or habit (PP, 126); it also runs awry of what he calls the "principle of parsimony in consciousness" (PP, 1108). Focused attention to bodily feelings "would be a superfluous complication" (ibid.) that distracts us from the true ends of our practical enterprises rather than aiding their realization. Of course, at an early stage of learning, the singer may need to think "of his throat or breathing; the balancer of his feet on the rope." But these forms of "supernumerary consciousness" are eventually best avoided in order to achieve true proficiency by concentrating on the ends – the right note or the pole one is balancing on one's forehead (ibid.). As James later puts it, "the end alone is enough"; "we fail of accuracy and certainty in our attainment of the end whenever we

---

[40] His four practical maxims on habit are (1) to acquire a new habit or be rid of an old, we must "*launch ourselves with as strong and decided an initiative as possible.*" (2) "*Never suffer an exception to occur till the new habit is securely rooted in your life.*" (3) "*Seize the very first possible opportunity to act on every resolution you make, and on every emotional prompting you may experience in the direction of the habits you aspire to gain.*" (4) "*Keep the faculty of effort alive in you by a little gratuitous exercise every day*" (PP, 127–130). James's account of the self as an amalgam of different selves, leads him to offer a formula for raising self-esteem (PP, 296–297), his account of the will as attention delivers a method to combat alcoholism (PP, 1169–1170). The maxim emerging from his account of emotion will be discussed later in this chapter.

are preoccupied with much ideal consciousness of the [bodily] means"
and the internal (or "resident") feelings they involve: "We walk a beam
the better the less we think of the position of our feet upon it. We pitch
or catch, we shoot or chop the better the less tactile and muscular (the
less resident), and the more exclusively optical (the more remote), our
consciousness is. Keep your *eye* on the place aimed at, and your hand will
fetch it; think of your hand, and you will very likely miss your aim" (PP,
1128).

James is right that in most practical situations, when our already
acquired habits are fully adequate to perform the actions and secure the
ends we desire, it does not seem helpful to focus attention on the bodily
means and feelings involved in such actions. But, in his ultimate example
to make this point, he nonetheless highlights the bodily means of keeping
the eye focused on the target, which may sometimes require attending
also to other bodily means that help secure the eyes' directional focus.
Moreover, as already noted, our habits often prove insufficient, either
because new situations require unfamiliar forms of action or because our
habits are simply defective, so that the desired action is either not performed successfully or is performed in a way involving excessive effort,
pain, or other negative consequences. In such cases, a careful attention
to our bodily means (and attendant feelings) of action can be very helpful, not only in improving the performance of the particular action on a
single occasion but also in constructing improved habits for performing
that action (and also other actions) in the future. Through such focused
awareness, we can learn to feel when we are contracting our muscles more
than is necessary and in places that conflict with the efficient execution
of the movement desired; and such knowledge can instruct us to make
the movement more successfully and with greater ease and grace. This
improved way of performing the movement and its attendant proprioceptive feelings can then be reinforced into a new and better habit of
action.[41]

[41] An abundance of clinical cases attesting to the success of this melioristic strategy can be
found in the literature relating to the Alexander Technique and the Feldenkrais Method.
Besides the writings of Alexander and Feldenkrais (some of whose works have already
been cited in this and earlier chapters), there is considerable secondary literature, more
extensive with the Alexander Technique which is the older method. See, for example,
Wilfred Barlow, *The Alexander Technique: How to Use Your Body Without Stress* (New York:
Knopf, 1973), whose second edition (Rochester, VT: Healing Arts Press, 1990) also contains Nikolaas Tinbergen's testimony (from his lecture in receiving the 1973 Nobel Prize
for Medicine) concerning the logical cogency of the Technique's core strategy and its

Recall the example of the batter. Though a batter should bat best when his attention is fixed on the ball and not on his own body, a slumping batter may discover (sometimes through an observant coach) that the way he places his feet and grips his toes, or the way he too tightly clenches the bat, puts him off balance or hinders movement in the rib cage and spine, and thus disturbs his swing and impairs his vision of the ball. At this point, conscious attention must be directed to the batter's own body and somatic feelings so that he can recognize the bad habits of stance and swing, inhibit them, and then consciously transform his posture, grip, and movement until a new, more effective habit of swinging the bat is established. Once it is established, then focused attention to these bodily means and sensations of swinging can be relinquished to sink back into the unattended background so that the batter can focus wholly on the ball he aims to hit. Nonetheless, since his very skill of somaesthetic awareness has itself also been reinforced by this exercise of introspection, it can be reapplied with greater ease and power in future cases where his habits prove inadequate, including a relapse into the earlier habit he has just corrected.

Pragmatism's melioristic respect for means should have made James more appreciative of the instrumentality of bodily consciousness in improving our habits and achieving our ends of action. But he followed the dominant tradition of philosophers who stress the dangers of somaesthetic introspection for practical life. Kant, for example, vehemently protested that the practice of examining such inner feelings "is either already a disease of the mind (hypochondria), or will lead to such a disease and ultimately to the madhouse." Such introspection of sensations, he argued, "distracts the mind's activity from considering other things and is harmful to the head." Moreover, "the inner sensibility that one here generates through one's reflections is harmful. Analysts easily get sick.... This inner view and self-feeling weakens the body and diverts it from animal functions."[42] In short, since focusing on one's inner bodily feelings is harmful to both mind and body, we should eschew such introspection.

practical success. See also Frank Jones, *Body Awareness in Action: A Study of the Alexander Technique* (New York: Schocken, 1976), which includes clinical accounts and experimental studies on the effects of heightened consciousness and conscious control.

[42] Immanuel Kant, *Anthropology from a Pragmatic Point of View*, trans. Victor Dowdell (Carbondale: Southern Illinois University Press, 1996), 17; and *Reflexionen zur Kritischen Philosophie*, ed. Benno Erdmann (Stuttgart: Frommann-Holzboog, 1992), 68–69 (my translation).

Sharing Kant's "tendency to hypochondria," and fearing "those intro-spective studies which had bred a sort of philosophical hypochondria" in his own mind, James concurs that "there is...no better known or more generally useful precept in the moral training of youth, or in one's per-sonal self-discipline, than that which bids us pay primary attention to what we do and express, and not to care too much for what we feel."[43] Since feelings and action are intrinsically connected (for feelings involve action and are deeply influenced by it), we can do better, James argues, by focusing simply on action to get a handle on our feelings, especially because feelings are far more elusive and harder to manage. To con-quer unwanted emotions (such as depression or sullenness or fear), we "must assiduously, and in the first instance cold-bloodedly, go through the *outward movements* of those contrary dispositions which we prefer to cultivate." For "by regulating the action, which is under the more direct control of the will, we can indirectly regulate the feeling, which is not." Thus to attain or regain cheerfulness, we should simply "act and speak as if cheerfulness were already there." "Smooth the brow, brighten the eye, contract the dorsal rather than the ventral aspect of the frame, and speak in a major key" (GR, 100; PP, 1077–1078). James repeatedly urged this method not only in technical and popular texts but also in private advice to his family, exhorting his homesick daughter Peggy to "bottle up your feelings," "throw up your arms 3 times daily and *hold yourself straight*." "My 'dying words,'" he wrote to his younger brother Robertson in 1876, "are, 'outward acts, not feelings!'"[44]

Though right to advocate the value of bodily actions for influencing our feelings, James fails to recognize the corresponding importance of somatic feelings for guiding our actions. We cannot properly know how to smooth the brow, if we cannot feel that our brow is furrowed or know what it feels like to have one's brow smooth. Similarly, those many of us habituated to poor posture cannot manage to hold ourselves straight

---

[43] William James, "The Gospel of Relaxation," in *Talks To Teachers*, 99; hereafter I refer to this essay as GR. On James's hypochondria, see Perry, TCWJ, who also cites James's mother's complaints about his excessive expression of "every unfavorable symptom" (361). On the "philosophical hypochondria" of "introspective studies," see James's letter to brother Henry of Aug. 24, 1872, in C1:167. Just as Kant publicly avowed his "disposition to hypochondria" in *The Conflict of the Faculties* [trans, Mary J. Gregor (Lincoln: University of Nebraska Press, 1992), 189], so James repeatedly confessed, in private correspondence, to being "an abominable neurasthenic." See, for example, his letters to F. H. Bradley and George H. Howison in C8:52, 57.
[44] C9:14; C4:586.

in a way that avoids excessive rigidity and arching of the back (which constrains our breathing and performance and will lead to pain) without a process of learning that involves sensitive attention to our proprioceptive feelings. This was a lesson that James's disciple John Dewey later inculcated, having learned it from the somatic educator-therapist F. M. Alexander. James's unfeeling insistence on vigorous dorsal contraction and stiff upright posture is thus a sure prescription for the kind of back pain he indeed suffered throughout his life, just as it is surely an expression of his puritan ethics more than a product of careful clinical research. If "action and feeling go together" (GR, 100), as James shrewdly remarked, they *both* need our careful attention for optimal functioning.

James feared that somaesthetic introspection would inhibit action and destroy the energies, spontaneity, and positive attitude he considered crucial for success in practical life. As mental "inhibition" undermines our "vitality," so "hyperesthetic" body sensitivity lowers one's "pain-threshold," thus heightening our inhibition to act and diminishing our energy.[45] We must instead free our action and even our thought "from the inhibitive influence of reflection upon them," James argues in "The Gospel of Relaxation" (GR, 109). "*Unclamp* . . . your intellectual and practical machinery, and let it run free; and the service it will do you will be twice as good" (ibid.). This advice to "trust your spontaneity" (ibid.) obviously builds on James's emphasis on the usefulness of habits. But what if our habits are flawed, as they very often are? To act spontaneously will simply reinforce these bad habits and the damage they cause. We cannot correct these bad habits without inhibiting their free flow, nor can we learn improved bodily habits without paying attention to the different somatic feelings that these new ways of using one's body involve. Because somatic inhibition and reflection are crucial in forming more fruitful and intelligent habits, they are tools rather than obstacles to practical life, though they can be misused (or overused) like any other tool.

Ironically, in the very same essay on relaxation, James blames bad bodily habits "of jerk and snap" as the source of "American over-tension" with its hurried "breathlessness" and "too desperate eagerness and anxiety." To counter these "*bad habits*" of "over-contraction" of our muscles, which in turn induces an "*over-contracted . . . spiritual life*," James urges "the gospel of relaxation" (GR, 103–105, 107) based on the work of the contemporary

---

[45] James, "The Energies of Men," 1225–1226, hereafter EM.

somatic and spiritual writer Annie Payson Call.[46] But how can we ensure that our muscles and breathing are "all relaxed" (GR, 104) without inhibiting our prior habit of over-tensing them and without attending to the different somatic sensations of muscular relaxation and excessive tension so that we can track the former and avoid the latter?

Besides the inconsistency of urging both spontaneity and the spurning of bad habits, there is an unresolved tension between the essay's gospel of relaxation or "ease" and its earlier touting of "muscular vigor," "athletic outdoor life and sport" as the key to overcoming inhibiting timidities and instilling better "spiritual hygiene" (GR, 102–103, 107). Such emphasis on robust muscular effort and striving is far more in tune with James's repeated advocacy of "the strenuous mood" of living with "hardihood" and "toughness" over "the easy-going mood" of relaxation and "moral holidays."[47] James seems to sense the problem of consistency when insisting that the needed relaxation involves a full moral letting go rather than a willful effort "to become strenuously relaxed" (GR, 112). One way to explain James's very uncharacteristic urging of moral and physical release (and its odd conjunction with athleticism) is to recall that the essay originated as a lecture to a school for women gymnasts, which was

---

[46] James refers primarily to her 1891 book, *Power through Repose*, though later invokes, with respect to moral relaxation, her later book *A Matter of Course*. James may have derived the phrase "gospel of relaxation" from the English evolutionary philosopher Sir Herbert Spencer, a frequent object of James's study and critical discussion. On a visit to America in 1882, Spencer commented in a Boston newspaper that overworked America had "too much of the 'gospel of work.' It is time to preach the gospel of relaxation." See Feinstein, 190.

[47] See "The Moral Philosopher and The Moral Life," and "The Moral Equivalent of War," in *The Writings of William James*, ed. McDermott, 627–628, 669, and "The Absolute and the Strenuous Life," in *The Meaning of Truth*, in *William James: Writings 1902–1910*, ed. Kuklick, 941. In the latter essay, James's overwhelming preference for the strenuous attitude is highlighted by his contrasting it to that of "sick souls" in need of "moral holidays," thus implicitly identifying the easygoing mood of relaxation with (mental or moral) sickness. James similarly argues for "strength and strenuousness, intensity and danger," and the "heroic life" of "human nature strained to its uttermost" as crucial elements for making life significant rather than flat and zestless (in "What Makes a Life Significant?" *Talks to Teachers*, 133–134). He likewise praises "the supreme theatre of human strenuousness" and "strenuous honor" in contrast to "unmanly ease" (in "The Moral Equivalent of War," 666, 669). True to his tolerant pluralism, James, however, acknowledged that some people find real joy in a simple life "of both thinking of nothing and doing nothing" and urged that we respect their forms of life and happiness (so long as they are not harmful), even if we find these forms "unintelligible" ("On a Certain Blindness in Human Beings," *Talks to Teachers*, 127, 129).

then repeatedly used as a talk for women's colleges.[48] An unabashed (if unconscious) sexist, James had no trouble affirming a double standard of strenuous living for men and relaxed ease for women that would help keep the latter happily at home where they could better care for the stress of their striving males.

Such explanations, however, do nothing to resolve the crucial problem of reconciling effort and relaxation, since men *and* women need to integrate both elements into their lives – not in terms of consecutive fits of frenetic activity and total collapse but ideally through performing the effortful with more relaxed ease. Relaxation per se was a difficult value for a puritan like James to embrace, but it could be recommended as a tool for better health and functioning, just as occasional "moral holidays" could be justified only as "provisional breathing-spells, intended to refresh us for the morrow's fight."[49] Conversely, as James knew from personal experience, relaxation could be pursued under the guise of illness, which would allow even a puritan to rest from normal responsibilities yet have his vigilant "*Arbeitsmoral*" conscience satisfied by a "work-schedule" of restful therapy at the spa.

Another problem is that James's essay exhorts us to relax but fails to instruct us how. Relaxation implies a proper degree of tonus, a balance of tension and release in the muscular system. But a person who does not know experientially what this state feels like and how, practically, to achieve it will find little help in the injunction to relax and will not know how to comply with it.[50] The fallacy of James's simple exhortation to relax all our muscles is not only that we need an appreciable degree of muscle contraction to hold ourselves functionally together but also that the only directly voluntary way to relax a muscle is by contracting its antagonistic one. Although James advises relaxation through slower breathing and a diminishing of unnecessary muscle contractions, he says nothing about

---

[48] This lecture to the Boston Normal School of Gymnastics concludes that "What our girl-students and woman-teachers most need nowadays is not the exacerbation, but rather the toning-down of their moral tensions" (GR, 112). James repeated the talk at Wellesley, Bryn Mawr, and Smith, and referred to it as his "female College address." See C2:389, C8:96.

[49] James, "The Absolute and the Strenuous Life," 941.

[50] I learned this from my clinical experience as a professional Feldenkrais practitioner. Many people I have worked with simply did not know what it felt like to release from certain chronic patterns of excessive contraction in their upper back, neck, and rib cage, and thus were unable to relax the muscles there until they were coaxed by bodily manipulations into the desired release from these contractions.

the means to achieve this, not even evoking the methods in fact described in Call's book.

The sole practical recommendation James ends up offering is just to give up trying and trust in God. The way to relax oneself, "paradoxical as it may seem, is genuinely not to care whether you are doing it or not. Then, possibly, by the grace of God, you may all at once find that you *are* doing it, and, having learned what the trick feels like, you may (again by the grace of God) be enabled to go on" (GR, 112). More than paradoxical, this method is excessively vague and overly reliant on supernatural providence. It is also, given the lecture's target audience, suspiciously sexist. Not only radical feminists will be shocked by James's call for women educators to slacken their striving, forsake critical attention to their feelings, and instead simply trust their spontaneous habits (largely the product of patriarchal domination) and their faith in the Divine Patriarch. Finally, since James's proposed method of relaxed trust in the divine also relies on attending to "what the trick feels like," it contradicts his claim that we should disregard examination of our feelings and instead concentrate only on action to regulate them.

To argue in James's defense that somatic philosophy need not pay more explicit attention to specific somatic methods would be inconsistent with his own pragmatic concern for the concrete. James's personal correspondence displayed an eager interest in expounding the details of many of the somatic regimes he tried, and his presidential address to the American Philosophical Association ("The Energies of Men") was largely devoted to advocating a systematic study of the specific means for increasing our energies by tapping more deeply into "our possible mental and physical resources," of which we normally use "only a small part" (EM, 1225). Such extension of our individual powers, James argued, would also bring wider benefits to society as a whole. If cases of second wind and more extraordinary displays of heroic endurance show that these deeper wells of energy can sometimes be found, then James pragmatically sought more reliable methods for drawing on these unfathomed powers in order to overcome the habitual limits of pain, fatigue, and vigor that inhibit our activity. Though "emotional excitement" and a sense "of necessity" often help "carry us over the dam" of inability, the essential catapult to these further energy levels, James maintained, is "an extra effort of will" (EM, 1226). The systematic exploration of our deeper powers should thus include the diverse means of strengthening the will to make those powers available. "This," he insisted, "would be an absolutely concrete study, to be carried on by using historical and biographical material mainly" (EM, 1240).

Yoga is the "methodical ascetic discipline" of will strengthening that James finds historically "most venerable" and richest in "experimental corroboration" (EM, 1230–1231), so his essay's central example focuses on a philosopher friend's fourteen-month experiment in hatha yoga, the yoga form that emphasizes somatic practices of posture, breathing, and diet. Quoting at great length from this friend's epistolary reports that analyze the yoga methods used and their effects, James confirms the extremely empowering transformation that his friend described. But he is surprisingly quick to reject attributing distinctive "value to the particular Hatha Yoga processes, the postures, breathings, fastings, and the like." They are nothing more, James claims, than "methodical self-suggestion" that altered "the gearing" of his friend's "mental machinery" and thus made his will more "available. . . . without any new ideas, beliefs, or emotions, so far as I can make out, having been implanted in him. He is simply more balanced where he was more unbalanced" (EM, 1234, 1236). This uncharitable and empirically ungrounded verdict is also highly inconsistent with James's pragmatic grasp of religious experience and his commitment to the influence of bodily actions on mental life. It is impossible that someone who underwent systematic training in hatha yoga practices would have not acquired any new ideas, beliefs, or emotions. At the very least, one would acquire all those ideas, beliefs, and emotions involved in performing those practices (of breathing, posture, somaesthetic awareness, and fasting) and in feeling that one had made progress in their performance.

Why, then, would James try to minimize the particular value of yogic body methods for strengthening the will by reducing them to a mere form of mental self-suggestion, "of mental influence over physiological processes" (EM, 1234)? Perhaps he thought his commitment to the exclusively mental nature of volition would be compromised by accepting that the will could be intrinsically strengthened by bodily means. In any case, hatha yoga (or Zen meditation) is not merely a matter of performing bodily postures and actions but of performing them with the proper mindfulness of rigorous concentration, as in the focusing of one's complete attention on one's breath. Such intense concentration on feeling one's breath and other bodily processes involves, however, the sort of somaesthetic introspection that James (and Kant) regarded as unproductive in practical life and psychologically dangerous.

But the facts show otherwise. Yoga, *zazen*, and other systematic disciplines involving somaesthetic introspection do not lead to the mental weakness, morbid introversion, and hypochondria that Kant and James

feared. Instead, they tend, as in the case of James's friend, to bolster
one's spirits and strengthen the individual's will and resiliency. Besides
the empirical evidence of long traditions of practice and testimony that
bear witness to the positive affects of these meditative disciplines, there
is now further confirmation from new scientific research in experimental psychology and neurophysiology. Clinical studies have demonstrated
that meditation training (including disciplines of sitting meditation, body
scan, and hatha yoga) can effectively reduce symptoms of anxiety, depression, and panic, thus generating more positive affect in the meditating
subjects.[51] Other experiments have established the neurological basis
of this positive power. Having determined that positive feelings and a
"resilient affective style" are "associated with high levels of left prefrontal
activation [in the brain] . . . and with the higher levels of antibody titres
to influenza vaccine," scientists have shown that subjects introduced to
an eight-week meditation training program display not only significantly
higher levels of left-sided anterior activation than the control group of
nonmeditators but also significant increases in antibody titers.[52] The
results clearly suggest that meditation improves not only our mood but
our immune function.

My own experience of Zen training in Japan has shown me how methodical somaesthetic reflection can also develop one's power of volition by
directing intensely focused consciousness to one's breathing or to other
somatic feelings (such as the contact of one's feet with the floor in walking
meditation). And this strengthening of volitional power can be explained
in terms of James's own theories, just as the admissibility of evidence
from personal observation would surely be granted by James's principles
of philosophizing from experience. Will power, as James insists, involves
keeping attention firmly fixed on an idea and resisting the mind's natural tendency to wander off through specific distractions introduced by
new sensations and our habitual interests and thought associations. We
are naturally and habitually inclined to devote attention to the outside

[51] See, for example, J. Kabat-Zinn et al., "Effectiveness of a Meditation-Based Stress Reduction Program in the Treatment of Anxiety Disorders," *American Journal of Psychiatry*, 149
(1992), 936–943; and "The Relationship of Cognitive and Somatic Components of Anxiety to Patient Preference for Alternative Relaxation Techniques," *Mind/Body Medicine*, 2
(1997), 101–109.
[52] See Richard J. Davidson et al., "Alterations in Brain and Immune Function Produced
by Mindfulness Meditation," *Psychosomatic Medicine*, 65 (2003), 564–570; and Richard
J. Davidson, "Well-Being and Affective Style: Neural Substrates and Biobehavioural Correlates," *Philosophical Transactions of the Royal Society*, Series B, 359 (2004): 1395–1411,
quotation on 1395.

world of flux and new perceptions, not to the constant and imminent experience of breathing. Even if we momentarily attend to our breathing, our thought almost immediately tends to move on to other things. It is thus extremely difficult to compel attention to remain focused wholly on the experience of breathing itself or indeed on any somatic process. Disciplines of sustained somaesthetic focusing can strengthen our will by training our attention to keep its concentration and resist its inclination to wander. Breathing and the body are wonderfully apt targets for such exercises of focusing attention because they are always there to focus on, while the mind typically ignores them in running off to more interesting or demanding objects. When I began my meditation training, it was hard for me to keep my focus for more than a single breath, but after continued, strenuous effort, I was able to sustain such concentration for much longer periods, yet do so with feelings of relaxed ease and pleasure. And my increased powers of attention could then be shifted beyond the breathing or meditative walking, so that everyday objects and familiar people were suddenly perceived with greater intensity, depth, and accuracy. My movement and action, like my perception, became sharper, surer, and more satisfying.

The strengthening of the will through somaesthetic awareness can also be explained in terms of James's key concept of habit. While breaking the habit of consciousness to rush off to other things it is prone to pursue because of familiar association patterns and entrenched interests, disciplined somaesthetic introspection also creates a habit (by sharpening an ability) of mindful control: the power to direct sustained attention to what consciousness is reluctant to focus lengthily on and would otherwise not long attend to. Once this power of attention is developed, it can be used to keep attention from drifting to the disturbingly morbid thoughts that sustained somatic reflection is presumed to generate. Such gloomy ruminations, in any case, have little to do with the careful monitoring and clear consciousness of actual bodily feelings that somaesthetics recommends (for certain contexts and occasions); they instead are vague, obscure, though powerful imaginations of disease and death, whose disturbing power rests largely on their obscurity.[53]

---

[53] Though much contemporary psychological literature still confirms a link between rumination and depression, recent studies insist on the need to distinguish between introspection that is depressive, obsessive, and focused on the negative (designated as rumination) and other, more positive, forms of introspection that are distinguished as self-awareness or self-reflection. See, for example, S. Nolen-Hoeksema, "Responses to Depression and Their Effects on the Duration of Depressive Episodes," *Journal of Abnormal Psychology*, 100

V

Perhaps James refused to advocate somaesthetic introspection for practical life because he was so psychologically disinclined to deploy it in his own life of action. Though effortful in some sense, somaesthetic reflection also calls for tranquillity and repose. This is because (as the Weber-Fechner law indicates) it is hard to notice subtle aspects of our breathing or muscle tone when engaged in vigorous, rapid movement. Outside his sickbed and armchair of introspective theory, tranquil slowness was not something James could readily muster. Notoriously volatile, restless, and impulsive, he was likened by his sister to "*a blob of mercury.*" His attention "was eagerly but *impatiently* interested" in what engaged him, so he loathed "prolonged application to the same task" and had to use his mind's wonderful quickness, mobility, and boldness to make up "for what it lacked in poise." James knew this and gladly characterized himself as "a motor," prizing dynamic energy and vigorous movement as part of his strenuous ideal.[54]

When James felt his motor in good form, he sought to increase its productive power by passionately working it at higher levels of performance, typically followed by some kind of physical or nervous breakdown. Even when ill, he firmly believed (at least till the last two years of his life) that the best remedy for his chronic ailments and poor spirits should be more vigorous exercise rather than thoughtful repose. Despite the many months James spent in rest cures throughout the spas of Europe, his comparative neglect of the valuable uses of slowness and energized repose is evident from his favored menu of practical somaesthetics, the actual body practices he most keenly pursued and cherished in his quest for health and the cultivation of his powers.

Though willing to try almost anything to augment his energy and cure himself, James clearly preferred methods that emphasized strenuous muscular effort and vigorous movement, even when chronic back pain and later heart disease should have militated against it. This preference reflects his heroic ethical ideals, his dynamic temperament, and the background ideologies of effortful puritan striving and machismo athleticism

(1991): 569–582; S. Nolen-Hoeksema and J. Morrow, "Effects of Rumination and Distraction on Naturally Occurring Depressed Mood," *Cognition & Emotion*, 7 (1993): 561–570; and P. D. Trapnell and J. D. Campbell, "Private Self-consciousness and the Five-Factor Model of Personality: Distinguishing Rumination from Reflection," *Journal of Personality and Social Psychology*, 76 (1999), 284–304.

[54] See Perry, TCWJ, 32–33, 66, 220.

(strikingly exemplified by James's contemporary Teddy Roosevelt) that were prominent at that time.[55] Weight lifting was an early favorite of James, but his deepest love was "rapid mountain-climbing," not only for its physical exercise but as his "main hold on primeval sanity and health of soul," his trusted "old resource of walking off tedium and trouble." Even after learning he had damaged his heart through impulsive excesses in climbing mountains, James continued to push himself with "uphill walking," complaining that he had to go slower than he liked but proudly happy that he could still make "a steep and slippery" climb.[56]

He disliked the sedentary nature of rest, regarding it almost as an immoral expression of lazy weakness but also fearing its damage to "digestion and nerve-strength" (C4:346; C9:157). Insufficiently appreciative of the values of leisure (and probably fearful of the listless morbidity he experienced in the rest cures of his youth), James would turn to rest only when too weak to cure himself by more strenuous means. In dealing with any experienced weakness, he seemed to prefer the hero's "bullying-treatment" of resolutely ignoring one's painful feelings and willfully exercising *over* the pain to vanquish it. In dealing with a sore foot, James proudly reports to his wife, he "triumphantly applied the bullying method . . . and walked it down" (EM, 1226; C8:389).

Too ill and fragile to serve in the Civil War (unlike two of his younger brothers), James compensated with a heroic ideal that was martial and dynamic, "a strong man battling with misfortune." "Keep sinewy all the while," and "Live *hard!*" were his ethical mottoes. "The impulse to take life strivingly," James firmly held, "is indestructible in the race."[57] This may be true but so is the impulse to repose, since rest is essential, even in a strong and striving life. We can also strive more effectively when

[55] Roosevelt was also diagnosed, in his youth, as neurasthenic but healed and transformed himself through rugged exercise and the rigorous willful quest for manly strength and toughness. See Tom Lutz, *American Nervousness – 1903* (Ithaca, NY: Cornell University Press, 1991).

[56] James seems to have first injured his heart in July 1898 while mountain climbing in the Adirondacks and trying to keep up with a group of much younger climbers (including some young women he especially admired). The heart damage became much more severe when he re-injured himself the next summer by getting hopelessly lost climbing in the same area of Mount Marcy and thus forced to scramble arduously for many hours before finding his way home. See C3:59, 64, 228, 345; C4:327; C8:390–391.

[57] From a diary entry cited by Perry, TCWJ, 225; C4: 409; C7:399; "The Sentiment of Rationality," in *The Will to Believe* (Cambridge, MA: Harvard University Press, 1979), 74. cf. "The Moral Equivalent of War" (662), where James writes, "Our ancestors have bred pugnacity into our bone and marrow, and thousands of years of peace won't breed it out of us."

our efforts, however forceful and swift, have a restful calm rather than
a frenetic nervousness about them. The Asian martial arts and archery,
the swinging of a baseball bat or golf club or stroking of a pool stick all
eloquently exemplify this point. Paradoxical as it sounds, the very effort
of maintaining an alert, animated, or active repose (as contrasted to a
passive collapse) can be a strenuous project in itself. I am not referring
only to the special meditative states of yoga or Zen noted earlier; there
are also projects of introducing more tranquil mindfulness in the tasks
we perform in everyday life, thus giving our actions (and being) a greater
sense of ease and grace. Because our habits are largely the misshapen
products of excessive busyness, tension, and pressure, this more relaxed
use of the self requires a strong-willed, strenuous effort of self-monitoring
and re-education, providing perhaps a *"moral equivalent* of war" – of battling one's own bad habits – that might meet even the Jamesian criteria of
heroic striving in the "theatre of human strenuousness."[58] He certainly
avowed that the task was difficult, when he eventually was convinced by
an unconventional Boston physician that he was systematically misusing
himself through excessive muscular effort in his everyday actions and
thought.

   Less than two years before his death, James began seeing a Dr. James
R. Taylor, whom he initially described as "a semi-quack homoeopathist"
(C3:376). Though continuing to complain about the cost of the frequent
visits and remaining skeptical about the benefits of the vapor inhalations, vibrations, and "homoeopathic pellets" that the doctor adminis-
tered (C3:386), James was clearly persuaded by Taylor's insightful diagnosis and re-educative instruction with respect to the damaging effects
of James's chronic tendency to excessive tension and muscular contractions (or "crispations") in his everyday life. The real benefit of Taylor's
treatment, explained James to his brother Henry,

> is to *re-educate* me as to my general way of holding myself in the current
> of life.... What tells in the long run ... is the 'pitch' at which a man lives,
> which may be a vicious and false one.... Suffice it that I have been racing
> too much, kept in a state of inner tension, anticipated the environment,
> braced myself to meet and resist it ere it was due (social environment chiefly
> here!), left the present act inattentively done because I am preoccupied
> with the next act, failed to listen etc, because I was too eager to speak, kept
> *up*, when I ought have kept *down*, been jerky, angular, rapid, precipitate, let

[58] James, "The Moral Equivalent of War," 666.

my mind run ahead of my body, etc, etc., and impaired my efficiency, as well as flushed my head, and made my tissues fibrous, in consequence. The everlastingly cumulative effect of his criticisms is sensible to me in an easier tone, better temper, less involvement of bodily 'crispations' in my thought processes, and in short a better attitude in general. (C3:386–387)

What James discovered, however late and reluctantly, was the unnoticed but deeply damaging effect of his spontaneous habits of impulsive strenuousness. He finally saw the crucial value of learning better self-use not by wrenching the will through strenuous activity but by careful, calm attention to relaxed, unhurried action. Six months before his death, he also seemed to discover the value of rest, when "a virulent cold" confined him to four weeks of "sedentary life" at his Cambridge home and left him feeling and working better than he had "for 'ages.'" But the entrenched habit of "overtaxing [his] heart" soon had James racing again to Europe, and to renewed illness. Yet, his very last letter to his brother Henry (written in June from the German cure resort of Nauheim) ultimately preaches the principle of moderate, unhurried motion and leisurely repose. Urging Henry not to "overdo the walking" since "moderation takes one farthest in the end," he also implores Henry not to rush hectically to visit him, but rather to "linger . . . & take the Continent in as broken stages as possible and each place leisurely. . . . My last word now is 'do not hurry hither!'" (C3:407–408, 424–425).

James learned his lessons too late and too imperfectly to reverse the damage his heart had already suffered. He never regained his health and died in August 1910. After the autopsy, his wife Alice recorded in her diary "Acute enlargement of the heart" and concluded "He had worn himself out."[59] It is useless to speculate to what extent James's life and work could have been improved had he more clearly grasped the limits of his somatic theory and practice and thus better monitored himself through somaesthetic reflection. Our attention is more usefully directed to probing the exemplary instruction that his texts and life provide, guided by the pragmatic project of overcoming their limitations. His pragmatist disciple, John Dewey, advances this project in significant ways.

[59] Cited in Gay Wilson Allen, *William James* (New York: Viking, 1967), 491–492.

6

Redeeming Somatic Reflection

John Dewey's Philosophy of Body-Mind

I

Though his sober, logical temperament was not prone to fervent hyperbole, John Dewey passionately exalted the human body as "the most wonderful of all the structures of the vast universe."[1] His *Experience and Nature* celebrates "body-mind" as an essential unity in which mental life emerges from the body's more basic physical and psychophysical functions rather than being superimposed on the soma by transcendent powers of reason emanating from a spiritual world beyond nature (LW1:199–225). Contesting the "contempt for the body, fear of the senses, and the opposition of flesh to spirit" that sadly dominates philosophy (even in the sensory field of aesthetics), Dewey's *Art as Experience* insists that "biological" factors form the "roots of the esthetic" and thus shape even our most spiritual experiences of fine art and imaginative thinking (LW10:20, 26).

Dewey, however, was not always so appreciative of the biological body. He began his career as a neo-Hegelian idealist, affirming a transcendent soul in contrast to the body and giving clear primacy to soul or spirit as the essential shaping force of life. Rather than understanding mind as emerging from bodily existence, he viewed the human body as the emergent creation and tool of a transcendent soul that makes itself immanent in the body in order to use it. In an 1886 essay, "Soul and Body," he claims, "The body is [the soul's] organ only because the soul has *made*

---

[1] John Dewey, *The Middle Works*, vol. 11 (Carbondale: Southern Illinois University Press, 1982), 351. References to the published writings of John Dewey will be to the Southern Illinois University Press editions of John Dewey's works, whose division of volumes into Early, Middle, and Later Works will be abbreviated here as EW, MW, and LW. Page numbers will be separated from volume numbers by a colon.

the body its organ . . . The body as an organ of the soul is the result of the informing, creating activity of the soul itself. In short, the soul is immanent in the body, not by virtue of the body as mere body, but because, being transcendent, it has expressed and manifested its nature in the body" (EW1:112–113).

Dewey even advocates this formative primacy of the transcendent soul with theological rhetoric endorsing ancient Christian doctrine: "Lo, see what the soul has done. It has tabernacled in the flesh and transformed flesh into its own manifestation. The body is the bodying forth of the soul. . . . Let it be no surprise that physiological psychology has revealed no new truth concerning the relations of soul and body. It can only confirm and deepen our insight into the truth divined by Aristotle and declared by St. Paul, and with good reason. *Das Wahre war schon längst gefunden*" (EW1:114–115). This backward-looking attitude – that the truth has already long been discovered and that Darwinian evolutionary theory and contemporary physiological research provide nothing to modify or challenge St. Paul's vilifying view of the flesh – is contrary not only to Dewey's subsequent celebration of the body but also to the progressive, scientific spirit for which he is justly famous.

What changed Dewey's vision of the body and its import for understanding the mind? One crucial factor was William James. Dewey's "official" biographical sketch (formulated by his daughters with his approval) clearly affirms, "William James's *Principles of Psychology* was much the greatest single influence in changing the direction of Dewey's philosophical thinking" from its earlier idealism.[2] Though insisting his philosophical inspirations derived from life experience rather than philosophical texts, Dewey made a special exception for James's "*Psychology*," crediting it as the "one specifiable philosophic factor which entered into my thinking so as to give it a new direction and quality." In particular, Dewey claimed that James's "biological conception of the *psyche*," whose "new force and value [was] due to the immense progress made by biology since the time of Aristotle," "worked its way more and more into all my ideas and acted as a ferment to transform old beliefs" (LW5:157).[3]

---

[2] Jane M. Dewey, ed., "Biography of John Dewey," in *The Philosophy of John Dewey*, ed. P. Schilpp and L. Hahn (LaSalle, IL: Open Court, 1989), 23; hereafter JD. I shall refer to William James, *The Principles of Psychology* (Cambridge, MA: Harvard University Press, 1983) as PP.

[3] Dewey further notes how "The objective biological approach of the Jamesian psychology led straight to the perception of the importance of distinctive social categories, especially communication and participation" (LW5: 159).

Once convinced that our mental and spiritual life was deeply rooted in the physiology and bodily behavior that shape human experience, Dewey applied James's biological naturalism with greater consistency than James himself to provide a more unified vision of body and mind. Challenging James's notion of a self (or ego) outside the realm of natural causal conditioning, he likewise rejected the idea that will was ever a purely mental affair, independent of the physical modalities of its efficacy and expression. While defending James's appreciation of the physiological aspect of emotions, Dewey provided a better-balanced theory that more clearly affirmed emotion's essential cognitive dimension while integrating both cognition and physiological reactions into a larger unity of behavioral response. In contrast to James's emphasis on the privacy of consciousness (PP 221), Dewey realized that the biological approach to mental life implied the essentially social nature of mind. This is because an organism's survival depends on interaction with (and incorporation of) its environment, and a crucial part of the human organism's environment is the society of other humans, without which a newborn human organism could never survive and acquire full human identity, including the mastery of a socially shared language in which one formulates one's most private thoughts. Finally, Dewey avoided the Jamesian inconsistency of deploying somaesthetic introspection in theorizing but rejecting it in practical life through an ardent advocacy of uninhibited spontaneity, habit, and pure will. Instead, Dewey wisely affirmed somatic reflection for both theory and practice.

Dewey's unifying improvements on James were partly due to his avowed "temperament" for making "logical consistency ... a dominant consideration" (JD, 45). But they also reflect the impact of another mentor whose influence may have been as inspirational as that of James. I refer to the somatic educator and therapist F. M. Alexander, whose ideas and practice Dewey frequently cited and tirelessly advocated (despite the skeptical objections of friends and colleagues). Dewey was very explicit about his debt to Alexander for not only improving his health and self-use and thus promoting his longevity,[4] but also for providing concrete "substance" to fill in the "schematic form" of his theoretical ideas. "My theories of mind-body, of the coördination of the active elements of the self and of the

---

[4] At the age of eighty-seven, Dewey wrote that without his sustained training "in Alexander's work ... I'd hardly be here today – as a personal matter." Letter to Joseph Ratner, July 24, 1946, cited in Steven Rockefeller, *John Dewey: Religious Faith and Democratic Humanism* (New York: Columbia University Press, 1991), 343.

place of ideas in inhibition and control of overt action required contact with the work of F. M. Alexander and in later years his brother, A.R., to transform them into realities" (JD, 44–45).[5]

Here again, Dewey was inspired to hyperbole. In one of the three prefaces he provided for Alexander's books, he boldly claimed: "Mr. Alexander has demonstrated a new scientific principle with respect to the control of human behavior, as important as any principle which has ever been discovered in the domain of external nature. Not only this, but his discovery is necessary to complete the discoveries that have been made about non-human nature, if these discoveries and inventions are not to end by making us their servants and helpless tools" (MW15:313). Though an outrageous overstatement (that ranks the Alexander Technique with Newtonian physics), it indicates that Dewey's philosophy of body-mind cannot be properly appreciated without understanding Alexander's views and methods.

This chapter therefore examines Dewey's somatic philosophy in terms of the Jamesian and Alexandrian pillars on which it is built. After showing how Alexander's teaching helped Dewey to improve on James and realize the practical value of somatic self-consciousness, I argue that Alexander's doctrine and influence were not entirely beneficial and that Dewey's somatic theory could have profited by distancing itself more clearly from some of Alexander's one-sided, rigidly rationalistic views and sustaining a more affect-respecting attitude that James advocated and Dewey generally shared.

II

Correcting the Jamesian Inconsistencies
In his *Principles of Psychology*, James emphasized the essential correlation of mental and bodily states and argued for a substantive bodily presence in the experience of mental phenomena usually thought to be wholly spiritual. But he still "allowed himself the conveniences of dualism," in which mind and body could be conceived as different kinds of things, however closely they interacted with each other.[6] He did so not only because dualism was the standard commonsense view that would make his

---

[5] JD, 44–45. Dewey continues: "My ideas tend, because of my temperament, to take a schematic form in which logical consistency is a dominant consideration, but I have been fortunate in a variety of contacts that has put substance in these forms" (45).

[6] Ralph Barton Perry, *The Thought and Character of William James*, abridged edition (Nashville, TN: Vanderbilt University Press, 1996), 273.

book (commissioned as a teaching text) clearer and more palatable, but because he was unwilling to endorse a more thoroughgoing naturalism that would threaten his existentially crucial belief in free will and foreclose his fervent hope for human consciousness beyond the bounds of mortal bodily life. Even when he gave up dualism for his "radical empiricism" in which mind and matter are just different ways of parsing a fundamentally unified field of pure experience, James did not forsake his commitment to free will as something that can effectively intervene in the physical world to determine action but that is not conversely determined by that world's causal chains.

Once converted to James's embodied perspective, Dewey plied a more consistent nondualistic naturalism. Instead of speaking of body and mind as two different, separable things whose reciprocal influences could be traced and correlated, Dewey insisted on treating them as a fundamental unit, condemning their established division as a pervasive flaw that plagues both theory and practice. Though famous for criticizing all sorts of dualisms (such as means/ends, art/life, subject/object, theory/practice), Dewey claimed he did "not know of anything so disastrously affected by the tradition of separation and isolation as is this particular theme of body-mind" (LW3:27). Recognizing that linguistic tradition both reflects and reinforces this separation, he complained that "we have no word by which to name mind-body in a unified wholeness of operation" that characterizes human life. Convinced of "the necessity of seeing mind-body as an integral whole," Dewey willingly flouted conventional usage by lexicographically asserting their oneness through such locutions as "body-mind" and "mind-body" (ibid.).[7]

Our action is always both bodily and mental. Though acts such as eating and drinking are usually classified as merely physical, they are nonetheless permeated with social, cognitive, and aesthetic meanings. In certain ritual contexts, they even take on deeply spiritual significance. The ways that moods and thoughts affect eating, drinking, and digestion, and the ways these latter reciprocally affect our mental states, express a connection so intimate "that it is artificial" to speak of "an influence exercised across and between two separate things" (LW3:29). Rather than an interaction between a body and a mind, we have a transactional whole of body-mind. However, this fundamental ontological *union* of body-mind

---

[7] Though I sometimes use the expression "sentient soma" to highlight the fundamental body-mind union in human experience, one should construe "soma" as already implying life and some degree of purposive sentience, thus enabling us to distinguish soma from mere body (which can exist in a lifeless, unfeeling state).

does not entail that a satisfactory degree of harmonious *unity* in our behavior as body-minds is always present or guaranteed.[8] Angry or gluttonous thoughts can disrupt smooth digestion, just as digesting the wrong foods (or quantities) can disturb our mental harmony. Erotic activity – whose capacity for social, aesthetic, and even spiritual meanings defies its categorization as merely physical – can likewise suffer because of inadequate harmony between bodily conditions and imaginative thought processes (which themselves are rooted and reflected in bodily behavior).

In the forward-looking, melioristic spirit of pragmatism, Dewey sees body-mind unity less as an ontological given in which we can smugly rest than as a desired, progressive goal of dynamic, harmonious functioning that we should continually strive to attain. As with the unity of habit, "integration is an achievement rather than a datum" (MW14:30). Recognizing that the organism is shaped by its environment and that the human environment is deeply social, Dewey argues that the level of body-mind unity deeply depends on social conditions. Such unity can therefore be used as a measure of the quality of a culture: "the more civilized it is, the less is there some behavior which is purely physical and some other purely mental" (LW3:29). He thus decries society's sharp divisions between unthinking physical labor (that works as mechanically as the machines it deploys) and purely intellectual work that is cut off from "employing and directing physical instrumentalities to effect material changes." Both extremes reflect "maladjustment," "a departure from that wholeness which is health" (ibid.).

So, more important than new terminology to suggest body-mind unity, more urgent than metaphysical theories to counter dualism, Dewey affirms that "the integration of mind-body in action" is most crucially a practical question, "the most practical of all questions we can ask of our civilization," and one that demands social reconstruction as well as individual efforts to achieve better unity in practice. Without such reform,

---

[8] This distinction between fundamental ontological union and harmonious unity would justify the hyphen in body-mind, since this mark (called in French a *trait d'union*) suggests a union that is not always a seamless unity. Here is how Dewey at one point defines body-mind and functionally distinguishes the two elements in the union: "body-mind simply designates what actually takes place when a living body is implicated in situations of discourse, communication and participation. In the hyphenated phrase body-mind, 'body' designates the continued and conserved, the registered and cumulative operation of factors continuous with the rest of nature, inanimate as well as animate; while 'mind' designates the characters and consequences which are differential, indicative of features which emerge when 'body' is engaged in a wider, more complex and interdependent situation." (LW1:217)

"we shall continue to live in a society in which a soulless and heartless materialism is compensated for by soulful but futile and unnatural idealism and spiritualism" (LW3:29–30).

The primacy of the practical did not discourage Dewey from making theoretical interventions to contest the metaphysics of the body/mind division. One Deweyan strategy is to undermine the traditional dualism of physical versus mental by instead explaining human reality in terms of three interpenetrating "levels of increasing complexity and intimacy of interaction among natural events," levels he calls "physical, psychophysical, and mental" (LW1.200). The "psycho-physical" is not a special substance that opposes the physical; nor is it the addition of something purely psychic or supernatural that is merged with the physical, "as a centaur is half man and half horse" (LW1:196). Instead, it signifies the emergence of a more complex level of organization of physical materials and energies through which the organism generates purposive efforts to achieve the satisfaction of its survival needs. When sensory discriminations (which are necessary for achieving the organism's successful sequence of need, effort, and satisfaction) become more complex, they reach the level of feelings or basic sentience that higher animals, including humans, experience. Mind, in Dewey's view, is a still higher level of organization that emerges from psychophysical experience only when language comes into play, because language enables the organism's feelings and movements to be named, and thus objectified and given a determinate meaning that can be reidentified and deployed in communication. Mind remains in the realm of natural events, but Dewey's linguistic requirement for mind also places it squarely in the realm of culture. No inconsistency is involved in this double status. Just as mind is not opposed to but is rather an emergent expression of the human body, so culture is not the contradiction of nature but rather its fulfillment and reshaping.[9]

Despite James's revolutionary emphasis on the bodily dimension of emotion, his *Principles of Psychology* affirmed an exceptional group of

---

[9] We might resist Dewey's linguistic-conceptual threshold of mind because of our conviction that some animals and certainly human infants have a mental life without displaying discursive language. This objection could be mitigated by noting that Dewey's theory still grants them the sentient life (of feelings and sensations and voluntary action) that belongs to the psychophysical. Moreover, Dewey's language requirement might be relaxed to include forms of nonconceptual body language that higher animals and infants may be argued to possess. We would not, however, want to say that in developing from merely psychophysical behavior to discursive language use, an infant changes radically in ontological status. She remains a natural, sentient organism that always had linguistic thought as a possibility to be realized.

"subtle" emotions (those of "pure" aesthetic, moral, and intellectual pleasure and displeasure) that are "almost feelingless," wholly "*cerebral*" and
"cognitive" and thus not dependent on feelings of "the bodily sounding board" (PP, 1082–1086). Dewey's reconstruction of James's theory of
emotion corrects this anomalous suggestion of a purely spiritual, bodiless
emotion that would imply a real division of mind from body. Contesting
James's characterization of pure philosophical pleasure as a merely cerebral satisfaction of cognitive rightness, Dewey points to the "revivals of
motor discharge and organic reinforcement" that sustain and heighten
the smooth flowing "sense of abundance and ease in thought" that James
identified with purely mental satisfaction. When intellectual activity is
functioning at its highest and purest, Dewey argues, "thinking becomes
really whole-hearted: it takes possession of us altogether" – body and
mind.[10]

Dewey finds a disturbing residual dualism not only in James's distinction between purely intellectual and robustly bodily emotion but also in
the Jamesian manner of contrasting the cognitive content of an emotion
with its physiological cause or expression. Rather than understanding
emotion as a combination of distinct cognitive perceptions and bodily
reactions, Dewey argues for a more basic unity of purposive behavior that
underlies both the cognitive and bodily dimensions of emotion. These
dimensions are only identified and individuated as such when behavior
(always an interaction with an environment) becomes problematic rather
than frictionless. When smoothly driving a car in traffic, we do not have
distinct perceptions of oncoming cars plus fears of the possible damage
they could cause in hitting us. Only when presented with a breakdown in
smooth interaction – as when a car suddenly crosses into our lane – do we
have a distinct emotion of fear coupled with a distinct perception of the
object of that fear as it hurtles toward us and we must decide how to avoid
it. We do not first have an idea of the car and then a feeling of fear, according to Dewey. Rather "*the idea and the emotional excitation are constituted at
one and the same time*" from the relevant "mode of behavior" (here the
driving) which "*is the primary thing*"; "*indeed, they* [idea and physiological
excitation] *represent the tension of stimulus and response within the coordination which makes up the mode of behavior*" (EW4:174). In short, mental and
bodily reactions are not two different things in search of a philosophical
synthesis but are instead analytical abstractions already enveloped in the
primal unity of purposive behavior.

[10] John Dewey, "The Theory of Emotion," EW4:157.

Such unity of voluntary action, Dewey maintains, should never be divided into a purely mental act of chosen purpose (performed through an allegedly disembodied agency of free will) which is then followed by a separate bodily execution of that purpose. James, we recall, had affirmed this dualistic account in his *Principles of Psychology*, claiming that in explicit acts of will "volitional effort lies exclusively within the mental world. The whole drama is a mental drama" (PP, 1168). He readily granted that science requires the methodological presumption that everything (including our choices) can in principle be explained or predicted in terms of causal conditions, "that the world must be one unbroken fact, and that prediction of all things . . . must be ideally, if not actually, possible." However, James argued, there is a contrary and ultimately overriding "*moral postulate about the Universe*" that is essential to our entire conception of ethics and action and that demands free will. It is "the postulate that *what ought to be can be, and that bad acts cannot be fated, but that good ones must be possible in their place*" (PP, 1177). We not only feel the exercise of free will in our choices, James insisted, but without it, "the whole sting and excitement" in choice of action would disappear; "life and history" would simply be "the dull rattling off of a chain that was forged innumerable ages ago," and moral responsibility would be nullified by determinism's causal chains (PP, 429).

Dewey shrewdly responds that this negatively portrayed alternative to free will is not scientific determinism (which involves causal conditions and correlations that are probabilistic, uncertain and changing) but instead a "theological *pre*determinism" that construes causality in old-fashioned terms of "a productive agency or determining force" (modeled on the idea of an independent ego such as God). The "uncertainty" of causal connections and results in our probabilistic world of flux should be enough to provide our actions with the sense of excitement.[11]

The idea of free will existing entirely outside the realm of causal connections is not merely inconsistent with science but also inadequate and unnecessary for explaining the ethical sense of free and meaningful choice. If free choice of a hot or cold drink meant a choice wholly unconditioned by material factors, then it would require disregarding one's established preferences, habits, current desires, bodily state, and environing physical and social conditions. Such freedom of choice would simply be the "freedom of indifference" or arbitrary randomness, not the meaningful exercise of will that defines ethical action (EW4:93). Besides, how could such choice be the *individual's* free will, for it is unconditioned

---

[11] John Dewey, "The Ego as Cause," EW4:91, 94.

by all the conditions that define one's individuality as an agent? But if choice is meaningful and important to ethical life precisely because it is guided by a person's conditions and desires, then choice or will cannot be unconditionally free.

Choices and freedoms are not unreal merely because they are conditioned. We experience our choices as free, Dewey argues, "because the presence in consciousness of alternative ends with the reflection which that calls out, *is* freedom" of a sort (EW4:95). And such freedom, though not devoid of causal conditions, allows for a distinctively future-looking sense of moral responsibility. By treating people as responsible and thus assigning them praise or blame for their actions, they can be influenced to make better use of reflection and judgment in making better choices. "Causes for an act always exist, but causes are not excuses . . . It is as causes of future actions that excuses and accusations alike must be considered . . . For morals has to do with acts still within our control, acts still to be performed." The moral issue is "prospective," a question "of modifying the factors which now influence future results," and our practices or "schemes of judgment, of assigning blame and praise, of awarding punishment and honor, are part of these conditions" (MW14:17). As Dewey elsewhere puts it, "Holding men to responsibility may make a decided difference in their *future* behavior; holding a stone or tree to responsibility is a meaningless performance" because there is no comparable influence on choice and conduct (LW3:94).

III

Alexander, Habit, and the Need for Somatic Reflection
We have explored the logical, ontological, and ethical arguments Dewey brings to show the incoherence of a Jamesian free will outside the realm of natural causal conditioning, thus suggesting a form of "soft determinism" that affirms real choice while recognizing its conditioned character. A second axis of critique more specifically challenges the Jamesian view that will is an exclusively mental affair intrinsically independent of bodily means but simply deploying them after the act of will is successfully achieved in its pure mentality. Here Dewey relies heavily on F. M. Alexander's insights concerning the power of bodily habits and the indispensability of somatic means in willed action.

Voluntary action is not a product of isolated moments of purely mental decision; it relies on the habits of feeling, thinking, acting, and desiring that make us the selves we are. Walking is a complicated mechanical matter involving the coordinated movement of many bones and muscles while maintaining balance. But in normal circumstances, our ordinary habits of walking simply respond to our desire to go somewhere without requiring any special conscious act of willing, with every step, the complex series of lifting, forward, and lowering movements of each hip, leg, and foot, along with the necessary attendant movements of the pelvis. In the vast bulk of voluntary behavior, our unreflective habits spontaneously perform our will. Indeed, as Dewey remarks, because "habits are demands for certain kinds of activity . . . , they *are* will," and their "projectile power" of "predisposition . . . is an immensely more intimate and fundamental part of ourselves than are vague, general, conscious choices." Habits thus "constitute the self . . . They form our effective desires and they furnish us with our working capacities. They rule our thoughts, determining which shall appear and be strong and which shall pass from light into obscurity" (MW14:21–22).

Habits cannot be purely mental and autonomous, since they always incorporate aspects of the environment. Your habitual way of walking depends not only on your particular physical structure (itself partly shaped by habits of nutrition and movement that shape muscle and eventually even bone) but also on the surfaces on which you walk, the shoes you walk in, the exemplars of walking you witness and attune yourself to, and the situational purposes that frame your customary gait (rushing to work through crowded streets versus leisurely strolling barefoot on the sand).[12] Habits of thought must likewise incorporate features of the environment that are necessary or worthwhile to think about and address through action. Moreover, since habits are formed over time, they also embody environmental histories and thus can persist even when the original conditions are no longer present, as we sadly know from victims of past abuse and oppression.

If will is constituted by habits, and if habits always incorporate environmental features, then it follows that will cannot be an entirely autonomous and purely mental affair. Willing cannot be a disembodied act because it requires some sense of deploying the available means or affordances of the environmental context of action, which includes our bodily resources. Willing (rather than merely wishing) to walk means somehow engaging our habits and means of bodily movement, even if we are deprived (for

---

[12] If the habits that constitute the self also incorporate the environment, it follows that the self is partly an environmental product. Our bodies, just like our thoughts, incorporate our surroundings, going beyond conventional body boundaries to meet our essential needs of breathing and nutrition. The ethical and social consequences of this point are discussed toward the end of this chapter.

example, through injury) of the habitual use of our legs and our muscular efforts are expressed only in other places.[13] Dewey credits Alexander for providing the clearest explanation of how bodily habits are indispensable for effective voluntary action but also enormously destructive in deceptively frustrating our will.

Who was Alexander, and what were the origins and principles of his somatic theory and practice? Born in Australia in 1869, he began his career as an actor but mysteriously kept losing his voice, though only when performing and despite his having normal vocal cords. Finding no help or explanation from medical experts, Alexander systematically studied his speech behavior in a mirror, and eventually came to see that his voice problems in acting were due to assuming a habitual declamatory posture in the head and neck area that constrained his breathing and thus strained his voice. He described this posture (which he used in acting but not in ordinary speech) as a "pulling back of the head." To his far greater surprise, Alexander then discovered that his conscious decision *not* to pull back his head was completely ineffective against his ingrained habit to do so, thus demonstrating that his habitual, embodied will was a more basic and powerful part of him than his conscious mental decision (or so-called act of will), even when that conscious desire was accompanied by strong muscular efforts to keep the head forward. To his further dismay, Alexander noticed (again through the use of mirrors) that even when he felt he was keeping it forward, he was actually reverting to his habit of pulling back the head. In short, he realized his sensory awareness of his own posture and movement was extremely inaccurate. He then studied others and found that most people similarly suffer from "debauched *kinaesthetic* systems" whose faulty "sense-appreciation" and lack of somatic self-awareness seriously hinder their performance by making them the unconscious victims of unthinking habits of bodily misuse.[14]

---

[13] Experiments have indicated that the mind's own sense of willed effort relies on motor commands and is physiologically expressed. Merely representing to oneself mentally the performance of an action one intends to perform, without actually performing it, activates muscular and other physiological responses related to such an effort of action, including "changes in cardiac rate." Even to localize an object in space that one wants to reach involves the simulated experience of the "muscular sensations" of "the movements that would be necessary to reach it." See Alain Berthoz, *The Brain's Sense of Movement*, trans. G. Weiss (Cambridge, MA: Harvard University Press, 2000), 31–32, 37.

[14] See F. M. Alexander, *Man's Supreme Inheritance*, 2nd ed. (New York: Dutton, 1918), 22, 89. Alexander best describes the process of self-examination and self-correction that led to the discovery of his theory and technique in the third of his books, *The Use of the Self*

Alexander further observed that eagerness to attain a desired but problematic end automatically prompts habitual actions to achieve that end, without our even realizing that we are then falling back into the original bad habits that have already been frustrating our efforts to achieve it. "When the end is held in mind, . . . habit will always seek to attain the end by habitual methods" (MSI, 204). Moreover, our focusing on the desired ends (which, when habits are well adapted to those ends, are indeed all we need to focus on) distracts us from attending to what we are really doing in our bodily posture and performance and therefore prevents us from seeing how this actually thwarts what we want to do. Our avid desire for "end-gaining" thus contributes to our distorted "sensory appreciation" (our flawed somaesthetic awareness), while diverting our attention from the needed "means-whereby" the action could be performed properly (CCC, 151–153; US, 29–30).

Alexander concluded that a systematic method of careful somatic awareness, analysis, and control was needed for improving self-knowledge and self-use: a method to discern, localize, and inhibit the unwanted habits, to discover the requisite bodily postures or movements (the indispensable "means whereby") for best producing the desired action or attitude, and finally to monitor and master their performance through "conscious control" until ultimately a better (i.e., more effective and controllable) habit could be established to achieve the willed end of action (MSI 181–236). The elaborate method he developed – emphasizing heightened somatic self-awareness and conscious control through inhibition, indirection, and a focus on "the means whereby" as crucial, provisional ends – became the famed Alexander Technique.

Moving to England in 1904 to promulgate this technique (and acquiring such famous students as George Bernard Shaw and Aldous Huxley), Alexander subsequently introduced it to America when he came to New York City in 1914, vigorously touting his theory not simply as a body therapy but as a general educational philosophy for improving the use of one's entire self, which, he argued, could better not only individual lives but society as a whole. The mass of kinaesthetic malfunctions and related somatic-psychic ailments (backaches, headaches, loss of vitality, nervousness, mental rigidity) that plague contemporary

(New York: Dutton, 1932). His first book was *Man's Supreme Inheritance*, whose first edition was published in England in 1910. This was followed by *Constructive Conscious Control of the Individual* (New York: Dutton, 1923). References to these books hereafter will use the abbreviations US, MSI, CCC. Alexander's final book, essentially a reformulation of earlier ideas, was *The Universal Constant in Living* (New York: Dutton, 1941).

culture, Alexander explained as resulting from a systematic mismatch between our somatic tendencies developed through slow processes of evolution and the very different modern conditions of life and work in which we are forced to function. Rejecting a regression to primitive life, he instead sought a method for people to rationally and consciously adjust their behavior to today's new and ever more quickly changing conditions rather than relying on unconscious, haphazard forces to shape such adaptations. The ordinary process of habit formation can no longer be trusted for adjusting to new conditions, because it is so slow, unsystematic, and uncertain. Given the rapid rate of contemporary change, even if we are lucky to develop a good new habit unreflectively, it could easily be rendered obsolete by the time it is successfully achieved. We thus need a systematic method for the intelligent reconstruction of habit through the guidance of what he called "constructive conscious control."

Alexander's key themes of habit, evolution, meliorism, body-mind unity, and respect for means and education for rationally reconstructing self and society were already clearly congenial to Dewey, who soon became an ardent advocate of Alexander's views, having been overwhelmingly won over by his practical technique as a somatic educator-therapist. Dewey (at the age of 57) first met Alexander in 1916 through a Columbia philosophy colleague Wendell Bush and soon began taking lessons in the technique. Having long suffered from eyestrain, back pains, and a painfully stiff neck, Dewey claimed "that Alexander had completely cured him, that he was able to read and to see and move his neck freely."[15] Unlike James, who died only two years after meeting his own postural self-use guru (Dr. James Taylor), Dewey benefited from Alexander's work for decades. Taking lessons from both Alexander and Alexander's younger brother, Dewey continued to reaffirm (even as late as 1946) that his "confidence in Alexander's work [was] unabated" and that his sustained health was deeply indebted to "their treatment."[16] What could be more convincing to a pragmatist philosopher of embodiment than undeniable, enduring practical improvements in somatic functioning and the resultant surge of psychic energy and mood?

In *Human Nature and Conduct* (1922), Dewey makes Alexander's somatic insights the core of his crucial chapter on "Habits and Will,"

---

[15] Corliss Lamont, ed., *Dialogue on John Dewey* (New York: Horizon Press, 1959), 27.

[16] See Dewey's letter to Joseph Ratner, July 24, 1946, cited Rockefeller, *John Dewey*, 343. Dewey also took lessons from other teachers of the technique who were trained by Alexander and his brother. See Frank Jones, *Body Awareness in Action: A Study of the Alexander Technique* (New York: Schocken, 1976).

where he expounds Alexander's critique of the common presumptions that our will can work "without intelligent control of means" and "that [habitual bodily] means can exist and yet remain inert and inoperative" (MW14:22). It is "superstition" to assume "that if a man is told to stand up straight, all that is further needed is wish and effort on his part, and the deed is done. [Alexander] pointed out that this belief is on a par with primitive magic in its neglect of attention to the means which are involved in reaching an end." Such belief blocks progress "because it makes us neglect intelligent inquiry to discover the means which will produce a desired result, and intelligent invention to procure the means. In short, it leaves out the importance of intelligently controlled habit." Falsely implying "that the means or effective conditions of the realization of a purpose exist independently of established habit and even that they may be set in motion in opposition to habit," this blind faith in our postural proficiency also assumes that the proper means already "are there, so that the failure to stand erect is wholly a matter of failure of purpose and desire" (MW14:23–24).

Relying on the lessons he learned from Alexander, Dewey instead argues, "A man who does not stand properly forms a habit of standing improperly, a positive, forceful habit." Hence to assume "he is simply failing to do the right thing, and that the failure can be made good by an order of will is absurd.... Conditions have been formed for producing a bad result, and the bad result will occur as long as those conditions exist. They can no more be dismissed by a direct effort of will than the conditions which create drought can be dispelled by whistling for wind" (MW14:24). Habits must intervene not only in the "execution" of our wishes, but even in "the formation of ideas" that convert vague desires into concrete acts of will. An explicitly concrete will to stand erect, in contrast to a mere abstract "wish" to achieve such posture, always involves some embodied idea – a proprioceptive notion or kinaesthetic feeling (however implicit, unnoticed, vague, partial, or misguided) – as to how one becomes and feels erect. And such "an idea gets shape and consistency only when it has a habit back of it." For even if "by a happy chance a right concrete idea or purpose...has been hit upon," the person's entrenched bad habit will tend to override it and frustrate its execution. Thus, Dewey concludes with Alexander, "Only when a man can already perform an act of standing straight does he know [in a concrete proprioceptive sense] what it is like to have a right posture and only then can he summon the idea required for proper execution. The act must come before the thought, and a habit before an ability to evoke the thought at will. Ordinary psychology reverses the actual state of affairs" (MW14:25–26).

Failure to recognize the essential bond between will and habit "only leads to a separation of mind from body" that undermines the "scientific" status (in Dewey's scare quotes) of both "psycho-analysis" and the theories of "nerve physiologists." While the former wrongly "thinks that mental habits can be straightened out by some kind of purely psychical manipulation without reference to . . . bad bodily sets," the latter falsely believe "that it is only necessary to locate a particular diseased cell or local lesion, independent of the whole complex of organic habits, in order to rectify conduct" (MW14:27). This scientific critique not only of psychoanalysis (for which Dewey had little regard – largely because of its emphasis on the unconscious, the sexual, and the past) but also of neurophysiology (which he clearly respected) should be understood in the light of his repeatedly ardent yet beleaguered defense of the scientific status of Alexander's work, whose persistent failure to win mainstream scientific acceptance was surely a great disappointment for Dewey, if not also an embarrassment.[17]

In William James, advocacy of non-embodied free will is complemented by the admonishment that somatic introspection constitutes a distraction and danger for practical life. So in pursuing a course of action, just "trust your spontaneity," he urges, and let habit work for you. Not only do "we walk a beam the better the less we think of the position of our feet," but reflective somatic consciousness also has an "inhibitive influence" on our will that frustrates action, undermines "vitality," and lowers our "pain-threshold" thus diminishing our efficacy and energy.[18] However, once we recognize that will is deeply enmeshed in habit, we should appreciate how inhibition can help us overcome the bad habits that express (and

---

[17] See Jones, *Body Awareness in Action*, 104–105, who also describes how some of Dewey's colleagues "smiled at" the philosopher's "naïve" adherence to Alexander's theory considering it a lapse of judgment or even a "superstition" (98). Admitting that Alexander made no "imposing show of technical scientific terminology of physiology, anatomy and psychology," Dewey construed this as a virtue of intellectual "sincerity and thoroughness" that did not compromise the work's scientific status. He argued instead that "Alexander's teaching is scientific in the strictest sense of the word," demonstrated by "its consequences in operation . . . [that can] be verified experimentally by observation" and by the way those consequences are shown to logically derive from his theory's "general principles"; it thus "satisfies the most exacting demands of scientific method" (MW15:311, 313).

[18] William James, PP, 1128; "The Energies of Men," in *William James: Writings 1902–1910*, ed. Bruce Kuklick (New York: Viking, 1987), 1225–1226. *Talks To Teachers on Psychology and To Students on Some of Life's Ideals* (New York: Dover, 1962), 109.

reinforce) themselves in spontaneous behavior and that frustrate our will. Besides restraining habitual reactions, inhibition provides a space for reflective consciousness prior to action so that habits can be monitored and corrected. Similarly, once we recognize that the will is essentially embodied, we can see how somaesthetic reflection provides a valuable tool for improving voluntary action and thus enhancing practical life. Convinced, through Alexander's work, of these central lessons, Dewey radically diverges from James by extolling the practical merits of reflective somatic consciousness and its valuable inhibitory functions, even though, like James, he was personally wary of the dangers of introspection.[19]

Dewey echoes Alexander's ambitious argument that cultivating somatic self-consciousness is necessary for "promoting our constructive growth and happiness" because it is essential to improving self-use and because self-use is essential to our use of all the other tools at our disposal. "No one would deny that we ourselves enter as an agency into whatever is attempted and done by us.... But the hardest thing to attend to is that which is closest to ourselves, that which is most constant and familiar. And this closest 'something' is, precisely, ourselves, our own habits and ways of doing things," through our primal agency of body-mind. To understand and redirect its workings requires attentively self-reflective "sensory consciousness" and control. Modern science has developed all sorts of powerful tools for influencing our environment. But "the one factor which is the primary tool in the use of all these other tools, namely ourselves, in other words, our own psycho-physical disposition, as the basic condition of our employment of all agencies and energies" also needs to be "studied as the central instrumentality" (MW15:314–315). For without "the control of our use of ourselves," Dewey concludes in his introduction to Alexander's *The Use of the Self,* "the control we have gained of physical energies ... is a perilous affair," and improved somatic self-awareness is necessary for this intelligent self-control of self-use (LW6:318).

If reflective somaesthetic consciousness is essential for understanding and correcting habits and thus improving self-use, then inhibition proves an equally crucial tool for such reform, since we need to inhibit the problematic habits in order to provide the opportunity to analyze and

---

[19] Confessing to a friend that "being too introspective by nature, I have had to learn to control the direction it takes," Dewey expresses particular unease about "autobiographical introspection ... as it is not good for me." See his letter to Scudder Klyce, cited in Rockefeller, *John Dewey, 318.* Dewey's idea of controlling the direction of introspection suggests the useful distinction between disciplined somatic reflection for self-knowledge and uncontrolled personal ruminations about one's life.

transform them into better ones. Otherwise, these entrenched habits will continue to be reinforced in our spontaneous unreflective behavior. Alexander therefore emphasizes "the process of inhibition as a primary and fundamental factor in [his] technique": "the inhibitory process must take first place, and remain the primary factor"; "preventive orders" are the "primary" orders whose restraint and undoing of old habits provides the necessary clearing for teaching new and better habits or modes of action (CCC, 152, 161,186). Alexander indeed regards our "intellectual powers of inhibition" as what "marks the differentiation of man from the animal world" and underlies the human capacities of "reasoning" and freedom (MSI, 35). What we uncritically presume to be the freedom of spontaneous action is in fact enslaved by chains of habit that prevent us from acting otherwise, even from deploying our bodies in other ways to perform the very same kind of action but better or differently.

True freedom of will thus involves freeing it from spontaneity's bondage to unreflective habit, so that one can consciously do with one's body what one really wants to do. Such freedom is not a native gift but an acquired skill involving mastery of inhibitory control as well as positive action. As Dewey puts it, "True spontaneity is henceforth not a birth-right but the last term, the consummated conquest, of an art – the art of conscious control," an art involving "the unconditional necessity of inhibition of customary acts, and the tremendous mental difficulty found in not 'doing' something as soon as an habitual act is suggested" (MW11:352; LW6:318). These inhibitory difficulties, which he first came to recognize through his Alexander training, Dewey described as "the most humiliating experience of [his] life, intellectually speaking" (LW6:318).

Inhibition's crucial role in freedom finds more recent support from experimental studies in neuroscience (introduced by Benjamin Libet) showing that motor action depends on neurological events that occur before our conscious awareness of deciding to make a movement, even though we feel that our conscious decision is what initiated the movement.[20] One experiment shows that, on average, 350 milliseconds (ms) before the subjects were conscious of deciding, or having an urge, to flick

[20] See Benjamin Libet, "Unconscious Cerebral Initiative and the Role of Conscious Will in Voluntary Action," *Behavioral and Brain Sciences*, 8 (1985): 529–66, quotations from 529, 536; "The Neural Time-Factor in Perception, Volition, and Free Will," *Revue de Métaphysique et de Morale*, 2 (1992): 255–272; "Do We Have Free Will?" *Journal of Consciousness Studies*, 6 (1999): 47–57; "Can Conscious Experience Affect Brain Activity?" *Journal of Consciousness Studies*, 10 (2003): 24–28; and P. Haggard and B. Libet, "Conscious Intention and Brain Activity," *Journal of Consciousness Studies* 8 (2001): 47–63.

their wrists, their brains were already engaged in preparing the motor processes of making the movement (such brain activity known as "readiness potential"). It then took an average of about 200 milliseconds from the conscious decision to perform the movement to the actual act of moving, of which time, just before the flick, there is up to about 50 milliseconds of neural activity descending from the motor cortex to the wrist. If voluntary acts of movement are indeed initiated "by special unconscious cerebral processes that begin . . . before the appearance of conscious intention," then how can we speak of conscious control of movement and conscious exercise of free will? Libet, however, affirms such conscious voluntary powers, precisely through our inhibitory ability to "veto" that act between its conscious awareness and actual implementation: "the final decision to act could still be consciously controlled during the 150 ms or so remaining after the conscious intention appears" and before its "motor performance." Free will, on this account, amounts essentially to a free "won't." Though the general concept of voluntary action and free will should not be limited to this inhibitory model (with its focus on unsituated "abstract" experimental movements and a razor time-slice of 150 ms for decision), Libet's findings lend scientific support to Alexander's emphasis on inhibition for exercising conscious constructive control in motor performance.

Not only essential in restraining problematic habits, inhibition is also necessary for the very effectiveness of somatic reflection that allows us to observe our behavior accurately so that we can inhibit the problematic habit and replace it with a superior mode of response. We cannot reliably change our actions if we do not really know what we are actually doing, yet most of us are very unaware of our habitual modes of bodily behavior. Which foot do you use when taking your first step in walking; which of your legs bears the most weight in standing; on which buttock do you more heavily rest in sitting; where do you initiate the action of reaching to pick up a cup – in your hand, elbow, shoulder joint, pelvis, head? We are not at all inclined to pay attention to such things, because as active creatures striving to survive and flourish within an environment, our sustained attention is habitually directed primarily to other things in that environment that affect our projects rather than to our bodily parts, movements, and sensations. For good evolutionary reasons, we are habituated to respond directly to external events rather than analyze our inner feelings; to act rather than to carefully observe, to reach impulsively for our ends rather than holding back to study the bodily means at our disposal. Inhibitory power is therefore needed even to break our habits of attending to other things so that we can sustain a focus on reflective somatic consciousness.

Such consciousness can better discern underlying somatic sensations and unnoticed movements when it is free from the influence of effortful action, since such action (like any strong stimulus) provides its own strong sensations that raise the threshold needed for other somatic factors to be detected. This point, articulated in the Weber-Fechner law of psychophysics, is obvious from ordinary experience. We hear sounds in the silence of night that we cannot detect in the noisy bustle of rush hour. It is much harder to notice the slight pressure of the hat you are wearing as you vigorously shovel snow than when you are calmly at rest. The same principle underlies *zazen* meditation. Performed while simply sitting quietly (and thus often characterized by its masters as "just sitting" – *shikan taza*), its position of tranquil absence of effortful, end-seeking action allows one to concentrate more clearly, fixedly, and exclusively on one's breathing and thus cease the mind's habits of associative thinking.[21] Of course, *zazen* paradoxically requires its own effort of concentration and mindful inhibitory control to achieve its meditative activity of inaction that master Dōgen describes as "sitting fixedly, think of not thinking," just as Alexander work involves effortful thinking about not acting.[22] Inhibition is especially difficult when dealing with thoughts of action, since the very thought of an action naturally tends to elicit that action.

How exactly does the Alexander Technique deploy inhibition in its reconstruction of habits and mastery of conscious control? Its distinctive educational use of inhibition is not directed only narrowly to the particular action of misuse that needs correcting but is instead instilled as a general principle that can be applied also to other actions and thus globally guides the proper use of self that the teacher wishes to instill in the student. Take the case of a golfer who habitually takes his eye off the ball by lifting his head. His Alexander teacher will not simply tell him to inhibit his head lifting and ask him to swing while inhibiting that lifting. She will instead instruct him positively about how to position his neck and head when swinging and then tell him that when she subsequently gives him these guiding orders to hold himself in that way when swinging, "he must not attempt to carry them out"; "on the contrary, *he must inhibit the*

---

[21] As Dōgen puts it, "to seek the pearl [of enlightenment], we should still the waves" because the pearl will be hard to see in turbulent water. See *Dōgen's Manuals of Zen Meditation*, trans. Carl Bielefeldt (Berkeley: University of California Press, 1988), 183.

[22] Ibid., 181.

desire to do so in the case of each and every order which is given to him" (CCC, 152–153). Rather than react in the commanded way, the student "must instead project the guiding orders as given to him whilst his teacher, at the same time, by means of manipulation, will make the required head readjustments and bring about the necessary co-ordinations, in this way performing for the pupil the particular movement or movements required, and giving him the new reliable sensory appreciation and the very best opportunity possible to connect the different guiding orders before attempting to put them into practice" (CCC, 153).

This method, moreover, trains the student more deeply and extensively to inhibit the tendency of direct "end-gaining" that encourages bad habits and is so detrimental to self-observation and self-use, while instilling in its place the habit "of attending instead to the *means whereby* this 'end' can be attained" (CCC, 153; cf. US, 28–33). By asking the student to rehearse but *not* to follow the guiding orders, the teacher also diminishes the performance anxiety of the student who in most cases will have a habit of feeling psychologically pressured when asked to perform any end of movement that is assigned to him by his teacher, who in the context of instruction is an authority figure. Relaxed from the demand to perform, the student can better concentrate calmly on the postural means and how they feel when the teacher provides them to the student through her physical manipulations. Through this attentive training he will eventually learn how to project to himself these guiding orders or means. Once these directions seem sufficiently digested, the teacher will then instruct the student that the guiding orders can be responded to through actual performance of the act commanded. The student will then continue to project the guiding directions to himself but at the same time will pause for a critical moment of decision on the basis of which he would either implement the action as directed, or refrain from it, or would instead perform a completely different action, all the while projecting the guiding directions. In this way, "the means whereby" can be clearly distinguished, pursued, and appreciated as a (provisional) goal or end rather than being totally subordinated to the initial end of action, preoccupation with which encourages the bad "end-gaining" habits that foster misuse of the self.

Based on his own experience of self-transformation and his subsequent work with others, Alexander claims the initial focus for such training of postural coordination should be in the head and neck area. For it is there he identifies the "primary control of the use of the self, which governs the working of all the mechanisms and so renders the control of the complex human organism comparatively simple." "This primary control," Alexander continues, "depends upon a certain use of the head and neck in relation to the use of the rest of the body, and once the pupil has inhibited the instinctive misdirection leading to his faulty habitual use, the teacher must begin the process of building up the new use by giving the pupil the primary direction towards the establishment of this primary control" (US, 32). As explained above, the pupil will then project this direction but not act on it; instead, he will let the teacher's hands bring about the corresponding desired posture or movement which "though unfamiliar at first, will become familiar with repetition" (ibid.). Once this primary control is established, the fundamental key to coordination has been achieved, so the teacher can then give further directions to the pupil (e.g., how to use his wrists in swinging). But the pupil "*must keep the primary direction going*, while he projects" these secondary directions "and while the teacher brings about the corresponding activity" (US, 33). As long as the primary control is maintained, Alexander asserts, the individual will be able to use himself more consciously and skillfully, thus enabling him to learn with greater speed and ease whatever specific modes of somatic "means whereby" he or his teacher discovers. The insistent focus on the primary control is why the Alexander Technique does not deploy the body scan, since focusing elsewhere would be "detracting from the primary control, namely, monitoring the head-neck relation."[23]

Alexander equated "this primary control" with Rudolph Magnus's important discovery (in 1924) of an anatomical "central control" in the brain (US, 32) that governed the righting reflex and all other reflex postural coordinations, a mechanism Magnus called the *Zentralapparat*.[24] Though having frequently emphasized the importance of head and neck posture in his earlier work, Alexander had not used the term "primary

[23] Though I noticed this from my own experience with Alexander work, I am quoting in confirmation from an e-mail message (March 26, 2003) from Galen Cranz, an Alexander practitioner who also inquired for me among her colleagues. Cranz is the author of a fine book, *The Chair: Rethinking Culture, Body, and Design* (New York: Norton, 2000), which applies Alexander's principles to provide a rigorous critical analysis of this common instrument of sitting, which though seeming so innocent can be surprisingly injurious to our posture and health.

[24] Rudolph Magnus, *Körperstellung* (Berlin: Springer, 1924). Alexander did not know German and had to rely on explanations and translations from his medical friends for his impression of this book, which was not published in English translation until 1987 as *Body Posture: Experimental-Physiological Investigations of the Reflexes Involved in Body Posture, Their Cooperation and Disturbances* (Springfield, VA: National Technical Information Service, 1987). My parenthetical page references are to this English edition, hereafter K.

control" until Magnus's theory became well known. He thus may have introduced this term precisely to give his own theory more scientific credibility through identification with Magnus's research, of which he never demonstrated a substantive understanding. Dewey, always concerned with the scientific respectability of Alexander's work, was keen to endorse this identification, while also suggesting that Alexander's discovery was prior and more powerfully potent through its *personally experienced* knowledge. "Magnus proved by means of what may be called *external* evidence the existence of a central control in the organism. But Mr. Alexander's technique gave a direct and intimate confirmation in personal experience of the fact of central control long before Magnus carried on his investigations. And one who has had experience of the technique *knows* it through the series of experiences which he himself has. The genuinely scientific character of Mr. Alexander's teaching and discoveries can be safely rested upon this fact alone" (LW6:317).

Magnus defines the *Zentralapparat* as "a complicated central nervous apparatus that governs the entire body posture in a coordinated manner" and that is located "in the brain stem, from the upper cervical cord to the midbrain . . . This is the apparatus on which the cerebral cortex plays, as complicated melodies are played on a piano" (K, 653). It provides, in other words, the basis of unreflective postural stability and reflex coordination that enables the higher purposive action that "can be carried out only when the cerebrum is intact" (K, 4). There are obvious resemblances between Alexander's notion of primary control and Magnus's *Zentralapparat*, for both focus on the head and neck area and serve as a primary coordinative control on which further coordinative behavior needs to be based. But there are also clear differences between the two notions. Magnus identifies an *anatomical mechanism* in the brain stem, while Alexander is speaking of a *behavioral use* of holding a certain postural relation between the head and neck and the rest of the body. Magnus's control is concerned with *automatic, unthinking reflexes*, while Alexander's is instead a function of *reflective conscious control* that highlights rational thinking, distinctively conscious inhibition, and methodical awareness of one's will in deliberative action, all of which go beyond the *Zentralapparat* because they require the intact cerebral cortex.[25]

[25] Magnus notes that without an intact cerebral cortex, an animal with a functional *Zentralapparat* can right itself, walk instinctively, and give reflex responses to external stimuli but cannot initiate voluntary action, which Magnus calls "spontaneous movements"; "external stimuli are required every time to set the animal in motion" (K 4).

IV

Discomforts of Alexander's Postural Theory

Though never seriously engaging the research of Magnus and other scientists, Alexander's work was touted by Dewey as cognitively superior to theirs because it treats the whole live organism in real-life situations – that is, "ordinary conditions of living – rising, sitting, walking, standing, using arms, hands, voice, tools, instruments of all kinds," while physiologists study isolated body parts or actions in "artificial" laboratory conditions. In the same way, the anatomist's mere theoretical knowledge of muscle coordination is contrasted with Alexander's concrete performable expertise of achieving and teaching coordination, which, Dewey claims, is knowledge "in the full and vital sense of that word" (LW6:316–317). This defense, however, does not vindicate Alexander's failure to seriously address current science pertaining to posture, movement, and mind. There is no reason why a practical, experiential somatic approach cannot also express, explain, and enrich itself by usefully deploying the best of contemporary scientific knowledge, as we find, for example, in the work of Moshe Feldenkrais, which is rich in explanations based on anatomy, physiology and psychophysics.[26] A pragmatic pluralism should encourage such interdisciplinary expression. Most damning, however, is Alexander's stubborn refusal to pursue (or even allow) the exploration and testing of his theories through standard scientific techniques of experimentation and analysis. This attitude – that flies in the faith of Alexander's commitments to rationality and flexible open-mindedness – eventually exasperated even Dewey, though he expressed his frustration only privately.[27]

If inhibition and the primary control constitute two key pillars of Alexander's Technique, his work also rests on a commitment to the supreme value and potentially all-pervasive power of rational consciousness, an ideal of total conscious control. Expressing Alexander's evolutionary vision of human progress through conscious "reasoning inhibition," it

---

[26] See, for example, Moshe Feldenkrais, *Body and Mature Behavior: A Study of Anxiety, Sex, Gravitation and Learning* (London: Routledge and Kegan Paul, 1949).

[27] For example, in a letter to Frank Jones, Dewey describes Alexander's negative attitude to scientific testing as the product "of early obstinate prejudices – whose formation or persistence is readily understandable on any theory except his own." See Jones, *Body Awareness in Action*, 105. A recent biography of Dewey indicates that Dewey succeeded in convincing the Macy Foundation to fund a scientific investigation of the Alexander Technique but that the Alexander brothers refused to cooperate and opposed the initiative. See Thomas C. Dalton, *Becoming John Dewey: Dilemmas of a Philosopher and a Naturalist* (Bloomington: Indiana University Press, 2002), 233.

fuels the meliorist passion of his project: "there is no function of the body that cannot be brought under the control of the conscious will . . . and I claim further that by the application of this principle of conscious control there may in time be evolved a complete mastery over the body, which will result in the elimination of all physical defects" (CCC, 44; MSI, 56). Such "complete conscious control of every function of the body," he insists, involves no "trance" (MSI, 41) but rather requires using one's reflective, inhibiting consciousness to attain a heightened somatic self-awareness that presupposes the possibility of observing every bodily function. This possibility is crucial, because by Alexander's principles, we can consciously control only that of which we are conscious, for otherwise we cannot observe and inhibit it.

Realizing that life would be impossibly unwieldy if we had to reflect on every movement, Alexander grants the value of positive habits working unreflectively beneath our focused consciousness. But he stresses that the essence of such positive habits is their always remaining accessible for consciousness to monitor and revise. His whole project of reconstructing habit is aimed at transforming ineffective, "unrecognized," and thus uncontrollable habits into habits that are effective and adaptable because they are essentially governed by "conscious control," even though not constantly held in the focus of reflective self-consciousness. Though "working quietly and unobtrusively" beneath the conscious level, proper habits may be checked and altered by conscious control "at any moment if necessary" (MSI, 90–92). Thus, Alexander insists his "method is based . . . on the complete acceptance of the hypothesis that each and every movement can be consciously directed and controlled" (MSI, 199).[28]

Yet how could such total transparency ever be possible? Not only have we noted the practical difficulties of sustaining attention and perceptual acuity for a detailed, accurate body scan, but the very figure/ground structure that is essential to any focused consciousness implies that there will always be something in the somatic background of consciousness that

---

[28] Perhaps one could, in principle, consciously but indirectly control somatic functions of which we are not conscious, if such functions are linked in an essential and stable way to functions that we are indeed conscious of and can consciously control. In the section "Notes and Instances," toward the end of *Man's Supreme Inheritance*, Alexander seems to recognize this option of indirect control, while admitting that "it may not be possible to control directly" every body part (e.g., "each separate part of the abdominal viscera") and body function (e.g., "the lower automatic functions"). Yet, he does not question that one can be directly conscious of all these parts and functions. See MSI, 291–292.

Shusterman's counter-argument

structures that consciousness but does not appear as an object within its field. Even if every particular somatic element were in principle available for such attentive awareness and control (itself a questionable hypothesis), some bodily part or function will always escape our attention as we focus on some other or attend to something else.

Dewey recognized such limitations of conscious reflection when he emphasized the indescribable, reflectively ungraspable immediacy of qualitative feeling as the essential glue that binds an experience together but cannot be attended to as one of its elements, since that immediately experienced quality is precisely what shapes the very attention to those elements that enables our awareness and identification of them as elements. Such immediate feelings, Dewey insists, are *had* but not known, yet underlie our every effort of thinking and knowing.[29] Habit's unreflective "mechanism is indispensable," because "if each act has to be consciously searched for at the moment and intentionally performed, execution is painful and the product is clumsy" (MW14:51). Reason and consciousness, moreover, cannot be regarded as autonomous entities for controlling habit because they themselves emerge from habits and have no real existence apart them. For Dewey, "habits formed in process of exercising biological aptitudes are the sole agents of observation, recollection, foresight and judgment: a mind or consciousness or soul in general which performs these operations is a myth...Concrete habits do all the perceiving, recognizing, imagining, recalling, judging, conceiving and reasoning that is done" (MW14:123–124). And they also do the work of inhibiting other habits. It is therefore wrong, Dewey argued, to oppose habit to reason and conscious control. The real opposition is between "routine," unintelligent habit and "intelligent or artistic habit" that "is fused with thought and feeling," between blind, fixed habit and "flexible, sensitive habit" (MW14:51–52). The art of somatic reflection and conscious control is thus itself a refined, intelligent habit emerging from and coordinating a background of countless other habits that constitute the developing bundle of "complex, unstable, opposing attitudes, habits, impulses" we call the self. "There is no one ready-made self behind [a person's] activities," and no single self-consciousness that can monitor them all (MW14:96).

[29] See John Dewey, "Qualitative Thought," in LW5:243–262; and *Logic: The Theory of Inquiry,* LW12:73–76. For critical discussion of his arguments that such qualitative immediate feeling provides the underlying unity necessary for the coherence of *all* our thinking, see my *Practicing Philosophy* (New York: Routledge, 1997), 162–166.

I have this book

It is disappointing that Dewey did not challenge the ideal of total transparency and conscious control in his discussions of Alexander's work. His celebration of Alexander's theory of "primary control" and its identification with Magnus's *Zentralapparat* is likewise unfortunate. "This discovery . . . of a central control which conditions all other reactions," Dewey rejoices, "brings the conditioning factor under conscious direction and enables the individual through his own coordinated activities to take possession of his own potentialities" (LW6:319). But the central control of Magnus was not at all a matter of "conscious direction" or "the consummated conquest . . . [of] the art of conscious control" (MW11:352); it was an instinctive, unconscious mechanism deployed even by animals suffering from substantial brain damage, so long as the key area in their brain stem was functionally intact.

More troubling than its differences from Magnus are the inherent limitations in Alexander's idea of primary control, an insight marred by overstatement. Though the posture of the head and neck is extremely important for our sensorimotor functioning, it is far from clear that the particular "primary direction" advocated by Alexander as the essential primary control – that is, keeping the head forward and up – is always the most indispensable, primal, and dominant factor for effecting all our movements. In many positions of untroubled rest, there is obviously no need to hold the head forward and up to achieve the regularity of our movements of breathing, and still more obviously no need for conscious control of this position. Even in consciously willed movements, such as rolling oneself over in bed, the postural orientation of the pelvis (or other body parts) can be equally or more important than holding the head forward and up; indeed for some movements (like swallowing), pulling the head back can be more advantageous.

I am not here contesting the primal importance of the head and neck area for proper posture and sensorimotor functioning. This area houses not only the brain, the organs of vision, hearing, taste, and the vestibular system of the inner ear (that provides for stability of posture and gaze) but also the first two cervical vertebrae (the atlas and axis), whose articulations and attached ligaments and muscles are what enable us to raise, lower, and rotate the head, thus affording greater scope for the sensory organs of our eyes, ears, nose, and mouth. Alexander's insistence on keeping the head forward and up is brilliantly insightful for postures and movements concerned with holding ourselves erect and balanced, in which sensory mechanisms in the head and neck are of crucial importance. But other parts of the body's nervous system – notably receptors of touch on the skin – also play a significant role in such matters of balance and body orientation, as recent neurophysiological experiments have shown. "Haptic information from hand contact can have a profoundly stabilizing effect on body posture," even overriding or correcting deficiencies in the vestibular and visual nervous system that would otherwise cause one to fall.[30] Sensory cutaneous input from the foot's plantar region and pro-prioceptive input from the ankle also have been shown to guide posture, so that stimulation of these areas can create whole-body tilts.[31]

In short, rather than absolute reliance on one central position of head and neck, human mastery of upright postural control relies on "the integration of multisensory information" from a variety of body areas.[32] This not only provides some redundancy of postural information that enables an individual to function when one sensory channel is blocked or impaired. The complex combination of partially overlapping sensory inputs with respect to posture also allows for more comparative feedback on body orientation and hence a more accurate, fine-tuned system for postural control. Somatic philosophy and reconstructive therapy should respect such pluralism.

One practical corollary is that somatic consciousness must not always be narrowly or primarily focused on Alexander's primary control. We should instead direct it to whatever bodily parts and postures require attention in order to achieve functional adjustment. This, I think, is why body scans are particularly useful. Working on the primary control of keeping the head forward and up will not automatically release a rigid rib cage or a frozen pelvis or increase the flexibility of stiff ankles and chronically contracted toes. Conversely, working on these other areas can often be good preliminaries for making adjustments to head and neck posture. As I know from my Feldenkrais practice, if the head and neck

---

[30] See J. R. Lackner and Paul A. DiZio, "Aspects of Body Self-Calibration," *Trends in Cognitive Science*, 4 (2000): 279–288, quotation, 282. Lackner and his colleagues also showed the contribution of tactile sensations of other body parts in bodily orientation. Their "rotisserie" experiments demonstrated that when subjects were deprived of ordinary visual and vestibular clues by being rotated horizontally on a machine in the dark, the pressure of touch to different body parts created very different senses of bodily orientation. For example, pressure on the buttocks induced the sensation of sitting and spinning, pressure to the feet of tipping up and rotating vertically. See also Berthoz, *The Brain's Sense of Movement*, 106, who notes how the postural righting reflex of animals can be inhibited by pressure to its flank.

[31] See A. Kavounoudias, R. Roll, and J.-P. Roll, "Foot Sole and Ankle Muscle Inputs Contribute Jointly to Human Erect Posture Regulation," *Journal of Physiology*, 532.3 (2001), 869–878.

[32] Ibid., 870.

area of a given individual is already associated with pain, stress, and rigidity because of its history of misuse, injury, and hypertension, then an immediate focus of intense attention or manipulation there is likely only to heighten that person's tension, anxiety, or pain. This would undermine our therapeutic and educational aims of releasing the problematic tension and bringing clearer awareness of what such relaxation feels like and how it can be induced. In such cases, it is more prudent to begin by directing somatic attention to less-sensitive areas of the body, where the individual being treated can experiment (in a zone of greater comfort) with the adjustments and sensations of relaxation and flexibility. Once these methods and feelings become familiar, they then can be more easily extended to the more problematic head and neck area.

The living, moving body constitutes a multifaceted, complexly integrated, dynamic field rather than a simple, static, linear system. Though some body parts are more basic or essential than others in motor control, somaesthetic attention should not be confined to a single body region or relationship defined as the "primary control." It requires the pragmatic pluralism that James most strongly stressed and that Dewey generally advocates.

The Alexander Technique is especially focused on upright posture, and Dewey shares an appreciation of its crucial importance.[33] There is no contesting that this posture has essentially shaped human experience and even modified our anatomy. Our ability to stand not only frees the hands to explore objects haptically, to carry and manipulate things, to gesture, and to develop tools. It also greatly extends our range of vision, whose increased distance perception provides for foresight and thus promotes planning and reflection. By liberating us from total absorption in what is of immediate concrete contact, it further provides the possibility for abstraction, symbolization, and inference. Moreover, by making us less dependent on the sense of smell and on carrying with the mouth, erect posture enabled humans to develop facial structures and muscles that are more capable of articulate speech, which in turn tremendously enhanced

---

[33] Besides his engagement with Alexander's work on erectness, Dewey was very closely involved with the empirical research of the developmental psychologist Myrtle McGraw concerning children's acquisition of erect locomotion. This relationship is presented in great detail in Dalton, *Becoming John Dewey*, chs. 9 and 10, who claims that Dewey regarded "the mastery of erect locomotion" as what "gave birth to inquiry" by providing the primal neurological resources for developing consciousness, reconstructive, equilibrium-oriented problem solving, and also providing "stride and pace [which] furnished rudimentary methods of measurement" (200, 208).

our capacities of thought and behavior. If being upright helped generate human language and rationality that mark our evolutionary advantage over lower animals, it also seems linked to our ethical transcendence that is enabled by thought and language.

The idea of physical, cognitive, and moral improvements through superior posture and self-use constitutes the core of Alexander's vision. Erectness and elevation are also key features of his practical technique.[34] His "primary control" of keeping the head "forward and up" (MSI, 284; CCC, 180) is thus emblematic of his avid commitment to humanity's continuing evolutionary progress: *up* from the lowly, impulsive, unthinking animal existence of our origins and *forward* to ever-increasing transcendence toward perfection through rational inhibition and conscious control. His radically rationalist ideal rejects any reliance on emotions or spontaneous feelings for guiding behavior. Activities that stimulate emotional excitement are therefore condemned as cognitive and moral dangers, even when such activities include the fine arts. Branding the arts of "dancing and drawing . . . as the two D's, . . . two forms of damnation when employed as fundamentals in education," he also cautions against music's emotional excitement whose "overexaltation of the whole kinaesthetic system" tends to undermine the control of the reasoning faculties (MSI, 124–125).

Though granting these artistic "artificial stimuli may be permissible" for moderate use by "the reasoning, trained adult," Alexander contends they are far too dangerous for educating children, since they speak most powerfully to the most primitive, savage parts of us. "Now music and dancing are, as every one knows, excitements which make a stronger emotional

---

[34] In contrast to comparable somatic disciplines such as Feldenkrais Method and Bioenergetics, the Alexander Technique concentrates on exercises of ascent and positions of verticality. Though many Alexander practitioners today work on people by having them lie on a table (a position that usefully avoids certain problems of ordinary gravitational pressure and accustomed habits of posture, movement, and thought), purist versions of the Technique eschew the use of prone positions, which were shunned by F. M. Alexander and his brother A.R. For they thought such positions were not very conducive to heightened awareness, control, and rationality, instead suggesting the unconscious surrender of hypnosis and psychoanalysis. In Alexander's somatics of verticality and ascent, a cardinal sin is "pulling down," and the Technique's signature exercise is to have the pupil effortlessly raise herself to standing from an erect sitting position in a chair by concentrating her consciousness on the somatic "means whereby." When performed correctly, this exercise (sometimes described as having "thought [one's] way out of the chair") gives a sense of effortlessly transcending the lowering forces of gravity by exercising the rational, elevating powers of mind. See Jones, *Body Awareness in Action*, 6–8, 71, 76; and my comparative analysis of the Alexander, Feldenkrais, and Bioenergetic methods in *Performing Live* (Ithaca, NY: Cornell University Press, 2000), ch. 8.

appeal to the primitive than to the more highly evolved races. No drunken man in our civilisation ever reaches the stage of anaesthesia and complete loss of self-control attained by the savage under the influence of these two stimuli" (ibid.).[35] If these remarks sound like lofty rationalism masking a repressive, irrational racism, Alexander is also ready to lift the mask and more explicitly assert: "The controlling and guiding forces in savage four-footed animals and in the savage black races are practically the same;...the mental progress of these races has not kept pace with their physical evolution." Such preposterous claims are offered as evidence that evolutionary progress in mental, social, and cultural matters cannot be achieved if we simply rely on "subconscious guidance and control" (MSI, 72).

Here again Dewey disappointingly fails to distance himself from Alexander's excessive claims.[36] In his introduction to the book that contains these claims Dewey basically affirms Alexander's educational critique that free emotional self-expression is a danger as damaging as the rigid "inculcation of fixed rules" (MSI, 144). What education instead requires, Dewey concludes, is neither repressive "control by external authority" nor "control by emotional gusts," but instead "control by intelligence" (MW11:352), a more subtle, supple version of Alexander's idea of control "dictated by reason" (MSI, 135–136). Those "interested in educational reform," Dewey insists, should "remember that freedom of physical action and free expression of emotion are means, not ends, and that as means they are justified only in so far as they are used as conditions for developing power of intelligence" (MW11:352).[37]

[35] Alexander later claims, "The lower the stage of evolution, within certain limits, the greater the appeal of music and dancing"(MSI, 165).

[36] Dewey clearly did not share Alexander's radical racism. His political engagement as one of the founders of the National Association for the Advancement of Colored People in 1909, showed an admirable commitment to African Americans. But he did not give race much philosophical attention, apart from an essay "Racial Prejudice and Friction" (MW13:242–254). Some of Dewey's writings display a sharp division between the mind of civilized and "savage peoples" that today might be regarded as racist, even though he attributed the difference not to native gifts but to the "backward institutions" of so-called savage society (MW9:41). A case for aspects of racism in Dewey is brought by Shannon Sullivan, "Re(construction) Zone," in *Dewey's Wake: Unfinished Work of Pragmatic Reconstruction*" ed. William Gavin (Albany: SUNY Press, 2003), 109–127.

[37] Perhaps motives of friendship and gratitude swayed Dewey from criticizing Alexander's one-sided emphasis on inhibitive, reflective, rational body consciousness, but it would anyway have resonated strongly with Dewey's personal tendency to strictly control his passions. It is noteworthy that Dewey wrote this particular critique of freely expressed "physical action" and "emotional gusts" at the very time he was struggling to keep in

Whether or not these Deweyan claims support Alexander's objections to dance and music as free emotional self-expression, they certainly suggest a disturbingly sharp (un-Deweyan) contrast between means and ends that subordinates physical action and emotion as *mere means* justifiable only by their subservience to more rational ends of developing greater intelligence. No wonder Deweyan pragmatism was often attacked (most notably by Randolph Bourne and Lewis Mumford) for being too instrumentally rationalistic and unfriendly to art's imaginative emotional expression. This critique eventually spurred Dewey to respond with his masterpiece *Art as Experience*, in which he insists that the mere fact that something serves as means does not entail that it cannot be enjoyed as an end. The same meal that functions as a means of nourishment, the same poem that aims to evoke love or patriotism, can also be appreciated as an end of aesthetic enjoyment. Emotional expression and unimpeded action can likewise be enjoyed and valued for their own sake and not merely as means to develop intelligence, though any such valuation must always face the test of future consequences to determine whether its values are lastingly valuable and not just fleetingly valued.

Fortunately, Dewey elsewhere affirms that the flourishing of conduct *and* thought requires the multiple resources of spontaneous feelings and unreflective habits, not just reflective conscious control. Our unthinking instincts, feelings, and habits cannot, on the whole, be unserviceable for coping with our needs and environment, because they are largely products of those demands and conditions, whether deriving from genetically generated tendencies honed by evolutionary selection or through unreflectively acquired habit based on the experience of our environment. Since habits incorporate our environments they cannot be radically out of touch with them. But, as Alexander astutely argues, in today's increasingly complex and quickly changing world, environments are altered (or simply switched through travel) at rates far too rapid for effective unreflective readjustment of habit. Moreover, since different environments

check his own passionate bodily desires for the young Polish writer Anzia Yezierska, who sought and courted him, inspiring an outburst of poetry wherein he sadly described himself as a "choked up fountain." See the poem "Two Weeks" in *The Poems of John Dewey*, ed. Jo Ann Boydston (Carbondale: Southern Illinois University Press, 1977), 16. Elsewhere in this poem about his relationship with Yezierska, Dewey expresses his bodily desire and its repression by his "cold heart" and "clear head": "I see your body's breathing/The curving of your breast/And hear the warm thoughts seething./ . . . While I am within this wonder/I am overcome as by thunder/Of my blood that surges/ . . . Renounce, renounce;/The horizon is too far to reach./All things must be given up./Driest the lips, when most full the cup" (15–16).

breed different and often conflicting habits, conscious control through somatic reflection will sometimes be necessary to adjust and coordinate these conflicts. Finally, the natural fit of human habits, feelings, and environment is only a rough and general one. In most individuals, there are habits and associated feelings (especially those formed through environments, tasks, and experiences that are stressful and problematic) that involve disharmonies, distortions, and maladjustments and that consistently hinder performance and impair our self-use, corrupting even our perceptual faculties so that "sensory appreciation is confused, perverted and falsified" (LW1:228) or (as Alexander puts it) "debauched" (MSI, 22).

Here then is the core practical dilemma of body consciousness: We must rely on unreflective feelings and habits – because we can't reflect on everything and because such unreflective feelings and habits always ground our very efforts of reflection. But we also cannot entirely rely on them and the judgments they generate, because some of them are considerably flawed and inaccurate. Moreover, how can we discern their flaws and inadequacy when they are concealed by their unreflective, immediate, habitual status; and how can we correct them when our conscious, reflective efforts of correction spontaneously rely on the same inaccurate, habitual mechanisms of perception and action that we are trying to correct?

V

Provisional Conclusions

There is no apparent answer that neatly resolves these issues, nor an honest and elegant way to sidestep them, so we must resort to pragmatic and piecemeal strategies. The most sensible practical attitude toward our habits and sensory feelings is (to borrow an old Hebrew maxim) "respect and suspect." We rely on them until they prove problematic in experience – whether through failures in performance, errors in judgment, feelings of confusion, physical discomfort and pain, or through the dialogical experience of hearing from others that one is doing something awkward, peculiar, or detrimental. At that point, we should examine more closely our unreflective behavior. But to discern exactly which habits are misguiding us, which precise dimension of a habit needs correction, and which sort of correction is called for requires rigorous practical work in critical somaesthetic self-consciousness. In such work, established disciplines of systematic somatic reflection are most helpful.

Every method has its limitations, so given the diversity of human needs, problems, aims, contexts, and temperaments, it would be foolish to advocate one method as always superior or always helpful. Our toolbox of somatic disciplines must be pluralistic. Trained teachers of these methods clearly play an indispensable role, because, besides their professional skills, they have a critical distance (both literally and figuratively) from the subject's habit that allows them to see it more clearly and recognize alternative ways of performing the same bodily act. Though Alexander displayed his singular genius in teaching himself, even he required mirrors. To learn improved self-use typically requires the help of others.

There is also a larger lesson to be learned here – the self's essential dependence on environmental others. Alexander's perfectionist rhetoric about "*Man's Supreme Inheritance*" of "reasoning intelligence" suggests an extremely proud and narrow individualism fueled by a haughtily hubristic humanist faith. The advocacy of conscious control of the self to achieve total mastery of every bodily function so as to "rise above the powers of all disease and physical disabilities" and ensure not only "physical perfection" but also "the complete control of our own potentialities" implies that the individual's "reasoning, deliberate consciousness" can establish itself as the all-powerful, fully autonomous, self-sufficient master of body, mind, and behavior (MSI, x, 11, 236). Concomitant with celebrating the individual's autonomous power there is blame for the individual who fails to realize this potential of "perfect health, physical and mental": that person "should realise the responsibility is his and his alone. He must be made aware that such defects arise from his own fault, and are the outcome of his ignorance or wilful neglect" (MSI, 155, 188).[38]

Despite our evolutionary progress of rational transcendence (including the technological advancements that some regard as rendering us posthuman cyborgs), we still essentially and dependently belong to a much wider natural and social world that continues to shape the individuals we are (including our reasoning consciousness) in ways beyond the control of our will and consciousness. As oxygen is necessary for the functioning of consciousness in the brain, so the practices, norms, and language of society are necessary materials for our processes of reasoning

---

[38] Alexander later reaffirms this point: "I am prepared to prove that the majority of physical defects have come about by the action of the patient's own will operating under the influence of erroneous preconceived ideas and consequent delusions, exercised consciously or more often subconsciously, and that these conditions can be changed by that same will directed by a right conception implanted by the teacher" (MSI, 216).

and evaluation. It is not moral perfectionism but blind arrogance to think otherwise.

Although touting Alexander's discovery as the "central control which conditions all other reactions . . . and enables the individual through his own coordinated activities to take possession of his own potentialities" (LW6:319), Dewey's humanism is generally far removed from Alexander's individualist hubris. Indeed Dewey highlights the individual's fundamental dependence on larger environmental factors by defining the self in terms of habits and by insisting that habits must engage and assimilate the environments in which they function, particularly those environmental elements that support or enable their functioning (what J. J. Gibson terms "affordances"). If the self's action, will, and thinking are governed by habit, and if habits necessarily incorporate environmental elements, then the self essentially relies on such environmental elements.

The upshot for somatic philosophy is that one's body (like one's mind) incorporates its surroundings, going, for example, beyond the conventional body boundary of the epidermis to satisfy its most essential needs of breathing and nutrition. Our bodies (like our thoughts) are thus paradoxically always more and less than our own. As Dewey pithily puts it, we "live . . . as much in processes across and 'through' skins as in processes 'within' skins" (LW16:119). The semipermeable boundary of our skin is a natural somatic symbol for the merely semiautonomous status of our selfhood. Being constituted by its environmental relations, the self is ultimately defined by Dewey as "transactional." He prefered this term to "interactional," which he thought implied greater separation and independence (see LW16:112–115).[39] Though such terms as "transactional self" and "transactional body" suffer from unseemly mercantile associations (reinforcing lamentable stereotypes of pragmatism as avidly commercialist), they do convey the sense of a dynamic, symbiotic individual that is essentially engaging with and relating to others and is in turn essentially reliant on and constituted by such relations.

This vision of the symbiotic body should inspire greater appreciation for the environmental others (human and nonhuman) that help define

---

[39] Dewey explains his transactional perspective on man as treating "all of his behavings, including his most advanced knowings, as activities not of himself alone, nor even as primarily his, but as processes of the full situation of organism-environnment" (LW16:97). Shannon Sullivan deftly deploys Dewey's transactional notion with special attention to feminist issues in her *Living Across and Through Skins: Transactional Bodies, Pragmatism, and Feminism* (Bloomington: University of Indiana Press, 2001), which also includes a chapter on somaesthetics from a feminist, "transactional" perspective.

and sustain it. There are also corollaries for somatic self-consciousness. Reflective awareness of our bodies can never stop at the skin; we cannot feel the body alone, apart from its environmental context. So in developing increased somatic sensitivity for greater somatic control, we must develop greater sensitivity to the body's environmental conditions, relations, and ambient energies. In our bodily actions, we are not self-sufficient agents but stewards and impresarios of larger powers that we organize to perform our tasks. As Emerson wisely observed, "we do few things by muscular force, but we place ourselves in such attitudes as to bring the force of gravity, that is, the weight of the planet, to bear upon the spade or the axe we wield. In short, . . . we seek not to use our own, but to bring a quite infinite force to bear."[40]

Emerson's point, though eminently American and pragmatic in its attention to the indispensable value of means and natural instrumentalities, also expresses a crucial insight of the Asian philosophical traditions that so deeply inspired his spiritual sensibility. The relational self acquires and deploys its powers only through its enabling relations; in the terms of classical Chinese thought, the exemplary individual's virtue, or *ren* (often translated as "humanity"), depends on his recognition, integration, and practice of the wider encompassing Dao.

This relational symbiotic notion of the self inspires a more extensive notion of somatic meliorism in which we are also charged with caring for and harmonizing the environmental affordances of our embodied selves, not just our own body parts. Such a cosmic model of somatic self-cultivation is expressed in the Confucian ideal of forming one body "with Heaven and Earth and all things." As the great neo-Confucians Cheng Hao and Wang Yangming affirm: "The man of humanity [*ren*] regards Heaven and Earth and all things as one body. If a single thing is deprived of its place, it means that my humanity is not yet demonstrated

---

[40] Emerson, "Art," in *Society and Solitude* (New York: Houghton Mifflin, 1904), 42. See also his "Civilization," in ibid., 27: "You have seen a carpenter on a ladder with a broad-axe chopping upward chips from a beam. How awkward! at what disadvantage he works! But see him on the ground, dressing his timber under him. Now, not his feeble muscles but the force of gravity brings down the axe; that is to say, the planet itself splits his stick." Emerson typically emphasizes the natural cosmic forces, like gravity, that bring to genius a power beyond "our own" personal force. But we should also include the powers of society and cultural tradition as part of the more-than-personal "infinite force" that comes together to galvanize and transfigure a mere individual into a genius. For more on this topic, see my "Genius and the Paradox of Self-Styling," in *Performing Live*, ch. 10.

to the fullest extent."[41] From its very outset, the Confucian direction of self-perfection toward virtue and finally to sagehood aimed at "the unity of man and Heaven or Nature" as its highest ideal, pursuing this quest to "form a trinity with Heaven and Earth" through the indispensable medium of the body – a natural, heavenly gift whose full realization requires the virtuous wisdom of the sage. As Mencius says, "The functions of the body are the endowment of Heaven. But it is only a Sage who can properly manipulate them."[42]

By enabling us to feel more of our universe with greater acuity, awareness, and appreciation, such a vision of somaesthetic cultivation promises the richest and deepest palate of experiential fulfillments because it can draw on the profusion of cosmic resources, including an uplifting sense of cosmic unity. Enchanting intensities of experience can thus be achieved in everyday living without requiring violent measures of sensory intensification that threaten ourselves and others. And if we still prefer more dangerous psychosomatic experiments of extreme intensity, our somaesthetically cultivated sensory awareness should render us more alert to the imminent risks and also more skilled in avoiding or diminishing the damage.

[41] See Wang Yangming, "Instructions for Practical Living," in *A Source Book in Chinese Philosophy* ed. and trans. Wing-tsit Chan (Princeton, NJ: Princeton University Press, 1963), 675 (where he also explicitly cites Cheng Hao on this point), 685, 690; and Cheng Hao himself in Chan, 530.
[42] See *The Doctrine of the Mean*, in Chan, *A Source Book in Chinese Philosophy*, 108; and W. A. C. H. Dobson, *Mencius* (Toronto: University of Toronto Press, 1963), 144.

Select Bibliography

Abrams, J. J. "Pragmatism, Artificial Intelligence, and Posthuman Bioethics: Shusterman, Rorty, Foucault." *Human Studies*, 27 (2004): 241–258.

Alexander, F. M. *Constructive Conscious Control of the Individual*. New York: Dutton, 1923.

——. *Man's Supreme Inheritance*. New York: Dutton, 1918.

——. *The Universal Constant in Living*. New York: Dutton, 1941.

——. *The Use of the Self*. New York: Dutton, 1932.

Ames, R. T., and Henry Rosemont, Jr. (translators). *The Analects of Confucius: A Philosophical Translation*. New York: Ballantine, 1998.

Ascher, Carol. *Simon de Beauvoir: A Life of Freedom*. Boston: Beacon, 1981.

Bair, Deirdre. *Simone de Beauvoir: A Biography*. New York: Summit, 1990.

Barlow, Wilfred. *The Alexander Technique: How to Use Your Body Without Stress*. New York: Knopf, 1973. Second edition, Rochester, VT: Healing Arts Press, 1990.

Bataille, Georges. *Eroticism*. Translated by Mary Dalwood. London: Penguin, 2001.

Baudelaire, Charles. *The Painter of Modern Life and Other Essays*. Translated by Jonathan Mayne. London: Phaidon, 1964.

Beauvoir, Simone de. *All Said and Done*. Translated by Patrick O'Brian. London: Penguin, 1977.

——. *Brigitte Bardot and the Lolita Syndrome*. Translated by Bernard Frechtman. New York: Arno Press, 1972.

——. *Force of Circumstance*. Translated by Richard Howard. London: Penguin, 1968.

——. *La Vieillesse*. Paris: Gallimard, 1970. Translation: *The Coming of Age*. Translated by Patrick O'Brien. New York: Putnam, 1972.

——. *Le deuxième sexe*. 2 vols. Paris: Gallimard, 1949. Translation: *The Second Sex*. Translated by H. M. Parshley. New York: Vintage, 1989.

——. *Memoirs of a Dutiful Daughter*. Translated by James Kirkup. New York: Harper, 1974.

——. *Must We Burn de Sade*. Translated by Annette Michelson. London: Peter Nevill, 1953.

——. *The Ethics of Ambiguity*. Translated by Bernard Frechtman. New York: Citadel Press, 1964.

——. *The Prime of Life*. Translated by Peter Green. London: Penguin, 1965.

P 93 — ——— 217 ———
Brigitte Bardot and the Lolita
Syndrome 1972 ——

Beere, P. A., et al. "Aerobic Exercise Training Can Reverse Age-Related Peripheral Circulatory Changes in Healthy Older Men." *Circulation*, 100.10 (1999): 1085–1094.

Bergoffen, Deborah. *The Philosophy of Simone de Beauvoir: Gendered Phenomenologies, Erotic Generosities*. Albany: SUNY Press, 1997.

Berthoz, Alain. *The Brain's Sense of Movement*. Translated by Giselle Weiss. Cambridge, MA: Harvard University Press, 2000.

Böhme, Gernot. "Somästhetik – sanft oder mit Gewalt?" *Deutsche Zeitschrift für Philosophie*, 50 (2002): 797–800.

Bordo, Susan. *Unbearable Weight: Feminism, Western Culture, and the Body*. Berkeley: University of California Press, 1993.

Bourdieu, Pierre. *The Logic of Practice*. Translated by Richard Nice. Cambridge: Polity Press, 1990.

———. *Pascalian Meditations*. Translated by Richard Nice. Stanford, CA: Stanford University Press, 2000.

Brown, Peter. *The Body and Society: Men, Women, and Sexual Renunciation in Early Christianity*. New York: Columbia University Press, 1988.

Butler, Judith. *Gender Trouble: Feminism and the Subversion of Identity*. New York: Routledge, 1990.

———. "Sexual Ideology and Phenomenological Description: A Feminist Critique of Merleau-Ponty's Phenomenology of Perception." In *The Thinking Muse: Feminism and Modern French Philosophy*. Edited by Jeffner Allen and Iris Marion Young. Bloomington: Indiana University Press, 1989.

Carrette, Jeremy. *Foucault and Religion: Spiritual Corporality and Political Spirituality*. London: Routledge, 2000.

Chan, Wing-tsit (translator). "The Doctrine of the Mean." In *A Source Book in Chinese Philosophy*. Edited by Wing-tsit Chan. Princeton, NJ: Princeton University Press, 1963.

———. "The Great Learning (Ta-Hsueh)." In *A Sourcebook in Chinese Philosophy*. Edited by Wing-tsit Chan. Princeton, NJ: Princeton University Press, 1963.

Cole, Jonathan, and Barbara Montero. "Affective Proprioception." *Janus-Head*, 9 (2007): 299–317.

Cranz, Galen. *The Chair: Rethinking Culture, Body, and Design*. New York: Norton, 2000.

Dalton, Thomas C. *Becoming John Dewey*. Bloomington: Indiana University Press, 2002.

Damasio, Antonio. *Descartes' Error: Emotion, Reason, and the Human Brain*. New York: Avon, 1994.

Davidson, Richard J., et al. "Alterations in Brain and Immune Function Produced by Mindfulness Meditation." *Psychosomatic Medicine*, 65 (2003): 564–570.

———. "Well-Being and Affective Style: Neural Substrates and Biobehavioural Correlates." *Philosophical Transactions of the Royal Society*, Series B, 359 (2004): 1395–1411.

Dennett, Daniel. *Consciousness Explained*. Boston: Little, Brown, 1991.

Descartes, René. *The Philosophical Writings of Descartes*. 2 vols. Translated by J. Cottingham, R. Stoothoof, and D. Murdoch. Cambridge: Cambridge University Press, 1984–1985.

Dewey, Jane. "Biography of John Dewey." In *The Philosophy of John Dewey.* Edited by P. Schilpp and L. Hahn. LaSalle, IL: Open Court, 1989.

Dewey, John. *John Dewey: The Early Works: 1882–1898.* Edited by Jo Ann Boydston. 5 vols. Carbondale: Southern Illinois University Press, 1969–1972.

———. *John Dewey: The Middle Works: 1899–1924.* Edited by Jo Ann Boydston. 15 vols. Carbondale: Southern Illinois University Press, 1976–1983.

———. *John Dewey: The Later Works: 1925–1953.* Edited by Jo Ann Boydston. 17 vols. Carbondale: Southern Illinois University Press, 1981–1990.

———. *The Poems of John Dewey.* Edited by Jo Ann Boydston. Carbondale: Southern Illinois University Press, 1977.

Diogenes Laertius. *Lives of Eminent Philosophers.* 2 vols. Translated by R. D. Hicks. Cambridge, MA: Harvard University Press, 1991.

Dobson, W. A. C. H. *Mencius.* Toronto: University of Toronto Press, 1963.

Dōgen, Zenji. *Dōgen's Manuals of Zen Meditation.* Translated by Carl Bielefeldt. Berkeley: University of California Press, 1988.

Donne, John. *John Donne: The Complete English Poems.* Edited by A. J. Smith. London: Penguin, 1971.

Eliot, T. S. *To Criticize the Critic.* London: Faber, 1978.

Emerson, Ralph Waldo. "Art." From *Essays: First Series* (1847). In *Ralph Waldo Emerson.* Edited by Richard Poirier. Oxford: Oxford University Press, 1990.

———. "Art." In *Society and Solitude* (1870). New York: Houghton Mifflin, 1904.

———. "Civilization." In *Society and Solitude* (1870). New York: Houghton Mifflin, 1904.

Eribon, Didier. *Michel Foucault.* Cambridge, MA: Harvard University Press, 1991.

Feldenkrais, Moshe. *Awareness Through Movement.* New York: Harper and Row, 1977.

———. *Body and Mature Behavior: A Study of Anxiety, Sex, Gravitation, and Learning.* London: Routledge and Kegan Paul, 1949.

———. *The Case of Nora: Body Awareness as Healing Therapy.* New York: Harper & Row, 1977.

———. *The Potent Self.* New York: HarperCollins, 1992.

Foucault, Michel. *Dits et Ecrits.* Edited by D. Defert and F. Ewald. 2 vols. Paris: Gallimard, 2001.

———. *Discipline and Punish.* Translated by Alan Sheridan. New York: Vintage, 1979.

———. *Foucault Live: Collected Interviews.* Edited by Sylvère Lotringer. New York: Semiotext(e), 1996.

———. *History of Sexuality.* 3 vols. Translated by Robert Hurley. New York: Vintage, 1980–1988.

———. "Introduction." In *Herculine Barbin: Being the Recently Discovered Memoirs of a Nineteenth Century Hermaphrodite.* Translated by Richard McDougall. New York: Pantheon, 1980.

———. "On the Genealogy of Ethics: An Overview of Work in Progress." In *Michel Foucault: Beyond Structuralism and Hermeneutics.* Edited by Hubert Dreyfus and Paul Rabinow. Chicago: University of Chicago Press, 1983.

———. "Technologies of the Self." In *The Essential Works of Michel Foucault, 1954–1984.* Edited by Paul Rabinow. Vol. 1. New York: New Press, 1997.

———. "What Is Enlightenment?" In *The Essential Works of Michel Foucault, 1954–1984*. Edited by Paul Rabinow. Vol. 1. New York: New Press, 1997.

Francis, Claude, and Fernande Gontier. *Simone de Beauvoir: A Life, a Love Story.* Translated by Lisa Nesselson. New York: St. Martin's Press, 1985.

Gallagher, Shaun. *How the Body Shapes the Mind.* Oxford: Oxford University Press, 2005.

Guerra, Gustavo. "Practicing Pragmatism: Richard Shusterman's Unbound Philosophy." *Journal of Aesthetic Education,* 36 (2002): 70–83.

Hadot, Pierre. *Philosophy as a Way of Life.* Edited by Arnold Davidson. Oxford: Blackwell, 1995.

Haskins, Casey. "Enlivened Bodies, Authenticity, and Romanticism." *Journal of Aesthetic Education,* 36 (2002), 92–102.

Higgins, Kathleen. "Living and Feeling at Home: Shusterman's *Performing Live.*" *Journal of Aesthetic Education,* 36 (2002): 84–92.

Horkheimer, Max, and Theodor Adorno. *Dialectic of Enlightenment.* Translated by John Cumming. New York: Continuum, 1986.

Husserl, Edmund. *Ideas Pertaining to a Pure Phenomenology and to a Phenomenological Philosophy.* Translated by R. Rojcewicz and A. Schwer. Boston: Kluwer, 1989.

Hwang, E. J., et al. "Dissociable Effects of the Implicit and Explicit Memory Systems on Learning Control of Reaching." *Experimental Brain Research,* 173 (2006): 425–437.

Innis, Robert. *Pragmatism and the Forms of Sense: Language, Perception, Technics.* University Park: Pennsylvania State University Press, 2002.

James, William. "The Absolute and the Strenuous Life." In *The Meaning of Truth,* in *William James: Writings 1902–1910.* Edited by Bruce Kuklick. New York: Viking, 1987.

———. *The Correspondence of William James.* 12 vols. Edited by I. K. Skrupskelis and E. M. Berkeley. Charlottesville: University Press of Virginia, 1992–2004.

———. "The Energies of Men." In *William James: Writings, 1902–1910.* Edited by Bruce Kuklick. New York: Viking, 1987.

———. *Essays in Radical Empiricism.* Cambridge, MA: Harvard University Press, 1976.

———. "The Gospel of Relaxation." In *Talks to Teachers on Psychology and to Students on Some of Life's Ideals.* New York: Dover, 1962.

———. "The Moral Equivalent of War." In *The Writings of William James.* Edited by John McDermott. Chicago: University of Chicago Press, 1977.

———. "The Moral Philosopher and The Moral Life." In *The Writings of William James.* Edited by John McDermott. Chicago: University of Chicago Press, 1977.

———. "On a Certain Blindness in Human Beings." In *Talks to Teachers on Psychology and to Students on Some of Life's Ideals.* New York: Dover, 1962.

———. "The Physical Basis of Emotion." In *Collected Essays and Reviews,* 351. New York: Longmans, 1920.

———. *The Principles of Psychology.* Cambridge, MA: Harvard University Press, 1983.

———. *The Varieties of Religious Experience.* New York: Penguin, 1982.

———. "What Is an Emotion?" *Mind,* 9 (1884): 188–205.

———. "What Makes a Life Significant?" In *Talks to Teachers on Psychology and to Students on Some of Life's Ideals*. New York: Dover, 1962.

———. *The Will to Believe*. Cambridge, MA: Harvard University Press, 1979.

Janiri, L., et al. "Anhedonia and Substance-Related Symptoms in Detoxified Substance-Dependent Subjects: A Correlation Study." *Neuropsychophysiology*, 52 (2005): 37–44.

Jay, Martin. "Somaesthetics and Democracy: Dewey and Contemporary Body Art." *Journal of Aesthetic Education*, 36 (2002), 55–69. Reprinted in his *Refractions of Violence*. New York: Routledge, 2003.

Jeanson, Francis. *Simone de Beauvoir ou l'enterprise de vivre*. Paris: Seuil, 1966.

Johnson, Mark. *The Body in the Mind: The Bodily Basis of Meaning, Imagination, and Reason*. Chicago: University of Chicago Press, 1987.

Jones, Frank. *Body Awareness in Action: A Study of the Alexander Technique*. New York: Schocken, 1976.

Kabat-Zinn, J., et al. "Effectiveness of a Meditation-Based Stress Reduction Program in the Treatment of Anxiety Disorders." *American Journal of Psychiatry*, 149 (1992): 936–943.

———. "The Relationship of Cognitive and Somatic Components of Anxiety to Patient Preference for Alternative Relaxation Techniques." *Mind/Body Medicine*, 2 (1997): 101–109.

Kamel, G. W. Levi. "The Leather Career: On Becoming a Sadomasochist." In *S&M: Studies in Dominance and Submission*. Edited by Thomas S. Weinberg. Amherst, NY: Prometheus Books, 1995.

———. "Leathersex: Meaningful Aspects of Gay Sadomasochism." In *S&M: Studies in Dominance and Submission*. Edited by Thomas S. Weinberg. Amherst, NY: Prometheus Books, 1996.

Kant, Immanuel. *Anthropology from a Pragmatic Point of View*. Translated by Victor Dowdell. Carbondale: Southern Illinois University Press, 1996.

———. *The Conflict of the Faculties*. Translated by Mary J. Gregor. Lincoln: University of Nebraska Press, 1992.

———. *Reflexionen zur Kritischen Philosophie*. Edited by Benno Erdmann. Stuttgart: Frommann-Holzboog, 1992.

Kavounoudias, A., R. Roll, and J.-P. Roll. "Foot Sole and Ankle Muscle Inputs Contribute Jointly to Human Erect Posture Regulation." *Journal of Physiology*, 532.3 (2001): 869–878.

Knoblock, John. *Xunzi: A Translation and Study of the Complete Works*. 3 vols. Stanford: Stanford University Press, 1988–1994.

Krüger, Hans-Peter. *Zwischen Lachen und Weinen*. 2 vols. Berlin: Akademie Verlag, 1999–2001.

Lackner, J. R., and Paul A. DiZio. "Aspects of Body Self-Calibration." *Trends in Cognitive Science*, 4 (2000): 279–282.

Lakoff, George, and Mark Johnson. *Philosophy in the Flesh: The Embodied Mind and Its Challenge to Western Thought*. New York: Basic Books, 1999.

Lau, D. C. *Tao Te Ching*. London: Penguin, 1963.

Leddy, Thomas. "Shusterman's *Pragmatist Aesthetics*." *Journal of Speculative Philosophy*, 16 (2002): 10–16.

Libet, Benjamin. "Unconscious Cerebral Initiative and the Role of Conscious Will in Voluntary Action." *Behavioral and Brain Sciences*, 8 (1985): 529–566.

———. "Do We have Free Will?" *Journal of Consciousness Studies*, 6.8–9 (1999): 47–57.

Lutz, Tom. *American Nervousness – 1903*. Ithaca, NY: Cornell University Press, 1991.

Magnus, Rudolph. *Body Posture [Körperstellung]: Experimental-Physiological Investigations of the Reflexes Involved in Body Posture, Their Cooperation and Disturbances*. Translated by William R. Rosanoff and edited by A. van Harreveld. Springfield, VA: National Technical Information Service, 1987.

Malcolm, Norman. *Wittgenstein: A Memoir*. Oxford: Oxford University Press, 1958.

Mead, George Herbert. *Mind, Self, and Society*. Chicago: University of Chicago Press, 1962.

Mei, W. P. (translator). *The Ethical and Political Works of Motse*. London: Probsthain, 1929.

Merleau-Ponty, Maurice. *In Praise of Philosophy and Other Essays*. Translated by John Wild, James Edie, and John O'Neill. Evanston, IL: Northwestern University Press, 1970.

———. *Phénoménologie de la perception*. Paris: Gallimard, 1945. Translation: *Phenomenology of Perception*. Translated by Colin Smith. London: Routledge, 1962.

———. *Signs*. Translated by Richard C. McCleary. Evanston, IL: Northwestern University Press, 1964.

———. *The Visible and the Invisible*. Translated by Alphonso Lingis. Evanston, IL: Northwestern University Press, 1968.

Moi, Toril. *Feminist Theory and Simone de Beauvoir*. Oxford: Blackwell, 1990.

———. *Simone de Beauvoir: The Making of an Intellectual Woman*. Oxford: Blackwell, 1994.

Monk, Ray. *Ludwig Wittgenstein: The Duty of Genius*. London: Penguin, 1991.

Montaigne, Michel de. *The Complete Works of Montaigne*. Translated by Donald Frame. Stanford: Stanford University Press, 1965.

Mullis, Eric. "Performative Somaesthetics: Principles and Scope." *Journal of Aesthetic Education*, 40 (2006): 104–117

Myers, Gerald. *William James: His Life and Thought*. New Haven, CT: Yale University Press, 1986.

Nehamas, Alexander. *Nietzsche: Life as Literature*. Cambridge, MA: Harvard University Press, 1985.

———. "Richard Shusterman on Pleasure and Aesthetic Experience." *Journal of Aesthetics and Art Criticism*, 56 (1998): 49–51.

Nietzsche, Friedrich. *The Will to Power*. Translatedd by Walter Kaufmann and R. J. Hollingdale. New York: Vintage, 1967.

Nolen-Hoeksema, Susan. "Responses to Depression and Their Effects on the Duration of Depressive Episodes." *Journal of Abnormal Psychology*, 100 (1991): 569–582.

Nolen-Hoeksema, Susan, and J. Morrow. "Effects of Rumination and Distraction on Naturally Occurring Depressed Mood." *Cognition & Emotion*, 7 (1993): 561–570.

Nussbaum, Martha. *The Therapy of Desire*. Princeton, NJ: Princeton University Press, 1994.

O'Shaughnessy, Brian. "Proprioception and the Body Image." In *The Body and the Self*. Edited by J. L. Bermúdez, A. Marcel, and N. Eilan. Cambridge, MA: MIT Press, 1995.

Pascal, Fania. "Wittgenstein: A Personal Memoir." In *Recollections of Wittgenstein*. Edited by Rush Rhees. Oxford: Oxford University Press, 1984.

Perry, Ralph Barton. *The Thought and Character of William James*. 2 vols. Boston: Little, Brown, 1935.

———. *The Thought and Character of William James*, abridged edition. Nashville, TN: Vanderbilt University Press, 1996.

Plato. *Complete Works*. Edited by John Cooper. Indianapolis, IN: Hackett, 1997.

———. *Timaeus*. Translated by H. D. P. Lee. London: Penguin, 1965.

Porphyry. "On the Life of Plotinus and the Arrangement of His Work." In *Plotinus: The Enneads*. Translated by Stephen MacKenna. London: Penguin, 1991.

Rahula, Walpola (translator). "The Foundations of Mindfulness." In his *What the Buddha Taught*. New York: Grove Press, 1974. Reprinted in *A Sourcebook of Asian Philosophy*. Edited by John Koller and Patricia Koller. Upper Saddle River, NJ: Prentice Hall, 1991.

Reich, Wilhelm. *The Function of the Orgasm*. Translated by Vincent R. Carfagno. New York: Farrar, Straus and Giroux, 1973.

Rimer, J. T., and Y. Masakazu. *On the Art of the Nō Drama: The Major Treatises of Zeami*. Princeton, NJ: Princeton University Press, 1984.

Rochlitz, Rainer. "Les esthétiques hédonistes." *Critique*, 540 (May 1992): 353–373.

Rockefeller, Steven. *John Dewey: Religious Faith and Democratic Humanism*. New York: Columbia University Press, 1991.

Rousseau, Jean-Jacques. *Emile: Or, on Education*. Translated by Allan Bloom. New York: Basic Books, 1979.

Rywerant, Yochanan. *The Feldenkrais Method: Teaching by Handling*. New York: Harper and Row, 1983.

Schiller, Friedrich. *On the Aesthetic Education of Man*. Translated by E. M. Wilkinson and L. A. Willoughby. Oxford: Clarendon, 1982.

Seigfried, Charlene Haddock. "*Second Sex*: Second Thoughts." In *Hypatia Reborn: Essays in Feminist Philosophy*. Edited by Azizah Al-Hibri and Margaret Simons. Bloomington: Indiana University Press, 1984.

Shusterman, Richard. "Aesthetic Experience: From Analysis to Eros." *Journal of Aesthetics and Art Criticism*, 64 (2006): 217–229.

———. "Asian *Ars Erotica* and the Question of Sexual Aesthetics." *Journal of Aesthetics and Art Criticism*, 65 (2007): 55–68.

———. "Entertainment: A Question for Aesthetics." *British Journal of Aesthetics*, 43 (2003): 289–307.

———. "Home Alone? Self and Other in Somaesthetics and *Performing Live*." *Journal of Aesthetic Education*, 36 (2002), 102–115.

———. "Interpretation, Pleasure, and Value in Aesthetic Experience." *Journal of Aesthetics and Art Criticism*, 56 (1998): 51–53.

———. *Performing Live: Aesthetic Alternatives for the Ends of Art.* Ithaca, NY: Cornell University Press, 2000.

———. *Practicing Philosophy: Pragmatism and the Philosophical Life.* New York: Routledge, 1997.

———. "Pragmatism and Criticism: A Response to Three Critics of *Pragmatist Aesthetics*." *Journal of Speculative Philosophy*, 16 (2002): 26–38.

———. "Pragmatism and East-Asian Thought." *The Range of Pragmatism and the Limits of Philosophy.* Edited by Richard Shusterman. Oxford: Blackwell, 2004.

———. *Pragmatist Aesthetics: Living Beauty, Rethinking Art.* Oxford: Blackwell, 1992. Second edition, New York: Rowman and Littlefield, 2000.

———. "Provokation und Erinnerung: Zu Freude, Sinn und Wert in ästhetischer Erfahrung." *Deutsche Zeitschrift für Philosophie*, 47 (1999): 127–137.

———. "Somaesthetics and Burke's Sublime." *British Journal of Aesthetics*, 45 (2005): 323–341.

———. "Somaesthetics and Care of the Self: The Case of Foucault." *Monist*, 83 (2000): 530–551.

———. "Somaesthetics and Education: Exploring the Terrain." In *Knowing Bodies, Moving Minds: Towards Embodied Teaching and Learning.* Edited by Liora Bresler. Dordrecht: Kluwer, 2004.

———. "Somaesthetics and *The Second Sex*: A Pragmatist Reading of a Feminist Classic." *Hypatia*, 18 (2003): 106–136.

———. "Thinking through the Body, Educating for the Humanites: A Plea for Somaesthetics." *Journal of Aesthetic Education*, 40 (2006): 1–21.

———. "William James, Somatic Introspection, and Care of the Self." *Philosophical Forum*, 36 (2005): 429–450.

Simons, Margaret. *Beauvoir and the Second Sex.* New York: Rowman and Littlefield, 1999.

Soulez, Antonia. "Practice, Theory, Pleasure, and the Problems of Form and Resistance: Shusterman's *Pragmatist Aesthetics*." *Journal of Speculative Philosophy*, 16 (2002): 1–9.

Spence, Alexander. *Biology of Human Aging.* 2nd ed. New York: Prentice Hall, 1994.

Spinoza, Benedict de. *The Ethics.* In *Works of Spinoza.* Translated by R. H. M. Elwes. New York: Dover, 1955.

Sullivan, Shannon. *Living Across and Through Skins: Transactional Bodies, Pragmatism, and Feminism.* Bloomington: Indiana University Press, 2001.

Svatmarama Swami. *The Hatha Yoga Pradapika.* Translated by Pancham Sinh. Allahabad, India: Lahif Mohan Basu, 1915.

Taylor, Paul. C. "The Two-Dewey Thesis, Continued: Shusterman's *Pragmatist Aesthetics*." *Journal of Speculative Philosophy*, 16 (2002): 17–25.

Thoreau, Henry David. *Walden.* In *The Portable Thoreau.* Edited by Carl Bode. New York: Viking, 1964.

Trapnell, P. D., and J. D. Campbell. "Private Self-consciousness and the Five-Factor Model of Personality: Distinguishing Rumination from Reflection." *Journal of Personality and Social Psychology*, 76 (1999): 284–304.

Turner, Bryan. *The Body and Society: Explorations in Social Theory.* Oxford: Blackwell, 1984.

Van Gulik, Robert. *Sexual Life in Ancient China: A Preliminary Survey of Chinese Sex and Society from ca. 1500 B.C. till 1644 A.D.* Leiden: Brill, 1974.

Veyne, Paul. "The Final Foucault and his Ethics," *Critical Inquiry*, 20 (1993): 1–9.

Vintges, Karen. *Philosophy as Passion: The Thinking of Simone de Beauvoir*. Bloomington, IN: Indiana University Press, 1996.

Wang, Yangming. "Instructions for Practical Living." In *A Source Book in Chinese Philosophy*. Translated and edited by Wing-tsit Chan. Princeton, NJ: Princeton University Press, 1963.

Watson, Burton. *The Complete Works of Chuang Tzu*. New York: Columbia University Press, 1968.

Welsch, Wolfgang. "Rettung durch Halbierung?: Zu Richard Shustermans Rehabilitierung ästhetischer Erfahrung." *Deutsche Zeitschrift für Philosophie*, 47 (1999): 111–126.

Whitlock, J. L., et al. "The Virtual Cutting Edge: The Internet and Adolescent Self-Injury." *Developmental Psychology*, 42 (2006): 407–417.

Wilson, T. D., and E. W. Dunn. "Self-Knowledge: Its Limits, Value, and Potential for Improvement." *Annual Review of Psychology*, 55 (2004): 493–518.

Wittgenstein, Ludwig. *Culture and Value*. Translated by Peter Winch. Oxford: Blackwell, 1980.

————. *Denkebewegung: Tagebücher, 1930–1932, 1936–1937*. Innsbruck: Haymon, 1997.

————. *Lectures and Conversations on Aesthetics, Psychology, and Religious Belief*. Oxford: Blackwell, 1970.

————. *Ludwig Wittgenstein: Cambridge Letters*. Edited by B. McGuinness and G. H. von Wright. Oxford: Blackwell, 1996.

————. *Philosophical Investigations*. Translated by G. E. M. Anscombe. Oxford: Blackwell, 1968.

————. *Tractatus Logico-Philosophicus*. Translated by D. F. Pears and B. F. McGuinness. London: Routledge, 1969.

————. *Zettel*. Translated by G. E. M. Anscombe. Oxford: Blackwell, 1967.

Xenophon. *Conversations of Socrates*. Edited by Robin Waterfield. Translated by Hugh Tredennick and Robin Waterfield. London: Penguin, 1990.

Young, Iris Marion. "Throwing Like a Girl." *The Thinking Muse: Feminism and Modern French Philosophy*. Edited by Jeffner Allen and Iris Marion Young. Bloomington: Indiana University Press, 1989.

Yuasa, Yasuo. *The Body: Toward an Eastern Mind-Body Theory*. Translated by S. Nagatomo and T. P. Kasulis. Albany: SUNY Press, 1987.

————. *The Body, Self-Cultivation, and Ki-Energy*. Translated by S. Nagatomo and M. S. Hull. Albany: SUNY Press, 1993.

Index

abortion, 99

Abrams, Jerold J., 29

action, x–xii, xiii, 19, 43, 54, 58–60, 62, 63–64, 67–70, 74–75, 85–86, 88–90, 96–97, 99, 108, 112, 165–169, 175–179, 183, 197–198, 212–215
  contextuality of, 118, 184–185
  voluntary, 43, 117–118, 122–123, 156–158, 188–194, 202

acuity, xiii, 3, 20, 38, 44, 153, 204, 216

adaptation, 143

Adorno, Theodor W., 27, 115

advertising, 6, 27–28

aerobics, 24, 29, 48

aesthesis, 1, 19, 43, 53

aesthetic, the, 1, 26

aesthetic experience, 42, 47, 124–126

aesthetic judgment, 112–113, 124, 134

aestheticism, 46–47

aesthetics, 11, 27–28, 84, 112–115, 123–127, 180, 184–185

AIDS (Acquired Immunodeficiency Syndrome), 31

ailments
  psychosomatic, 93, 96, 137, 158, 192
  somatic, 83, 106, 110, 136–137, 155

Al-Ghazzali, Abu Hamed, 43

alcoholism, 165

Alexander, Albert Redden, 183, 193

Alexander, Frederick Matthias, 11–12, 18, 62, 64, 122, 169, 182–183, 189, 191–204, 206–214

Alexander Technique, xi–xiii, 7, 12, 20, 24, 44, 63, 66, 122, 158, 166, 183, 189, 192–204, 206–214

guiding orders, 199–201
  primary control, 200–203, 206–209
  scientific testing and status of, 195, 203

alienation, 103, 106, 109
  somatic, 3, 27–28, 82–83

Allen, Gay Wilson, 179

altruism, 153

Ames, Roger, 18

anaesthesia, 210

anatomy, 137, 203, 208

anger, 20, 116, 146–148, 150, 185

anhedonia, 36, 38–39

animals, 186, 197, 206, 209

anorexia, 26

Anscombe, Gertrude Elizabeth Margaret, 112

anthropology, 129

antisemitism, 112, 128–129

anxiety, 20, 92–94, 121, 128, 137, 150, 169, 174, 200, 208

Aristippus, 17

Aristotle, 41, 181

art, x–xi, xii, 46–47, 114–115, 124–126, 136, 137, 180, 197, 209–211
  of living, 4, 37, 126

artist, 84, 124

asceticism, ix, 21, 37, 40, 44–46, 79, 141, 173

Ascher, Carol, 79

Asian body disciplines, xiii, 12, 63, 162

association, 124, 135, 153, 174–175, 199

athleticism, 176

athletics (or sports), 2, 28, 48, 86–89, 106–107, 130, 170

Feldenkrais Method, x, xiii–xiv, 7, 20, 24,
  25, 44, 63, 108–109, 121, 123, 155,
  158, 162, 166, 171
  Awareness Through Movement, 25, 26
  Functional Integration, 25
Feldenkrais, Moshe, 18, 22, 155, 203
feminism, 6, 9, 22, 23, 80, 83, 97, 99, 172,
  214
fitness, 102, 104–106, 136
flesh, x, xi, xii, 27, 30, 45, 47, 52, 60, 72,
  81–82, 85–86, 88–89, 91, 92–97, 104,
  110, 127, 132, 181
flexibility, 130, 207–208
focusing, 2–3, 26, 53–56, 62, 67–73, 145,
  151, 159–168, 175, 204–205
Foucault, Michel, 8, 9–10, 12, 15–16,
  18–19, 21, 23, 29–40, 42, 44–48, 49,
  62, 127, 130, 135, 139, 141
  on biopower, 21–22, 29
  on body consciousness, 38
  on death, 47
  Discipline and Punish, 44
  on drugs, 30, 36
  on pleasure, 9–10, 15, 30, 32–40, 47
  on sadomasochism, 29, 32–35
  on the self and self-styling, 35, 45–47
  on sex, 32–36
  and spirituality, 44–47
Francis, Claude, 79
freedom, ix, 28, 78, 88–89, 95–96, 98, 197,
  210
Freud, Sigmund, 81, 131
future, 14, 66, 84, 189

Gallagher, Shaun, 23, 64
Gehlen, Arnold, 9
gender, 23, 31, 34, 74, 90–91
genes, 48, 83, 211
genitalia, 29, 32–33, 93, 94, 105
genius, 59, 215
gesture, x, 49, 59, 60, 121, 124,
  208
Gibson, James Jerome, 214
Gibson, William, 12
glands, 12, 105
God, 45, 94, 172, 188
Gontier, Fernande, 79
grace, x, 64, 166, 178
gravity, 53, 98, 108, 215
Guerra, Gustavo, 29
Gulik, Robert van, 35

gymnastics, 88, 139, 170

habit, 3, 7, 69, 80, 130, 140–142, 165–167,
  172, 175, 182, 188, 204–205, 211–214
  bodily, xi, 2, 8, 13–14, 19–22, 65–67, 71,
    74, 78, 89, 122–123, 140, 169–170,
    178–179, 185, 189–201
  contextuality of, 141, 190–191, 214
  diagnosis and reform of, 62–63, 65, 67,
    70, 96, 130, 166–167, 169–170,
    193–201, 204
  formation of, 62, 130, 140–141, 193, 194,
    205
  intelligent/unintelligent, 205
  and mind, 140–142, 190, 195, 205
  power of, 189, 191
  and self, 190, 205
Hadot, Pierre, 15–16, 37, 46
hands, 53, 71–72, 118, 161, 166, 203, 207,
  208
happiness, xii, xiii, 19, 21, 39, 196
Haskins, Casey, 29
hatred, 127–131
head, x, 11, 21–22, 29, 52, 54, 64, 66, 70,
  108, 109, 118–119, 122, 132, 144, 152,
  154, 155, 157, 160, 191, 198, 199–202,
  206–209
head and neck area, 200–202, 206–208
headache, 136, 192
health, xi, 14, 17, 20, 23, 28–29, 80, 83,
  101, 104–108, 110, 129, 136–137, 171,
  176, 185, 193, 213
heart, 43, 107, 132, 144, 147, 160, 177, 179
hedonism, 19, 35–38, 40, 42, 43
Hegel, Georg Wilhelm Friedrich, 127
Helmholtz, Hermann von, 117
Higgins, Kathleen, 29
history, 23–24, 77, 83–84, 100, 128,
  188
Holocaust, 128
homeopathy, 139, 178
homophobia, 131
homosexuality, 9, 29–30, 33–35, 129, 131
Horkheimer, Max, 27
Howison, George H., 168
human nature, 84, 127
  ambiguity of, 3, 95
human rights, 127
humanism (and humanity), 213–216
Husserl, Edmund, 3
Huxley, Aldous, 192

48 the basic contemporary
cultural question - now
global -

How one has to create and care for
our embodied selves today?

Shadows is performing his
challenges an context

Chords the shadow
and lake

on the way into the Phenom
May 8 - 09
Hes. was closer in shadow
in lake —
w/m I meant moral